D1714586

No One Ever Asked Us . . .
A Postscript to Foster Care

No One Ever Asked Us . . .

A Postscript to Foster Care

Trudy Festinger

New York   Columbia University Press   *1983*

Library of Congress Cataloging in Publication Data

Festinger, Trudy.
　No one ever asked us.

　Bibliography: p.
　Includes index.
　1. Foster home care—New York (N.Y.)—Longitudinal
studies. 2. Young adults—Longitudinal studies.
I. Title.
HV875.652.N5F47 1983 362.7′33′0973 83-7705
ISBN 0-231-05736-9

Columbia University Press
New York Guildford, Surrey

Clothbound editions of Columbia University Press books are
Smyth-sewn and printed on permanent and durable acid-free paper.

Contents

Appendixes

Acknowledgments

This project would not have begun, and could not have been completed, without the encouragement, participation, cooperation, and support of many individuals and organizations. I want to thank each one of them and express my appreciation.

To begin with, my deep gratitude to all of the young adults, the subjects of this book. Their interest in participating and their willingness to talk about themselves and their experiences made the study possible, and was a constant source of encouragement. Many thanks also to the biological and foster families who supported our efforts.

A complex field study has numerous components. It relies on different forms of assistance during the many phases of its development. At its inception Carol Parry, then New York City Assistant Commissioner of Special Services for Children, actively supported the intent of the study. She urged me onward during periods when my enthusiasm waned in the face of serious misgivings about the task that lay ahead. She and her successor, Beverly Sanders, provided full cooperation. Barbara Blum, Commissioner of the New York State Department of Social Services, provided a contract that allowed project staff to review case records. My deep appreciation also extends to all of the executive directors, professional, and office staff of the voluntary and public agencies that participated. Thank you for sharing your ideas and questions, and for helping us with numerous chores when we were in your agencies. Above all, thank you for your trust and your patience.

During the two years of data collection, I was fortunate to have a nucleus of three dedicated full-time staff members. My research associate June Hendricks was responsible for training the staff for case record reviews and for the interviews, and she supervised numerous aspects of the research concerned with the location of the sample and with project management. She and Barbara Kreger, the research assistant, participated in all phases of data collection. June's tireless devotion and their combined dedication and dogged determination were essential. The project secretary Heidi Getzoff managed all aspects of the project office. I highly value all of this team's efforts and thank them for having put up with me.

Many others assisted in one or another phase of data collection, including Vito Bianco, Dennis Chestnut, Chris Gabettas, Ivan Gibson, Brenda Jones, Xavier Keyes, Marsha Martin, Daniel Montopoli, Helen Munoz, Kenneth Pinter, Lucius Priester, Rhona Robin, Paul Robinson, Reid Scher, Irene Shrier, Brenda Thompson, Diana Torres, and Sam Tsemberis. I appreciate all of their help.

The interviews and questionnaires were coded by Alan Reich and JoEllen Lynch. I appreciate the work of both and extend a special thanks to JoEllen for her help in statistical analysis of the data from the University of Michigan and for her assistance in developing a typology for open-ended questions.

The initial computer work was the responsibility of Leah Hass. Others from New York University who assisted included Bert Holland, Eugene Rodolphe, and Laura Scalia. At the University of Michigan David Klingel helped with special computer runs. During my sabbatical in Israel, Chaim Mano of Hebrew University provided valuable computer assistance.

A number of other people assisted in one important way or another. Robert Gundersen and several staff members of the Child Welfare Information Services, Inc., provided the foster care population listings. General population data were provided with the help of Angus Campbell and Richard Kulka at the Institute for Social Research, University of Michigan; other special data were provided by Richard Rosen and Emilie Wright of the New York State Division of Criminal Justice

Services Statistical Analysis Center; Thomas Su of the Human Resources Administration Division of Policy and Economic Research; Robert Scardamalia and Michael Batutis of the New York State Department of Commerce State Data Center; Patricia Pettiford of the Human Resources Administration Office of Research and Program Evaluation; and Lucille Grow of the School of Social Work, Yeshiva University. Without their ready cooperation, vital comparisons would not have been possible. Needless to say, how I used the data these people supplied and how I interpreted them are my own responsibility.

The final manuscript was typed by Evelyn Manning. It was a pleasure to work with someone who was not only precise, but also conscientious and cheerful.

My home base for the study was the New York University School of Social Work. I want to extend my deep appreciation to Dean Shirley Ehrenkranz and Associate Dean Oscar Rosenfeld for their cooperation and support. I also thank Abraham Doron and David Kleinman of the Paul Baerwald School of Social Work for arranging access to the computer facilities of Hebrew University.

This study could never have begun, let alone be completed, without substantial financial support. I was fortunate to receive such support from six private foundations: Edna McConnell Clark Foundation, Field Foundation, Foundation for Child Development, New-Land Foundation, New York Community Trust, and Robert Sterling Clark Foundation. I am deeply grateful to the many people at each foundation for their trust, and for their patience in waiting to see what I would produce. I hope their confidence was warranted.

Finally, on a more personal note, I was fortunate to have the support of Leon, Debbie, and Bobs, all of whom not only lived through the experience with me, but also tolerated it.

Introduction

This book is about a group of young adults who spent many years in foster care. What is foster care? One can think of it as "any kind of full-time substitute care of children outside their own home by persons other than their parents" (Encyc. SW 1977:114). The generic term includes care provided in foster family homes as well as in various forms of group settings, including group homes, group residences, and institutions. Such substitute care involves a change in the legal custody of children. In a broad sense, the term also encompasses other forms of surrogate care including adoption, which involves a change not only in legal custody, but also in legal guardianship. This book concerns the former—people who spent many years in foster homes and group settings.

Foster care facilities are intended to provide services for children who, for one or another reason, cannot be adequately cared for by their own families, temporarily or for an extended period. Foster care can, in a sense, be regarded as "the ultimate form of parental prosthesis" (Polansky et al. 1981:235). It is the actual operational response to the problem posed by the concept of *parens patriae* which "suggests that society has ultimate parental responsibilities for all children in the community" (Encyc. SW 1977:114). Society must therefore provide alternative, adequate care. Child welfare services are the formal instrument through which the community discharges these responisbilities.

The history of foster care is lengthy and has been well documented by others (see, for example: Bremner 1970; Bremner 1971; Bremner 1974; Kadushin 1980). The asylums of antiquity, the poor houses and provisions of apprenticeships embodied in the seventeenth-century Elizabethan Poor Laws, almhouses and institutions for dependent children in the eighteenth century, and exchanges of child labor for child care in the mid-nineteenth century all form part of the background of modern foster care. Institutional care of one sort or another predominated in that history, and continued to be the most common form of care formally provided in the United States in the first decades of the twentieth century. For example, it is estimated that in 1923 approximately 64 percent of the children in foster care were in institutions (SW Year Book 1933). During the 1920s and 1930s debates raged over the relative merits of institutional versus foster home care. By 1933 the proportion of children who were living in institutions had dropped somewhat, but still constituted a small majority (SW Year Book 1943). Because of increasing recognition of the importance of a family environment for children's development, bolstered by writings that overemphasized the deleterious effects of institutional care for young children (Bowlby 1951), the proportion of children in foster care living in institutions declined substantially over time. As a consequence, by 1977 an estimated 21% were living in group homes, group residences, and institutions in contrast to 79% who were in foster family homes (Shyne and Schroeder 1978).

An earlier competitive stance between "foster institutions" (SW Year Book 1933:186) and foster homes had given way to a view of the two forms of care as complementary resources, each "necessary and appropriate for different groups of children" (Kadushin 1980:586) and each occupying "a particular place in the total pattern of child-care services" (Kadushin 1980:586). Today group settings continue to be viewed as an important component of foster care. Ideally they are to be used when they best meet the needs of a particular child and family, but only after less restrictive alternatives have been explored and found wanting.

Over the decades of this century there have also been shifts in the number and rates of children in foster care. The rates declined after passage of the Social Security Act in 1935 since its provisions allowed more children to be maintained in their own homes. But in the 1960s and 1970s there was "a steady growth in substitute care as a result of increases in family disruption from all causes" (Kadushin 1980:320). An estimate for 1977 placed the number of children in various foster care facilities at 502,000 (Shyne and Schroeder 1978:110).

Foster care policies and practices have also changed over the years as the service, designed primarily to be a temporary arrangement, came under criticism for its failure to deal adequately with the future of many children. Although longitudinal studies show that foster care is actually a relatively temporary phenomenon for a majority of children (Kadushin 1978), it has become an unplanned long-term experience for some. Words like "drift" and "limbo" became short-hand phrases that were frequently applied to describe this situation. Most recently, efforts to address the problem of temporary care turning inadvertently into long-term care have emphasized new criteria for judging the performance of agencies that provide foster care. The thrust is in the direction of more efficient case management, stressing explicit case plans and goals, and time frames for their achievement. The phrase "permanency planning" has entered the foster care lexicon with a vehemence, on the assumption that a speedy return home or formal adoption produces a continuity and stability of relationships that will ultimately benefit the children.

In spite of these changes there have always been, and for the foreseeable future there will continue to be, those who will grow to adulthood in foster care. For some this occurs because there are no feasible alternatives (Derdeyn 1977), but for others the foster care field has, in a sense, gone most seriously awry. Yet amid all of the publicity about foster care, minimal attention has been paid to a small, but ever growing army of people who left foster care when they reached young adulthood. They are people who for one or another reason did not return home, nor were they adopted. The phenomenon is so common that it has even merited the label "aging out."

This book presents the results of a study of such a group some years after they were discharged from foster homes and group settings. I undertook this venture because virtually nothing is known about how such young adults fare in society. In view of so much criticism of the foster care system, it seemed important to try to understand what it ultimately produces. That was my major purpose. A knowledge void is a fertile atmosphere for untested notions to proliferate. Therefore, data were collected to assess various opinions that have, in some quarters, gained the status of facts by virtue of repetition. Are those who "graduate" from foster care problem ridden? Is their self-image damaged? Are they excessively dependent on public support? Are they unduly in trouble with the law?

There was a further reason for undertaking this study. Discussions about foster care and its assessment have most typically been carried on by interested professionals, sometimes by public officials, rarely by the biological or foster parents, but almost never by those about whom the arguments swirl—those who have firsthand information about life as a foster child. I hoped that everyone could learn from their perspective, not only about their foster care experience but also about their preparation for independence. I trusted that this would stimulate ideas about changes in the system that might be beneficial. In short, my final broad purpose was to offer former foster children an opportunity to speak.

No One Ever Asked Us . . .
A Postscript to Foster Care

Chapter One

HOW IT ALL BEGAN

Every once in a while someone asks me, "How do you become a humorist?" I always reply, "Well first you have to become a foster child—and after that it all comes naturally."

Art Buchwald
April 1972 (1973:vii)

Right now in New York City alone there are roughly 20,000 children in foster care. Most of them are living in foster homes; the rest are primarily in group homes, group residences, or institutions. Some will remain in foster care a brief period while others will have extended stays. Many will return to their families or be adopted, but there are also some who will remain in care, eventually to be discharged when they reach the age of 18 or, if attending college or vocational school, the age of 21. Once these adults are discharged, little is known about what happens to them, about how they manage their lives as young adults. A recent report pointed to this void by stating, "whether they were employed, living stable lives, drifting in the streets, or in trouble with the law are questions for which the foster care system presently provides no information or answers" (Task Force 1980:52). This book will try to fill the void, for it is about such a group of young adults some years after they left foster care.

In recent years there has been a startling similarity among the youths whose official discharge designation is "to own responsibility." For instance, in New York City between 1976 and 1980 roughly 850 to 1,100 young adults were so discharged each year (CWIS 1976–1980). Most of them, between 63% and 69%, had spent six or more years in foster care.

This number is a stern reminder that despite the many voices over the years that have advocated change, large systems are slow to respond. It underscores how human beings employed by the system have accommodated to its deficiencies much as a laborer or farmer will accommodate to the deficiencies of machines at hand. This number reflects an absence or breakdown of efforts to plan for children, and a failure to find permanent homes for them during earlier years. It also suggests that sometimes such plans or efforts, no matter how much pursued, may not succeed.

As long ago as 1909 there was a call for information about adults who were reared in foster care. At that time a report to President Theodore Roosevelt that embodied conclusions from the White House Conference on the Care of Dependent Children stated:

> One unfortunate feature of child-caring work hitherto is the scanty information available as to the actual careers of children who have been reared under the care of charitable agencies. This applies both to institutions which too frequently lose sight of the children soon after they leave their doors, and home-finding agencies, which too frequently have failed to exercise supervision adequate to enable them to judge of the real results of their work. It is extremely desirable that, taking all precautions to prevent injury or embarrassment to those who have been the subjects of charitable care, the agencies which have been responsible should know to what station in life they attain and what sort of citizens they become. Only in this manner can they form a correct judgment of the result of their efforts.
>
> (Bremner 1971:367)

Despite this call there are few recorded studies of the long-range impact of growing up as a foster child. On the other hand there have been many important studies of the more immediate short-range effects of foster care on the physical, psychological, and cognitive functioning of children of various ages. Although these short-range studies are not directly relevant, it is useful to note that Kadushin, following an extensive review, concludes that if foster families are selected with reasonable caution and provided with support, such care "is not injurious to the child's development" and that institutions for the dependent and neglected "were neither as harmful as had been feared nor as helpful as had been hoped" (Kadushin 1980:382, 610). The few studies of a long-range nature, those that focused on adults, have provided a mixed picture that may be as much a function of the variety of samples, approaches, and sometimes questionable methodologies as anything else. A brief look at the results of these will provide the flavor.

Past Studies

The first serious effort to collect first-hand information on a considerable scale was a study by Theis (1924). Interviews were arranged with more than 500 former foster children and their foster parents or relatives at the time the young adults were at least 18 years old. They had lived with foster parents for at least one year. In all, close to 75% of the sample were judged by "experienced supervisors" as "capable" at the time of their interviews. That is, they were considered law-abiding, sensibly managing their own affairs, and abiding by their communities' moral standards. Children who were five years of age or younger at the time of placement were more likely to be judged "capable" than those placed later. The outcome was also positively related to the quality of the relationship between the children and their foster parents.

More than ten years later Baylor and Monachesi (1939) reported a study of nearly 500 former foster children, based on visits "in the homes of people concerned," such as relatives and various independent references, in addition to contacts with employers. At the time of the follow-up the subjects ranged in age from 5 to more than 29, but it is not clear how long they had been in care or how old they were when discharged. Independent global ratings by the two authors suggested that among those aged 21 or above at the time of the follow-up, the behavior of 73.5% was judged to be "favorable," that is, they "had not misbehaved." Furthermore, 70.5% of these young adults were considered to be living in a "favorable" environment, "a situation marked by the absence of conditions and factors which, on the whole, were harmful."

About fifteen years later Salo (1956) published findings from a study in Finland. In this study the adult adjustment of 742 dependent and neglected children who had been placed in foster homes and institutions was compared with the adjustment of their 437 older siblings who had remained at home with their biological families. The length of placement was for "a minimum of half a year." At the time of the follow-up in 1952 members of the foster care group were, on the average, approaching 27 years of age, while their older siblings averaged 29 years. Indexes of maladjustment included economic dependence, criminal behavior, and excessive use of alcohol, based on information "provided by various authorities and supplemented by personal interviews as far as possible." At the time of the follow-up the adults who had been in foster care were occupationally "better placed in life" than the corresponding control group, and fewer were criminals and alcoholics. "Conjugal adjustment" did not differ. The foster care group showed less instability and "increased success in life." On the whole, foster family care resulted in more favorable outcomes than institutional placement. However, the author noted that the latter group "came from more difficult home conditions." The author concluded that the outcome of foster care was more positive than the effects of having remained in neglectful homes. It is unfortunate that the English summary provides no details about the length of care, the comparability of the comparison group, or the methods used to arrive at some of the conclusions.

Meanwhile in the mid-1950s another study of former foster children was completed in Holland (Van Der Waals 1960). A social worker at Tot Steun, a child caring agency, carried out extensive interviews with 160 young adults who were born between 1903 and 1920 and had been in care "for a considerable length of time." Their ages ranged from less than 2 to 14 at the time of placement, usually into rural areas in order to prevent contact between the children and their biological parents. Although there is no mention of it, one can assume that the children remained in care until adulthood. All had been placed in foster homes by a variety of concerned but untrained individuals, and most had several placements. At the time of the follow-up more than one-half of the adults "expressed strong negative feelings toward their former foster families." Most severed all contact with the foster parents after they came of age and "had kept no ties whatsoever with their own parents." Those whose biological mothers had kept in regular touch by writing and sending gifts, and who therefore felt accepted by their mothers, tended to be more accepting of their foster parents. The author further noted that, as adults, many "were rather well established" socially, and "few were unemployed or antisocial." However, "many felt unsuccessful, dissatisfied, and distressed . . . they felt that their life had not been worth living."

A study issued at about the same time in the United States (McCord, McCord, and Thurber 1960) reported on the connection between foster home placement and adult deviance. The subjects were all drawn from the Cambridge-Somerville Youth Study, a service program whose goal was delinquency prevention. Nineteen males who were placed in foster homes as a "last resort" during early adolescence when "all other measures had failed" were compared with another group of 19 males matched for such background factors as parental deviance and parental attitudes toward their sons. As these males were entering their early 30s the investigators reviewed records "from the courts, mental hospitals, and various private agencies in order to identify those individuals who had become alcoholic, psychotic or criminal." The authors reported that a "higher proportion of those who had been placed in foster homes had criminal records in adulthood." Their explanation admits the possibility of an imperfect match between those placed and those in the comparison group, notes the possibility of inadequate foster homes, but leans most heavily in the direction of suggesting that foster home placement in adolescence "may actually be harmful." To this writer such an interpretation seems extreme. Perhaps the results merely suggest that last resort placement—after all else has failed—may be a less than opportune time to place such adolescents. But to fault foster care because of the outcome commits the error of assuming that placement can somehow undo the damage wrought earlier.

In the 1960s a study from Scotland also reviewed figures on crime. Ferguson (1966) reported the results of a follow-up of 205 young adults born in the mid-1940s, all "children of the war." They had entered care between infancy and age 15. About two-thirds were placed with foster parents, while the rest were in children's homes or with relatives or guardians. Intelligence test results showed that a majority had scores below 90. All were discharged at age 18 and followed up several times thereafter until they reached 20 years of age. At that time their health was considered "very good." More of the women (24%) than men (4%) had married, and 92% of the men and 90% of the nonmarried women were described as being fully self-supporting. A majority (75%) of those from foster homes maintained contact with their foster parents. However, the author reported with some alarm that while few females had a run-in with the law, 31% of the males had been convicted by the courts at some time, including 15% with such a record since their discharge from care. More males who had ever been convicted or adjudicated delinquent had been shifted among foster homes, were regarded by their teachers as having "a poor temperamental quality," had poorer scholastic abilities, and had a generally lower I.Q. This last was considered a major factor in accounting for the conviction rate among males. Thus, the proportion from care who were convicted between the ages of 8 and 20 were quite similar to males their age from "special schools for the educationally subnormal" and differed from "lads who left ordinary schools at [the] earliest permitted age."

A recent study from Sweden also reported on criminality. Bohman and Sigvardsson (1980) reviewed the official records of a cohort of 329 males who were born in 1956–1957. At birth all their mothers had requested adoption. All together 93 were placed in adoptive homes before the age of 1; 118 were returned to their biological mothers and were reared by them; 118 boys were placed in foster care, most before 1 year of age, and almost all "grew up with their foster parents and a majority were subsequently legally adopted by them." These three groups were compared with each other and with control subjects, males born on the same days in the same towns. Comparisons were made at several points in time. For instance, at age 18 military enlistment procedures for 263 of the males showed that, on various tests of intellectual capacity, those from foster homes and those reared by their biological mothers functioned at a lower level than the controls. Both of these groups achieved lower scores than the adopted males. Furthermore, the official registers of alcohol abuse and criminality were reviewed, covering the period between age 16 and 22 or 23. Among those from foster homes 29.2% were registered for alcohol abuse or criminal offenses or both. This was a higher percentage than the controls (15.5%), the group reared by their mothers (16.5%), or the adoptees (18%). The authors noted that a variety of differences in the backgrounds of the various groups suggested the possibility of genetic factors at play, but they tended to interpret their findings as resulting from deficient preparation of the foster parents for placement, and from insecurities connected with being in foster care. No analysis was presented of a possible connection between lower intellectual capacity and other factors.

The results of this study are difficult to interpret. The biological backgrounds of the various groups differed consistently; they were most negative for those reared in foster care. It is plausible that a great deal of selectivity determined who was adopted, who was returned home shortly after birth, and who remained in foster care, particularly since all the biological mothers had requested adoption. In an earlier article, but not here, the issue of "negative selection" was noted (Bohman 1971). Such selectivity could have been a function of the social sufficiency of the biological parents or optimal characteristics of the children, or both. Thus, initial differences could easily have affected who became a member of which group in the first place, with obvious implications for the outcome years later.

To my knowledge there is only one other published study that systematically followed up young adults after their discharge from foster care on reaching legal maturity. Meier's survey (1962, 1965) presents material on 66 adults, most of whom were interviewed when they were 28 to 32 years old. They had all lived in foster homes in Minnesota for at least five years and had remained in guardianship until they "went on their own" in the late 1940s. Many had been reared in rural areas. All but one was white. Most of those who were interviewed were rated on their sense of well-being, or their "feelings of adequacy and pleasure," and their social effectiveness in various areas of life. The score on social effectiveness was based on interviewer ratings of the home surroundings, and housekeeping standards, employment and economic circumstances, health, support and care of children, and social behavior outside the family group. A large majority of the ratings were positive, and "with few exceptions these young men and women are self-supporting individuals, living in attractive homes and taking good care of their children." A majority had found places for themselves in their communities and were conforming to the social standards of those communities. Most continued to be in touch with their foster families. All of the women and 63% of the men had married and most had children, but the author notes that the women tended to express excessive doubts about themselves as mothers. A few comparisons with the general population are presented. A higher percentage of the women from foster care were living with a spouse than was the case of a comparable group of women at large, but at the same time broken marriages were somewhat more common for men and women from foster care. Overall there were no sex differences in the scores on social effectiveness and well-being, and for both men and women "impairment of the sense of well-being was more frequently found than was lack of social effectiveness," but sex differences were noted in a number of areas including a more positive feeling on the part of women about having been placed. Regular parental visiting was so limited that a link with the outcome could not be assessed except in a few instances. These showed no connection. Finally, factors often thought to have an important bearing on the outcome of foster care, such as the age at placement and the number of placements, were unrelated to the adult functioning of these former foster children.

It would be risky to draw general conclusions from these studies. Some were very limited in size and scope; many were quite impressionistic; and different studies yielded inconsistent results. Overall one might dare to say that over the more than 50 years spanned by these studies a majority of the adults from foster care were functioning satisfactorily in their communities. But what does this mean? Perhaps very little, for percentages quickly lose their concrete magic when countered with the awesome question: Compared with whom? Most of the studies suffered in this regard. Yet it is an understandable failing, for the problem of finding relevant comparison groups is an enormous one.

Goals of This Study

Many years have passed since most of the children in these studies were last in foster care. The field of foster care and our society have both changed. There are more children in foster care now than in the early 1960s, the ages of children entering foster care have shifted upward, a large group have spent many years in care, and increasing numbers of former foster children can now be found in our society. Yet this twenty-year period has witnessed an absence of studies of such adults in the United States. There is only one recent study that is even tangentially relevant to our issue here. Zimmerman (1982) attempted to follow-up 170 former foster children who had lived one or more years in a foster home in Orleans Parish. In 1980 interviews were conducted with 61 of them. At that time they ranged in age from 19 through 29 years. Only 18 of them had been discharged between the ages of 18 and 21, and no separate data are presented for these. The reason to mention this study is that Zimmerman states that the results "clearly indicated that youngsters in this study who remained in longterm foster care and were discharged upon reaching their majority are significantly better off than those who were in foster care for shorter periods of time and were returned to the custody of natural family members" (Zimmerman 1982: 90). The absence of recent relevant studies is at once curious and understandable, for as Fanshel pointed out:

> It has long been considered necessary for a proper evaluation of child welfare services to conduct studies that will determine how well children adjust after they have left the care of an agency. Because studies of this kind are extremely difficult to execute, reports of such undertakings are relatively rare in the professional literature. Follow-up studies pose many problems: location of the subjects, obtaining their cooperation, developing reliable and valid measures of their adjustment, and designating appropriate control groups with whom subjects can be compared. The complexity of attempting to link back to the foster care experience some of the variations in the child's current adjustment is also viewed as a formidable problem.   (1966:101)

Although Fanshel spoke here about children, identical obstacles must be faced by anyone who attempts to follow up a group of adults. Despite such complications, the dearth of such studies was troubling.

In areas where knowledge is limited, beliefs spring up to fill the void. And so deep inside many people there is a lurking suspicion—a thought that can change into a belief—that those who were reared in foster care must have ended up as damaged people. Such notions have even gained the unwitting support of some clinicians who cannot help but see, and may insist on seeing, the world through problem-colored glasses. Such ideas surface in social gatherings where one can be confronted by the "we know they are all emotionally damaged" or "it is clear they are overpopulating the jails" remark. The only thing clear was the likelihood that such ideas oversimplified very complex events, the possibility that such notions were wrong, and the fact that information was sorely needed before a discussion could begin. For all these reasons I embarked on this tortuous venture. The outcome . . . well, that's what this book is all about.

But first I must speak a bit about our approach. There were two broad goals. One was to provide a detailed picture of a group of young adults who were discharged from foster care on or after reaching the age of majority. I wanted to learn about their experiences since their discharge, to describe various aspects of their lives, and to hear their views of themselves and their lives. The second goal was to hear what they had to say about foster care, their thoughts about what might improve such care.

Numerous questions were subsumed under such broad purposes, questions that addressed the quality of the young adults' lives and that tested some professional notions and public beliefs. For instance, are former foster children footloose or have they become integrated in their communities? Have they married or established partnerships, or are they loners and prone to separation and divorce? Do they rear their own children or rely on others to do so? To what extent have they placed children in foster care? Have they pursued training? Are they self-supporting members of society or do they depend on public support? How many seek out biological family members or decrease such contact over time? Do they remain in touch with foster families and how close do they feel? What did it mean to be a foster child? Do former foster children maintain themselves within the law? What is their general physical and emotional state, their sense of well-being? To what extent do elements of the placement experience such as its length, the amount of shifting about, and family visiting make a difference in the long run? Are there different outcomes for those who left foster homes as opposed to group settings?

These are but a few of the questions I had. The rest will become self-evident. It is easy to ask questions but firm answers are often elusive. The overarching question of how these young adults turned out is too broad. Therefore, many components of their lives will be examined. The answers to some questions require making comparisons. I will compare different groups of young adults, all from foster care, such as those discharged from foster homes with those from group settings. But I will also make many comparisons with young adults in the general population in order to see whether and how those from foster care differ.

Both the objective and subjective components of the young adults' lives will be explored; one cannot understand people's sense of well-being from a knowledge of their objective circumstances alone. Although the objective facts of people's lives are important, they are but part of the whole picture. Knowledge about how people perceive their circumstances is also an important element, for as Campbell said so well:

> The mind does indeed influence our perception of the world, not without limits, to be sure, but to a sufficient degree that the correspondence between our objective conditions and our subjective experience is very imperfect. If we try to explain the population's sense of well-being on the basis of objective circumstances, we will leave unaccounted for most of what we are trying to explain.   (1981:1)

People's satisfaction with their lives can be looked at from a variety of perspectives. In large measure I concentrated on three dimensions, using Allardt's (1976) classification of basic

needs of "having," or needs related to material and impersonal resources; "loving," or needs related to love, companion-
ship, and solidarity; and "being," or needs denoting self-ac-
tualization and the obverse of alienation. The interviews with
the young adults incorporated many aspects of these three dimensions on the assumption that these would tap the central
components of their lives.

Study Methods

The basic group consisted of all people who were discharged from foster care in the New York metropolitan area
in 1975, who had been in care continuously for at least the
preceding five years, and who were 18 to 21 years old at the
time of discharge. After obtaining official permission from
Special Services for Children, New York City Human Resources Administration, I and my staff received from the Child
Welfare Information Service, Inc., a roster of more than 600
name codes, birth dates, and dates of discharge of persons
who met such specifications. They had been discharged from
48 child caring agencies. We had numerous meetings with
agencies in order to enlist their cooperation. At the very least,
we needed to decode the names. Furthermore, we wanted to
review the case records for background information and clues
that might help us find people. Because of the confidentiality
of such material and the concern of some agencies about legal
liability, a contract with the New York State Department of
Social Services was negotiated that allowed my staff access to
the closed records. All but a few of the agencies that were
approached agreed to participate, but not all were sought out
because of time and financial constraints. To make a long story
very short, the relevant records of 30 agencies, some with many
separate divisions, were reviewed. They included small agencies and large ones, voluntary agencies of all denominations
and public foster home divisions, and they covered a wide
range of geographic locations. Agencies with outlying divi-

sions were often helpful in assembling case records at a central location. Altogether 421 case records were read and coded, with every tenth case independently coded by two people in order to assess and maintain reliability. More than 100 items of background and placement information were sought in addition to any clues that would help us find the young adults. As an aside, many of the records were quite something to behold, consisting of volume upon volume, over a foot in height. Needless to say, they took hours to read.

We began with 421 people but excluded 21 as too emotionally disturbed, mentally retarded, or physically impaired for an interview. These people at discharge were, for example, diagnosed as psychotic, had I.Q. scores below 60, or were deaf and mute. We felt that an interview with these people would be too difficult, possibly disturbing, or that the material might not be understood, and so we did not attempt to locate them. We also learned that six of the young adults had died of natural as well as unnatural causes in the years following their discharge from foster care.

We then set out to find the remaining 394 people. Somewhat more than two-thirds of them (69.3%) had been discharged from foster homes; the rest (30.7%) were from group settings, that is, from group homes (8.9%), group residences (5.6%), and institutions (16.2%). It is difficult to describe this hair-raising process, for so much was happening at once, and so many techniques were used that an orderly picture cannot tell the story. We used mountains of telephone directories for an initial check of all names, including those of biological family members and foster families. This was helpful in some cases but more often resulted in a plethora of identical names at different locations, none of which coincided with addresses we knew about. We sent out letters to each young adult both directly and in care of others, often two or three letters per person at this early stage. These letters told them about the study but did not mention foster care, for we were mindful of confidentiality and knew that someone other than the young adult might read it (see sample in Appendix C). Forms and stamped envelopes were enclosed so that the young adults could let us know of their whereabouts if they were interested. Over the course of many mailings about one-fourth (23.6%) returned these forms. The process was prolonged. At first we were somewhat hesitant in our pursuit, worried about negative reactions. But with time and a large accumulation of returned letters with "addressee unknown" emblazoned on the envelopes, we became more aggressive. We sent letters to others in English and Spanish, to relatives, friends, colleges, and some former employers, asking for information about the young adults' whereabouts. Over time many thousands of letters were sent, for we had no way of knowing whether a nonresponse signified a lack of interest or a failure to reach the young adult. Post office records of forwarding addresses and letter carriers' memories sometimes helped. At the same time we attempted to locate people or verify addresses by telephone, using information services all over the country and directories that listed people by address. We were plagued by unlisted phone numbers. Sometimes neighbors, superintendents, and local shopkeepers were a help in our search. We developed an elaborate set of telephone procedures to address all manner of contingencies and worked out approaches to questions that might be asked. We role-played and trained each other. We never explained the details of the study until we were quite certain that we were speaking with the young adult we had in mind.

We also used a number of other methods in making our search. For instance the Human Resources Administration maintained records on all who had been placed in the voluntary agencies. We requested some of these, usually from the warehouse where closed records were stored. The 121 records thus reviewed sometimes provided new clues. The computerized public assistance file was another source that occasionally gave leads. Locator services used by the various armed forces also helped us find some people, especially those who were overseas. Finally, copies of motor vehicle license records were useful in some instances.

One final word needs to be said about the task of locating

people. Much of it had to be done at night and on weekends, as well as on holidays. It was a time-consuming job, taxing the morale of the staff and filled with frustrations. It required dedication, imagination, luck, and above all persistence. At the time we called a halt there were 58 people whose whereabouts were a complete mystery. We had some clues on 42, but were not sure of their precise location. For instance, some picked up mail at the homes of their foster or biological families, but we could never connect with them. Others made appointments with us but did not follow through; perhaps they were avoiding us. Yet others said they wanted to participate, but the questionnaire we sent, for example overseas, was returned "addressee unknown." Their army unit had moved! In addition to these 100, we located two persons who actually sent in their completed questionnaires, but too late for us to include their responses. Fifteen others who were found refused to participate. Thus, of the 394 we set out to locate, 277 (70.3%) participated in the study.

Overall there were very few differences between those who became respondents and those who did not. A majority, or 72.6% of the 277 respondents, in contrast to 61.5% of the 117 nonrespondents, had been discharged from foster homes rather than one of the forms of group care. We did not reach as many from group settings as from foster homes because we had fewer leads to pursue. Those from group settings who became respondents had a slight educational edge at the time of discharge over their counterparts who were nonrespondents. On the other hand numerous background and placement factors, such as age, contact with family members, and problems exhibited, did not distinguish the nonrespondents from the respondents.

A majority of the 15 nonrespondents who refused to participate gave some information about themselves. Almost all came from foster homes where they had resided for many years, and most were satisfied with their foster care experience. They were all employed or attending school, said they had never received public assistance, and most were single and said they felt happy. Some said that they were too busy to participate, a few did not want to give personal information to strangers, while others rejected the words "foster care." They felt their foster parents were simply their parents. While little can be said about such a small group, we mention them to counter the notion that one who refuses to participate of necessity has a poorer outcome. However, there were others who also refused but did so by evading us, and we have no information about them. Some of them may also have disavowed the idea of foster care, or perhaps misunderstood our broad interpretation of it. For instance, there were some from group settings who equated foster care with foster family care, who announced that they were "never fostered." All of these considerations, as well as others, may have affected participation. In the long run, however, our ability to find people was probably the main factor. For once we spoke with people, explained what we had in mind, and answered their questions, there was usually little hesitation about participating. There was, in fact, considerable interest, even enthusiasm.

The interview schedule* was developed and pretested on a number of volunteers who had once been in foster care. Primarily a structured instrument, it contained many questions that were identical with those asked in three national surveys in order to have a basis for making comparisons with people in the general population. Some items the young adults were asked to complete themselves. We hoped that this would lead to greater honesty in certain sensitive, personal areas. Interviews, whether face to face or on the telephone, were identical. A questionnaire was also developed. It contained many items from the interview schedule, but some areas could not be covered in as much depth and other areas were omitted entirely because they were too complex. For instance, the detailed material on contact with family members at various

---

*Available from the author on request. Write to: School of Social Work, New York University.

points in time would have taken too much space. Therefore, the number of respondents varies somewhat depending on the area addressed.

The young adults were given a number of options about participating. If they lived in or near New York City interviews could be scheduled at New York University or at another convenient place of their choosing. One hundred forty-two were interviewed at our offices and 44 elsewhere, usually in their homes. If they lived some distance away the choice was a telephone interview or a questionnaire. There were 55 telephone interviews, 30 completed questionnaires in the United States, and 6 returned questionnaires from overseas. These last were given no choice, for otherwise our telephone bills would have reached astronomical heights. Nevertheless, some who were overseas when we first located them asked for an interview on their return to the United States. Some of these respondents are part of the interviewed group. There were others who preferred an interview but it was impossible to arrange. They had no telephone and could not "borrow" one from an acquaintance, or the only telephone was in a hallway, or they had no access to one because they were in jail. In other words, questionnaires were sometimes a necessity rather than an option. Interviews were decidedly preferred by most of the young adults.

Our first interviews were conducted at the end of May 1979, but the bulk came later. Data collection continued through the first weeks of April 1980. Interviews were scheduled on any day of the week, including weekends, and at any hour, including the early evening. We offered some monetary compensation since we felt that people should be paid for their time. No doubt this was also an inducement to participate and may have skewed the sample somewhat toward those who felt in need of extra cash. In any event, we paid $10 in addition to transportation costs for those who actually traveled to our office and $5 to all others.

The interviewers were all provided with information about foster care and trained in the use of the schedule. Practice sessions included role playing until we were satisfied that each interviewer not only was attuned to the intent and precise wording of each question but would approach each person with care and sensitivity, and be prepared to elicit and handle the variety of facts and feelings that would inevitably emerge. Training was an ongoing process since all interviews were independently reviewed and ambiguities discussed soon after they were held. At times this led to another brief contact with the young adult in order to clarify some issue. It was also an ongoing process since new interviewers had to be trained from time to time. In addition to the 3 full-time staff members, 13 part-time interviewers worked with us. Most were graduate students in social work and psychology with considerable experience in interviewing.

We used so many interviewers because we were interested in matching interviewers and interviewees on the basis of sex and racial background (black, Hispanic, or white). This interest was sparked following discussions with a variety of survey researchers who thought it would not hinder, but could help, in making the respondents more willing to participate and more comfortable in the interview, even if the evidence on the issue of matching was not that clear-cut. Our philosophy was that anything that might help should be tried, even if it added severe complications to the management of the project. However, we did not have at hand, because we could not afford, interviewers of all descriptions on every day of the week. As it turned out, this would have been necessary for perfect matching. In any event, we matched on the basis of sex in 85.1% of the 241 interviews, on race in 69.7%, including a match on both sex and race in 61.8% of the interviews. About 7% of the interviews were matched on neither. In view of some of the problems we encountered, it is surprising that we succeeded so frequently. We were certainly perplexed the day a young man walked in dressed in woman's clothing. We do not know to what extent matching ultimately made a difference, for a test of this would have required random assignment to matched and unmatched conditions and we had no such arrangement.

Our impressionistic hindsight suggested that it was worth the effort. A slightly nagging question remained about the extent of the match on race. We had used information from case records in assigning interviewers, and this is reflected in the percentages given above, but as it turned out some of the young adults' self-designations did not correspond.

A few other things must be mentioned about our preparation for the interviews. What did each interviewer know about the person to be interviewed? The answer is essentially nothing except the individual's name, address, date of discharge from foster care, and name of the agency at that time. The interviewer was also informed of anything noteworthy that had transpired in arranging the appointment that might help the interviewer establish rapport. The point is that the interviewer was not privy to the coded case record material, and therefore did not know of the person's background. This was done for several reasons: to guard against any potential influence of this material on the manner in which questions were asked, to have the interviews as fresh as possible, and to protect the confidential contents of the records.

Operations such as this one need a name, and so we spent some time thinking about titles that might catch the attention of young people. Our secretary came up with one that fit the bill: WHAT'S HAPPENING: Young Adults in Society Today. This appeared on all of our stationery and various instruments. When we spoke with the prospective participants, we provided more details and answered their questions. We were prepared for all sorts of questions, most of which never materialized. At the time of the interviews we again reviewed our overall purpose. For instance, the young people were told that we were interested in the quality of life of those who had spent many years in foster care, that we would be asking about their current life and experiences in recent years, and about their feelings concerning a variety of things, including foster care. They were told that we wanted to know their ideas about what could help others now growing up away from their families. They were, of course, guaranteed total confidentiality. Similar information was printed on a consent form which they were asked to read and sign at the time of the face-to-face interview, or to mail to us prior to a telephone interview.

In the retelling the process sounds too smooth. Further problems arose after we had located people, made appointments on the telephone, and an interviewer awaited them at a particular time. Much to our dismay we quickly realized that this was unworkable because of too many missed appointments. A scheme was devised that included sending a reminder with relevant details of date, time, location, and the name of the interviewer. A map of the area with public transportation information was appended for those coming to our offices, for it became clear that many had never been to that part of the city. In addition, each person was telephoned one or two days before the appointment in order to confirm it. In spite of these reminders, people missed appointments. All together, including the week before these procedures were in place, 50 of the respondents missed an appointment, and a few missed two. Some others—14 in all—also did not appear at the scheduled time and never became participants.

What was going on? We immediately assumed that missed appointments signaled ambivalence, but then we began to recognize countervailing facts. For instance, home interviews and telephone interviews were rarely missed. This suggested that the strangeness of the location was partly responsible. But there were other factors as well. We were dealing with a young group who had other priorities, more important things to do, and whose attention could easily be diverted by other events that occurred. We had the sense that many did not realize that an appointment meant that someone would be waiting specifically for them. After all, many had probably experienced long waits in clinics. As a consequence some may have treated appointment times with indifference. In fact, they rarely called to cancel or to reschedule. Instead, some simply appeared on another day, unannounced. Others had to be reached again, and we do not know if they too would have shown up on their own if we had not pursued them. They were a minority but a fine example of how things did not work smoothly. In addition to missed appointments, there were more general problems with time. Lateness was common, and sometimes it meant delays of several hours. But they did come, most often by themselves, but sometimes accompanied by friends, or a spouse, or with their children in tow. We set up ad hoc waiting rooms and play areas, for we preferred the interviews to be private. For the vast majority no one else was present, except perhaps a child. And according to interviewer ratings, most of the young adults were friendly, interested, attentive, and involved.

Most interviews lasted from 1½ to more than 2 hours, but some were longer. In order to portray the lives of these young adults, there was much ground to cover in a limited time. Such a "one shot" approach has certain limitations. For example, when addressing people's feelings one is apt to tap the more manifest, as opposed to the latent content, and these may differ. Yet I agree with Polansky and his coauthors (1981) that while people's responses cannot be taken at face value, neither ought one automatically assume that all people distort their reports. We did not have the luxury of extended interviewing, but had to content ourselves with what the respondents could and would describe. But as Campbell (1981:18) wisely stated: "No doubt something is lost in this procedure, but a great deal is gained." What is lost in depth is gained in scope, since the focus can be on a more representative group of cases. A further shortcoming of a single interview is the variability of moods and feelings. No doubt, there are fluctuations that occur over time that are missed. This would be a problem in describing a particular individual, but does not pose a serious difficulty when averages are used, since such short-term swings or the possible influences of recent events tend to average out. Furthermore, we attempted to discourage reactions to a particular moment in time by prefacing certain key questions with a phrase such as "these days" or by providing a broader time frame.

Much of the ground we covered was factual, but naturally we were also interested in the young adults' subjective feelings about themselves, other people, and various aspects of their world. The factual material and their feelings about various parts of their lives are indivisible, for they are the multiple strands that in some complex combination address the question of how they fare. I will not disentangle all of these threads. I will, however, review various aspects of their lives and examine their linkage, or lack thereof, to the young adults' own subjective assessments of how they fare.

But what did I use as a measure of that subjective state, a state I will call their sense of well-being? After considerable study I decided to use a global measure whose reliability and construct validity had been extensively examined (Andrews and Withey 1976). It consisted of the average score of two administrations of the same item that asked "How do you feel about your life as a whole?" The two questions were separated by 10 to 20 minutes of interview time. In each instance the respondents were asked to select one of seven responses along a continuum that moved from "delighted" to "terrible." In the case of questionnaire respondents, the question was asked only once. It became quite clear in subsequent analyses that this global measure of well-being was intimately tied to two other measures—Rosenberg's (1965) 10-item self-esteem scale and a question that asked "Taken all together, how would you say things are for you these days—would you say they are very happy, pretty happy, or not too happy?" Both conceptually and from the standpoint of reliability, it made sense to combine these three measures into one score after appropriate conversions. The sense of well-being as used throughout this book refers to this index.

Problems of Interpretation

Again and again I will pose the question of what factors— whether from their background, the experiences in their foster care placement, or from their life at the time of our contacts—are associated with their sense of well-being. The search for the meaning of such connections often led me along a tortuous trail of subgroup analyses in order to gain a better understanding. An example can clarify what was involved. Imagine the following hypothetical finding: that young adults who were married had a more positive sense of well-being than those who were not. In order to understand this better it was important to examine whether this was equally true for males and females, for those with or without children, for those with or without fairly serious emotional problems at the time they were discharged from foster homes or group care, and so on. In principle, the task of tracing linkages was an endless one. Common sense and a sprinkling of knowledge were helpful guides, but no doubt some things were missed. In any event, in what follows I will not burden the reader with the details of this intricate search, except on rare occasion.

A few words of caution are in order. As associations are described, it is important to bear in mind the distinction between concomitance and cause. Meaningful associations are often simply part of a causal chain. An equally serious distinction is necessary between causal factors and consequences. The question here is what preceded what in time. For instance, when one examines placement experiences from case records, it is clear that these preceded the young adults' sense of well-being at the time of our contacts. But other time sequences are not so clear. Suppose one finds that those who feel closer to a sibling also have a better sense of well-being. While, on the one hand, it is quite plausible that their close relationship influenced their well-being, it is also possible that their better well-being influenced what they said about closeness. I will sometimes puzzle about such ambiguities. One last proviso is in order. In a study with many variables, some connections that are statistically significant can be purely chance associations. My approach was to look for consistencies and trends that made sense, rather than isolated events.

Internal "within sample" comparisons can tell one a great deal about the way in which different groups, all from foster care, varied in their sense of well-being some years after their discharge from foster care. Such analyses allowed me to raise and address questions about the relative impact of the foster care experience on, for instance, males when compared with females. Yet, even then, utmost care was, and is, required before any inference about impact is possible. That word concerns a very complex set of events in the past, of which the foster care experience was but one. Other aspects of the young adults' histories, including their genetic and psychosocial backgrounds may have influenced not only that experience but also their sense of well-being at the time of our contacts. In a study like this it is not possible to isolate the precise elements at work.

But the point here is that such "within sample" comparisons cannot shed light on the important question of how young adults from foster care fare vis-à-vis others who were not in foster care. Since the question of "as compared with whom" had dogged many past studies, several approaches were attempted here. One logical comparison group that we proceeded to identify consisted of siblings, close in age, who had not entered foster care. But since this potential roster dwindled because most siblings had been placed or had, for instance, left with an aunt for distant parts many years ago, this mode of approach was abandoned. Adoptees who were born and placed at about the same time as our sample, and who were alike on race and sex, were also sought as a potential comparison group. Such a list, consisting of 140 young adults, was identified at one "test" agency which also sent out letters to the adoptive families inviting the young adults to contact us in order to let us know of their interest in participating. A large number of these letters were returned to the agency with the notation "addressee unknown" or there was no response. Since we had no names or addresses, or access to any other information, it was not possible to attempt to reach this group in a manner similar to that employed with the sample from foster care. Some adoptees did wish to participate, but we did not proceed with this group because of my concern about self-selective biases. Hence, this approach was also abandoned. In the end, I relied on a series of comparisons with the same age groups from three general population surveys. Despite some problems with comparability, the possibility of examining a wide variety of areas where identical questions had been asked was fortunate. These analyses were augmented by comparisons with data furnished by several investigators and a number of New York State and New York City agencies. Thus, ultimately I was in a position to examine whether and how those who were in foster care differed from those who were not.

General Plan of the Book

To fully understand the present, one needs to know about the past. The young adults' background and experiences in foster care form a backdrop against which their current life can best be viewed. Part I of this book deals with that background and with the period they were in placement. It examines what aspects of the young adults' past are linked to their sense of well-being in the present. Part II moves into the present—the lives of the young people at the time of our contacts. A broad picture will be provided by singling out important sectors of their "current" experience, from both a factual and a subjective point of view. Connections with their sense of well-being will again be examined. Comparisons with older adults from foster care will permit one to see whether unusual changes occur with the passage of more years. And comparisons with the general population will deal with the issue of how the young adults fare. Finally, Part III concerns their view of foster care and their suggestions. At the outset of this study that was one objective. As it turned out, there was compensation for time gone by, for in the words of some: "They should listen to children more . . . this study should have been done years ago . . . the people in foster care should be believed and listened to . . . nobody ever asked us."

PART ONE

THE YOUNG ADULTS AT AND DURING FOSTER CARE PLACEMENT

Chapter Two

THE YOUNG ADULTS' PAST

Try not to think about your background, for it'll only hold you back
because you are now you . . . and it's you who has to be the one
to survive by yourself and have your own identity.

Questionnaire
March 1980

As background for what is to come, I will begin by describing
the young adults, their families, and what led to their placement. Except where noted, this information came from case
records. While these records were usually voluminous, the information about family background was often sparse and provided little documentation about the events of their life before
placement. I will report whatever was gleaned from them.
Throughout, the amount of missing information will be noted
so that the reader can judge what weight to atttach to the information.

In approaching the task of describing the young adults and
their families, a decision had to be made whether to describe
the total group or just those who were respondents. Two
factors were of major importance in making the decision. First,
very few differences were observed between those who were
and those who were not respondents. Second, it seemed desirable for the sake of clarity to maintain a steady focus on the
277 young adults who eventually became respondents. Therefore, I decided to concentrate on the latter, the sample, in the

discussion that follows, although instances of differences between this group and the nonrespondents will be pointed out.

The sample consisted of 161 (58.1%) males and 116 (41.9%) females. It is not clear whether males predominated because more were placed in foster care or more remained there until young adulthood. To begin to assess this, one would have to know the sex distribution of children placed in New York City during the years that our sample entered care. Unfortunately, such information was not available.

Ethnicity and Religious Preference

Although the young adults' self-designations as to ethnicity and religion are not strictly part of their background, they will be described because both are heavily influenced by that background. A description of the ethnic makeup of the sample involves some complications that are not readily apparent. One can talk about the young adults' ethnic background or their current self-perception, realizing that the two approaches do not necessarily yield identical results. Some youngsters, for instance, were never fully told about their ethnic background and relied on their own physical features for an ethnic designation. Others were placed cross-ethnically and grew up using the ethnic identification of their foster parents. Situations in which the youngster knew the ethnicity of only one parent were more common and resulted in various bases for self-designation.

Of the 277 mothers somewhat more than one-half (51.3%) were black, 27.4% were white, 20.2% were Hispanic, and a few were recorded as Oriental. Information was available on only 209 putative fathers. Of these 38.3% were recorded as black, 32.1% as white, 26.8% as Hispanic, and once again a small group as Oriental. Where information on both parents existed, it was clear that most unions were between people of the same ethnic group. Only 25 of the unions were known to be mixed.

The interviews and questionnaires gave us the opportunity

to ask the young adults how they perceived themselves. Most agreed with the case record material concerning one or both biological parents. However, young adults from interracial unions rarely regarded themselves as mixed; instead, they aligned themselves ethnically with one or the other parent. Thus a black-white mixture sometimes led to a white, and sometimes to a black self-designation. The important point here is that studies in the field of foster care will inevitably contain a certain amount of error in designating ethnicity unless the child's perspective is also included.

For our description in subsequent analyses we used the respondents' self-designations. As already mentioned, in most instances there were no discrepancies between the young adults' views and what was in the record about either a mother, a father, or both. For instance, if in the case record a mother was white, a father was black, and the young adult called himself black, that person was designated as black. However, eight cases could not be classified since the young adults did not know, or used a designation like "human," in response to our question. These were not included in our ethnic analyses. In addition two cases were omitted, perhaps mistakenly, because the self-designations were totally at variance with the case record material, as in the case of a young man who said he was black although the records indicated a white mother and a Hispanic father. In both instances the interviewers were skeptical of the validity of the subjects' responses. All together, 10 cases were excluded. The remaining 267 designated themselves as 51.7% black, 27.7% white, 19.1% Hispanic, and 1.5% Oriental.

The records contained the religious designations of 270 mothers. Of these 51.9% were Protestant, 40% were Catholic, 7.4% were Jewish, and a few were another religion such as Buddhist. Information on 174 fathers showed that 37.9% were Protestant, 48.2% were Catholic, 11.5% were Jewish, and the small remainder were of another religion. Most unions were between people of the same religion; only 23 were known to be mixed.

All but three of the young adults answered a question about

their religion. Of these 274, some 35.4% said they were of the Protestant faith (primarily Baptist), 33.2% stated they were Catholic, and 6.2% said they were Jewish. An array of other faiths were mentioned by 9.9% of the respondents, including Islam, Jehovah's Witnesses, Buddhism, the Pentecostal faith, and the Unification Church. The remaining respondents, some 15.3%, considered themselves to have no formal religious affiliation at the time of our interviews. This was equally true of both men and women, but occurred more among those from group care (23.7%) than among those from foster homes (12.1%).

Age of Parents at Birth and Placement

When the young adults in our sample were born their mothers (N = 265) were on the average about 26 years old and their fathers (N = 204) were on the average 32. There was considerable variation in age, with mothers ranging from 14 to 43 years and fathers ranging from 15 to 64. The males in our sample tended on the average to have younger parents than did the females. This can readily be seen in table 2.1. This peculiarity exists because females who did not respond had younger parents than did the respondents. In the overall population of 421 cases, of course, there were no differences between males and females in the parents' ages at birth.

By the time our sample came into placement, there were 28 whose mothers and 22 whose fathers had died. As for the rest, the mothers' average age was 30.2 years, and the fathers averaged 36 years of age. Once again there were large variations in the ages of each, as can be seen in table 2.1. Not shown in the table is the fact that those who were eventually discharged from foster homes had younger parents at the point of placement than did those who were discharged from group settings. The mothers of the former group averaged 28.8 years at placement, whereas the mothers of those discharged from group settings averaged 34 years of age when their children were placed. Fathers paralleled this differential and were in

Table 2.1
Age of Biological Parents at Birth and at Initial Placement

	(N)	Mean	S.D.	Minimum	Maximum
At Birth					
Male Respondents					
Age of mother	(151)	25.3	5.5	14	41
Age of father	(109)	30.9	9.1	15	63
Female respondents					
Age of mother	(114)	27.1	6.3	14	43
Age of father	(95)	33.5	10.2	15	64
At Initial Placement					
Male respondents					
Age of mother	(139)	30.1	7.5	14	53
Age of father	(99)	35.6	10.6	15	73
Female respondents					
Age of mother	(100)	30.4	7.4	14	48
Age of father	(87)	36.4	11.0	14	70

each instance an average of 6 years older than the mothers. There is no mystery in these numbers, for there was a strong relationship ($r = .60$) between the ages of the children and their parents at the time of placement, and the ages of the children at placement was an element in whether they were eventually discharged from a foster home or a group setting.

It is important to note in passing that the parents were generally not youngsters. Could this have had a bearing on why these young adults remained in placement? In the absence of parental age comparisons for children who did not remain in foster care, one does not know. Perhaps they were not very young because conditions such as neglect take time to develop and to be noticed. It is, therefore, likely that the situations that brought many children into placement had existed for some time and were part of the early history that preceded their placement.

Birth Weight

Information on birth weight could be valuable since very low weight could indicate nutritional deficiency or poor early prenatal care. Unfortunately, such information was available in only 88 of the 277 records. I have no firm idea about the reasons for its inclusion or omission. The fact that such information was much less likely to be available for those eventually discharged from a group setting than for those discharged from foster homes provided a hint. Since the latter tended to be younger at the time they were placed, and some in fact were infants, such information may simply have been more readily available at the time or more easily recalled by parents.

Of the 88 with information available, close to one-fourth (23.9%) had a birth weight below 5½ pounds. This tended to occur more among those who were eventually discharged from group settings (46.2%) than among those eventually discharged from foster homes (20%). Perhaps there was a link between low birth weight and subsequent problems, which in turn resulted in more of these youngsters being placed, eventually at least, in a group setting.

Education, Economic Support, and Employment of Parents

The case records yielded limited information on the education and work histories of the parents of our respondents. Of the 172 mothers where information was available, 18% were high school graduates and 3.4% had some college education. Thirty-two percent had some high school credits, and 46.5% had completed ninth grade or less. Close to 21% had not gone beyond grade school.

Information was available on only 83 fathers. Slightly more than 24% had completed high school and close to 5% had some college. Somewhat over 31% had some high school credits, and close to 40% had completed ninth grade or less. This included some 30% who had not gone beyond grade school.

Information on the parents' economic support at placement was available for 210 mothers and 130 fathers. About 41% of the mothers and 21% of the fathers were receiving some form of public assistance, social security, or benefits from the Veterans Administration. Some 27.2% of the mothers but only

1.5% of the fathers were financially dependent on their spouses or families. Some parents were residents of institutions such as hospitals, jails, or training schools at the time their children were placed. These accounted for the support of 21% of the mothers and 6.2% of the fathers. Finally, earnings were the economic mainstay of 11.4% of the mothers and 71.5% of the fathers at that time.

By 1975, when the 277 young adults were discharged from foster care, 75 of the mothers and 50 fathers were known to have died. Some parents had disappeared and information on the sources of economic support of others was missing. Thus, we had information on only 125 mothers and 64 fathers. Close to 61% of these mothers were receiving public assistance or some other public support, 15.2% were supported by husbands and other family members, and 5.6% were residents of institutions. Earnings were the principal support of 18.4%, who were working primarily in various service and clerical positions. As for that small group of fathers for whom there was information at the time our young adults were discharged, close to 30% were receiving public support, primarily some form of welfare, and 1.6% were residing in institutions. The rest (68.8%) were supported primarily by their own earnings, a majority of them service workers or operatives of various sorts.

On the whole, then, the biological families occupied the lower rungs of the socioeconomic ladder. They were families with limited educational backgrounds and scant financial resources. Their situation was similar to that described by others in the past (see, for example, Giovannoni and Billingsley 1970). It is, therefore, doubtful that the picture would have been altered if the gaps in information had been filled.

Marital Status of Parents

The records of 273 respondents contained only general information on the marital status of the mothers and putative fathers at the time our sample was born. At that time close to

58% were either married or living together in a common law relationship.

At the time the young adults were placed, information on the marital status of the respondents' mothers vis-à-vis the putative fathers was more detailed and was available in 231 case records. In 31.6% of these cases the parents had been married, but by the time of placement the mothers were separated, divorced, or widowed. About 23% were still married or living together with the fathers in common law relationships. In the remaining cases (45%) the mothers and putative fathers had never been married to each other and were now living apart.

By 1975, when the young adults were discharged from foster care, some of these 231 mothers were no longer alive and information was missing for others. The mother's relationship with the putative father was spelled out in 158 case records. Only 10.1% of these parents were living together in marital or common law relationships at that point in time. Somewhat more than 8% of the mothers were widows and the rest had separated or were divorced from the fathers of the young adults. Instability of the parents' relationships was the pattern rather than the exception.

The picture of the marital status of the mothers vis-à-vis the putative fathers is, however, not an adequate portrayal, for over time some mothers had married or were living in common law relationships with others. We had such information about 138 mothers who were alive at the time the young adults were discharged. Somewhat over 23% had never married; 27.5% were married or living in common law relationships; and slightly over 49% were separated, divorced, or widowed. Information on only 81 living fathers was available at the time of discharge. Close to 56% were married or living in common law relationships; 42% were separated, divorced, or widowed; and only a few had never married.

Unfortunately, the absence of so much information makes it difficult to draw any firm conclusions beyond those already mentioned. The young adults came from homes where the parents generally did not maintain ongoing relationships with each other over time. Although some of the mothers and fathers established relationships with others, this did not characterize the large majority.

Birth Order and Siblings

As pointed out earlier, when the young adults were born the parents were generally not youngsters themselves. In fact, only 21.7% of the 272 on whom we had information were first-born children, and close to 56% were the third or later arrival in the family. A few (2.9%) were the eighth or ninth child to be born.

Thus, a majority of the mothers already had children at the time the young adults were born, and many had given birth to additional children by the time the ones in our sample came into placement. Only about one in ten families had no other known children at that time. The rest had anywhere from 1 to 13 other children, with an average of 3.

Some of the siblings of the young adults in our sample were much older and living independently, some were living with relatives, and others had been placed in foster care. Many of the sample children came into care together with some siblings, and others joined brothers and sisters already in placement. Some siblings were separated from each other at the point of placement or were placed in the care of different agencies that did not discover this for years, if ever. There were so many diverse and complex situations that it would have been impossible to capture this in any accurate way without spending much more time than we had available. Our general impression was that when siblings or half siblings were placed at the same time, as many were, the tendency was to keep them together in the same agency and most often under the same roof.

Among those who had siblings there were very few—7% at most—who were the only ones in their families known to have ever been placed in foster care. The situation of those who were placed was, therefore, not unique. Yet only eleven sibling pairs, including four sets of twins, became a part of the sample of 277 respondents. There were perhaps others who were never identified. This could have occurred in situations where siblings were placed at different times, were under the care of different agencies, and had different surnames.

In any event most of the sample had other siblings, either older or younger, who were also in foster care at some point during the time the young adults were in placement. And in most instances at least some of them were in touch with each other. This is easily demonstrated by looking at their last years in foster care. During that time slightly over 70% of the sample had one or more brothers or sisters who were still in foster care, and 91% of these were in contact with at least one of their siblings.

The Whereabouts of Parents at Placement and Discharge

At the time the young adults were placed, about 10% of their mothers and 8% of their fathers had died, including a few situations where both parents were dead. The whereabouts of 10.1% of the mothers and over one-third of the fathers were unknown. About 54% of the mothers were living in the community in New York and a few (1.8%) lived elsewhere in the continental United States or Puerto Rico. About 18% were confined to mental institutions, some 5% were in correctional facilities, and several were living in foster care themselves. Most of the fathers (53.8%) also resided in the community, and 2.9% were known to be in institutional facilities.

By 1975, when the young adults were discharged, 27.1% of their mothers and 18.1% of their fathers were known to have died, including 5.4% where both were deceased. The whereabouts of close to 16% of the mothers and nearly 50% of the

fathers were unknown. About 3% of the mothers were confined to mental hospitals. The rest of the mothers and fathers
were residing in the community in the New York area, and a
small number were living elsewhere in the United States or in
Puerto Rico.

Although the whereabouts of the mothers was most often
known, there was meager information about the fathers. In
fact, the whereabouts of only 10 mothers, but of 81 fathers,
were unknown both at placement and at discharge. Some of
these parents may have appeared at some point during the
placement period and then disappeared again. Our review of
these large records could have missed such instances. Nevertheless, the fathers were more apt to drop out of the picture,
in some cases prior to placement. The mothers, on the other
hand, were not generally people who placed their children and
then disappeared for the remainder of placement, although
there may have been lengthy gaps between appearances and
precise information about place of residence was often lacking.

It is startling that by the time the young adults in our sample were 18 to 21 years old and were discharged, such a sizable number had at least one parent who was known to have
died. Obviously they hailed from families whose survival was
at risk, whether because of age, physical illness, or environmental hardships.

Caretakers Before Placement

No description of the young adults would be complete without some mention of their principal caretakers before they
were placed. The precipitating events that led to placement
were sometimes sudden, such as a caretaker's death or hospi-
talization, so that the living arrangements for a child could
shift rather abruptly in the days or weeks before the child entered foster care. First the children's principal caretakers prior

to the events that led to their placement will be described, and then their living arrangements at the time of placement will be examined.

Information was available on 244 children who had lived in the community, that is, had not been placed directly from a hospital after their birth. A large majority—close to 76%— had been cared for by their mothers or both parents together. A father was the primary child carer in only 3% of the cases. Relatives in conjunction with either or both parents accounted for the care of close to 10% of the children, and for 7% a relative alone was mainly responsible. The remaining 4.5% were cared for principally by others, such as neighbors or the parents' friends.

At the time of placement the children's primary caretakers differed somewhat. We had information about this on 276 children. Slightly more than 11% came into placement directly from hospitals or institutions where they had been born. Of the 245 living in the community, most (60.8%) were cared for by their mothers or both parents, and somewhat over 12% resided with their fathers. Some 18% were cared for by relatives and 9% by people outside of the family.

The shifts that had occurred in living arrangements prior to placement were thus primarily of two sorts. More of the children were living with their fathers and with people who were not family members, and fewer were with their mothers. In the main this was a function of the death of some mothers and the institutionalization of others.

Such a neat picture does not, however, adequately describe the helter-skelter child care arrangements and shifting scene that for some preceded placement. The records often conveyed the impression of families beset by circumstances beyond their control, or of adults unable or unwilling to cope with their situation or with themselves. In some homes there was a parade of caretakers, or none at all, or older children taking care of the younger ones when a mother or father was absent. For these youngsters the period prior to placement was often turbulent and filled with uncertainty.

Reasons for Placement and Court Involvement

A majority of the 277 young adults—some 66.8%—came into foster care on a voluntary basis, which is about the same percentage that has prevailed in New York City over the years. The remainder were placed through the Family Court, as it is now called, and were primarily the result of petitions of neglect (31%). Abandonment, abuse, and PINS petitions accounted for the remaining 2.2% of the cases.

We used these court reports and all recordings connected with each child's entry into care in order to classify the main reason for placement in each case. In many instances there was more than one reason for a child's placement. These additional reasons, often secondary to the central reason, were also classified; each will be discussed in turn.

The main reasons for the initial placements of the 277 young adults are presented in table 2.2 in the order of their frequency. It can readily be seen that four primary reasons—ne-

Table 2.2
Main Reason for Initial Placement

	Males (N = 161)		Females (N = 116)		Total (N = 277)	
	N	(%)	N	(%)	N	(%)
Neglect	34	(21.1)	33	(28.4)	67	(24.2)
Mental illness of primary child caring person	31	(19.3)	25	(21.6)	56	(20.2)
Unable or unwilling to cope	18	(11.2)	16	(13.8)	34	(12.3)
Abandonment, desertion	21	(13.0)	12	(10.3)	33	(11.9)
Physical illness	14	(8.7)	9	(7.8)	23	(8.3)
Death	10	(6.2)	7	(6.0)	17	(6.1)
Unable or unwilling to assume care	8	(5.0)	8	(6.9)	16	(5.8)
Incarceration	7	(4.3)	2	(1.7)	9	(3.2)
Behavior of child	7	(4.3)	2	(1.7)	9	(3.2)
Family conflict	7	(4.3)	0	—	7	(2.5)
Abuse	3	(1.9)	1	(0.9)	4	(1.4)
Retardation	1	(0.6)	1	(0.9)	2	(0.7)
Total	161	(100)	116	(100)	277	(100)

glect, mental illness, coping problems, and abandonment—were responsible for a majority (68.6%) of the placements. No material differences existed between the males and females. There were two foster home–group care differences that were not surprising. All who were placed early because no one would assume their care were eventually discharged from foster homes, while all who were placed because of behavior problems left group care.

The main reasons these young adults entered care are not so different from what has been reported by others, although differences in systems of classification make comparisons quite hazardous. Perhaps mental illness among the principal caretakers was more common in our sample (See, for example, Shyne and Schroeder 1978; Lash, Sigal, and Dudzinski 1980). Another distinction concerned child related problems, which were less frequently a precipitating factor in our sample. It has been noted that such children tend to come from a wider range of socioeconomic backgrounds and from families that are more apt to be intact (Kadushin 1980). Perhaps they remain in care for less extensive periods of time and are therefore less likely to be a part of a group that stays in foster care until young adulthood.

A fuller picture of what led to the placements can be gained by examining all of the reasons, both primary and secondary, that were classified. After all, in any one situation a combination of two or even more factors may have been important. Not all of the reasons shown in table 2.2 will be reviewed—just those that highlight the situation in these families at placement. For instance, neglect was a factor, whether primary or secondary, in 46.5% of the 277 sample cases. Mental illness of the primary caretaker was a factor in 35.4% of the cases, and 23.5% of the caretakers were physically ill. Family conflict was also apparent in a large group (24.2%) of cases. Finally, abandonment led to the placement of 19.8% of the youngsters, and for 9% there was some indication of physical abuse. We also noted instances where housing problems or severe financial strain contributed to the placement. Instances of severe overcrowding, eviction, fire, and the inability to obtain speedy financial aid were so classified. In 33.9% of the cases these added factors led to placement in foster care.

Clearly many in the sample came from family situations in which there was turmoil and some form of illness. In many situations children had been neglected and some had been deserted, abused, or both. Housing problems and severe poverty were often additional and important facts of their life before placement.

One important area has been omitted in the presentation so far, namely, alcohol and drug use as factors in the placement of the children. When heavy use by a parent or primary caretaker was mentioned, or when a child was born with withdrawal symptoms, we noted it. It is quite possible that here there is an undercount, especially with regard to drugs, since the intake staff did not routinely gather such information. On the other hand, a large proportion of our sample came into placement in the 1950s and early 1960s when drug use was not as prevalent as in more recent years. In any event, in 26.3% of the cases a parent or other primary caretaker was known to be a heavy user of alcohol, but in only 5% of the cases was a parent addicted to drugs. These factors also need to be added as contributors to the placement of the 277 young adults.

Mental Hospitals and Correctional Facilities

As noted earlier, a fair proportion of the sample came into placement as a result, at least in part, of their caretakers' mental illness. Many of the mothers and fathers were seriously disturbed at some point in their lives. To underscore this fact one can examine whether they were ever admitted to a mental hospital, excluding brief diagnostic evaluations. Once again we relied on any mention in the case records, and therefore may have an undercount again, particularly for fathers. Information was available on 256 mothers and 172 fathers. Some 7.6% of the fathers were known to have been admitted to a mental hospital at some time, as compared with 36.3% of the mothers. Some had been in such institutions on a number of occasions.

Unfortunately, we could not obtain precise information on when these mental hospital admissions occurred, or on how long they lasted. Some of the admissions took place prior to placement and some later. But we can surmise that a fair number of the young adults were exposed to a mentally ill parent as they were growing up, and that there must have been periods of time when a parent, particularly a mother, was less than available to nurture them.

Time served by parents in correctional facilities also must have interfered with such availability. Once again we had information about 256 mothers and 172 fathers. Some 20.4% of the latter and 16% of the former were known to have spent some time in a jail, prison, or house of detention.

Some parents had, of course, been in both mental and penal institutions, but they comprised only a small minority. All in all, then, 26.7% of the fathers and 49.2% of the mothers on whom we had any information had spent some time in either or both types of institutions while the young adults were growing up.

Although our picture of the parents is far from complete, the available material sheds some light on the young adults' backgrounds. It suggests that many of the parents experienced great pressures, whether internal, external, or both, in their lives. When that stress became too severe, and adequate support from relatives, friends, or the community was not available, not provided, or too late to be used, the situation disintegrated. And ultimately the children came into foster care.

Background and Sense of Well-Being

An important question has been omitted from this discussion so far. Was anything from the description of the young adults or their backgrounds associated with their sense of well-being at the time of our contacts with them? Only two factors stood out—their religious preference and the primary reason for their placement.

Actually there were no differences in the sense of well-being among those of different religions, but those who stated that they had no religious preference—whether discharged from a foster home or group setting—had a poorer sense of well-being than those who voiced a religious preference. One does not know which came first. Did those who claimed no preference eventually have a poorer outlook on life? Or did a poor outlook lead them to become more alienated from various social institutions, including an organized religion? It is also possible that the absence of a religious preference was a function of a generally critical outlook on life, and this in turn led them to describe themselves as less satisfied with their lives in general. If so, the young adults from foster care were similar in this respect to Americans in general (Campbell 1981).

The second factor connected with their sense of well-being was the main reason for their placement. It is likely that some contingencies that result in placement are easier for a child to accept than are others. Death and physical illness are most clear-cut, a consequence of circumstances beyond anyone's control, and perhaps easiest to accept. Mental illness is probably more difficult to accept because the caretaker seems physically healthy yet does not continue to care for a child; and factors such as abandonment, neglect, and unwillingness or inability to cope can be viewed as the most difficult for a child to accept since the parent not only is healthy but deserts the child physically or psychologically. It seemed plausible that if such a hierarchy of acceptance existed, it might ultimately have an impact on the sense of well-being of the young adults. Two assumptions were necessary, however. First, one had to assume that the children were or became aware of the reason why they were placed. The second assumption concerned the salience of the main reason for placement when secondary reasons clouded such a neat hierarchy because of inevitable overlaps. Yet, because I felt that the reason for placement could serve as a symbol of the young adults' background, I made both assumptions to gain a rough picture of its influence on their sense of well-being. It clearly had an impact. Those who were placed because of neglect or abandonment, or because their caretakers could or would no longer cope ultimately had a poorer sense of themselves and their lives than those who were placed for reasons that were more apt to have been seen as beyond immediate parental control (such as death, physical illness, or imprisonment). Those who were placed because of parental mental illness were in between. This was equally true of males and females, and of those discharged from foster homes or group settings.

It is noteworthy that this rough indicator of the children's background had a bearing on how they eventually felt as young adults. Yet the connection was by no means perfect, for there were some who had been deserted or neglected who felt relatively good about their lives, while some who were placed because of the death or illness of parents eventually felt relatively poorly. But on the average the connection was a statistically significant one. It probably tells us something indirectly about the effects of early family experiences if we can make the reasonable assumption that those who were placed because of neglect or desertion probably had been exposed to a less nurturing environment than those whose placement was necessitated by parental death or illness. The effect on the young adults' later sense of well-being was therefore probably a function of the impact of early experiences coupled with a greater difficulty in eventually finding an acceptable explanation for why they were placed. There were even some who as adults continued to feel that their placement had not been necessary. Although there were only 32 who felt that way, a majority (79.3%) of them had been placed for reasons such as neglect or desertion, and on the whole their sense of well-being as young adults was poorer than that of those who thought their placement had been necessary.

It is noteworthy that so few aspects of background were

connected with the young adults' sense of well-being. Perhaps the family characteristics we examined were in fact ultimately not so important. Perhaps the absence of connections was a function of the limited information available in the case records. There were gaps in the background material; the quality of the information varied; and potentially important areas of early history were often not mentioned. The records were much more apt to focus on the immediate events that led to the placement and on the history of that placement.

Chapter Three

PLACEMENT CHARACTERISTICS

We're not to be pitied . . . we just need a family . . . we're not
going to fall apart . . . people get used to many things . . . they
adapt . . . we should be treated special . . . but not too special.

Interview
January 1980

The young adults were all born between 1954 and 1957 and
were placed in foster care by 1970. A majority entered care
before 1963, as can be seen in table 3.1. Once placed, most
remained in care continuously until they reached the age of
majority. At a minimum they were in placement for the five
years immediately preceding their discharge in 1975. Most
were in placement much longer.

From 1954 onward the 277 young adults became a part of
each year's statistics on "children remaining in foster care."
Most others their age who were placed during those years did
not have the same fate; they were either adopted or returned
to their homes. Why not the 277 young adults? Did they differ
in some peculiar way? In the absence of any vital information
about the others, one cannot answer such questions.

Yet we do know that most of those in our sample were neither physically nor cognitively handicapped, nor emotionally
disturbed at the time they entered placement. We also know
that most were not free for adoptive placement. Rather, there
were those who had families with a strong interest in main-

Table 3.1
Year of Initial Placement

	Discharged From:				Total (N = 277)	
	Foster Home		Group Setting			
	M (N = 109)	F (N = 92)	M (N = 52)	F (N = 24)	N	(%)
1954–1958	49.5%	55.4%	21.2%	25.0%	122	44.0
1959–1962	30.3	27.1	15.4	25.0	72	26.0
1963–1966	15.6	10.9	19.2	33.3	45	16.2
1967–1970	4.6	6.5	44.2	16.7	38	13.7
	100.0%	99.9%	100.0%	100.0%	277	99.9

Note: in this and subsequent tables, M = males, F = females.

taining ties, others where the claim of such interest was never tested, and still others who were a product of drift and what Kadushin (1980) has called "a default in decision making."

A few historical facts will provide a perspective on their situation. One needs only to recall that the period during which many of the young adults were placed coincided with the early study by Maas and Engler (1959) that depicted children adrift in foster care, children described by the then director of the Child Welfare League of America (Reid 1959) as "orphans of the living." It was also a time when, in a well-publicized case in the New York courts (JCCA 1959), a child was ordered removed from foster parents because their relationship with the child was too close. It was a time when Boehm (1958) provided evidence of serious deterrents to the adoption of children and when New York State laws were such as to preclude freeing children for adoption unless there was clear proof of abandonment, which the courts generally did not recognize (Polier 1959). Remedial legislation that created a new legal category, the "permanently neglected child," did not become effective until 1959. Furthermore, the organization and some of the attitudes and practices of social agencies hindered, rather than encouraged, the adoption of children. Finally, adoption subsidies were not yet available and, unlike recent years, less emphasis was placed on finding permanent arrangements for children. In short, when these young adults came into placement a variety of factors converged to keep them in foster care, and they soon became the harder-to-place older ones. These factors, rather than any peculiar characteristics of the children themselves, were most likely at issue in their becoming a part of the annual "remaining in care" statistics.

A word of explanation should be given about the terminology to be used here. As already pointed out, a majority of the 277 young adults who became respondents had been discharged in 1975 from foster homes (72.6%). As for the rest, 8.3% came from group homes, 6.5% from group residences, and 12.6% from institutions. These three forms of group care no doubt vary in a number of ways. One distinguishing characteristic concerns the number of children they accommodate, with group homes having the smallest number and institutions the largest number of children at any one time. But individual institutions, for example, also differ from one another in a variety of ways, including their location, facilities, number and quality of staff, and the philosophy and quality of care they provide. The respondents were too few in number to make such distinctions in analyzing the material. There were even too few for a separate examination of those from group homes, group residences, and institutions, except on occasion. Therefore, in much of what follows these will be combined, and we will refer to "group settings" or "group care" in many comparisons of these 76 young adults with the 201 who were discharged from foster homes.

Age at Placement and Time in Care

At the time they were initially placed, the young adults ranged in age from infancy to 16 years, the median falling at 3.1 years. Close to 45% were under 3 years old at the time, and another 26.8% were 3 through 6 years old. About 94% were 12 or less at the time they were first placed.

Those who were older at placement were apt to spend more

of their time in, and to be discharged from, one or another group setting. This was in line with the prevalent notion that such older youngsters would benefit from an environment that permitted more distance from adults, that provided ample opportunity for interaction with a peer group, and that stressed the achievement of independence from the family group.

Those who were eventually discharged from foster homes were therefore on the average younger when they were placed than those who were discharged from group settings. The differences can readily be seen in table 3.2. The foster home group ranged in age from about one week to 13 years at the time they entered care, and their median age was 2.2 years. Some of those eventually discharged from group settings had been placed at birth, but they ranged in age to 16, and their

Table 3.2
Placement Characteristics

	Discharged From:							
	Foster Home				*Group Setting*			
	M (N = 109)		F (N = 92)		M (N = 52)		F (N = 24)	
	Mean	(S.D.)	Mean	(S.D.)	Mean	(S.D.)	Mean	(S.D.)
Age (yrs.) at initial placement	3.9	(3.4)	3.5	(3.5)	8.6	(4.9)	6.4	(4.4)
Age (yrs.) at final placement	4.3	(3.6)	4.0	(3.7)	9.4	(4.7)	7.7	(4.6)
Length (yrs.) of this placement	15.3	(3.8)	15.7	(4.0)	10.1	(4.8)	11.7	(4.5)
Length (yrs.) of total placement	15.4	(3.7)	16.0	(3.8)	10.3*	(4.8)	12.4	(4.2)
Age (yrs.) at discharge	19.6	(1.1)	19.7	(1.0)	19.4	(1.0)	19.3	(.9)
Number of shifts in care	2.6	(1.7)	2.1	(1.5)	2.0	(1.5)	3.2	(1.8)
Age (yrs.) at start of longest location	6.7	(4.0)	5.5†	(4.2)	11.0	(4.5)	8.8	(4.2)
Yrs. of longest location	11.1	(4.7)	13.0†	(4.7)	6.5	(3.5)	7.3	(3.1)

*Based on 50 cases because of missing information.
†Based on 91 cases because of missing information.

median age was 7.5 years at the time of placement. Actually one can think of those from group settings as consisting of two distinct groups: those initially placed into such settings because of their older age, and those who were initially placed in foster homes but subsequently transferred into group care. It is also clear from table 3.2 that males were on the average older than females at the time they came into placement. A larger proportion of them, therefore, were placed in, and discharged from, group settings.

Following initial placement, some young adults in the sample were discharged to their families, then they reentered foster care. This was true of 18 (9%) of those discharged from a foster home and 15 (19.7%) of those eventually discharged from a group setting. Usually this occurred only once. The time spent at home before returning to foster care was in most instances fairly short. For example, about two out of three of them were back in care within 23 months after their unsuccessful discharge.

These were all so-called final discharges that apparently did not work out. A few others returned home briefly on a trial basis. The main point here is that for a large majority the initial placement was synonymous with their final placement which continued until they were 18 to 21 years old.

There was, therefore, a strong inverse relationship between the young adults' age at original placement and the total time they spent in foster care. For those discharged from foster homes the average time in care was 15.7 years, with a median of 15.9 years; while those discharged from group settings averaged 11 years in care, with a median of 9.7 years. The total time in care for each group ranged from 5 years to 20 or 21 years.

Shifts and Types of Placements

I was lucky I wasn't moved a lot . . . my brother though was . . . like a little CARE package.

Interview
December 1979

You sometimes feel like a cereal box, going from shelf to shelf.

Interview
February 1980

If things don't work between you and the foster family, it's best to move.

Interview
August 1979

Much has been written about the desirability of placement stability and continuity. Changes in living arrangements are disruptive for a child and are thought to be emotionally burdensome. The impact of separation and possible feelings of rejection are among the dangers often cited. Lack of environmental consistency alone, even when ostensibly minor, can be confusing and a source of insecurity for a child.

The young adults in our sample had all been exposed to some disruption, some lack of constancy and consistency in the very process of being placed. Even prior to that time the environment had for many not been a stable haven, and for most of them their placement experience added further instability.

I sought to document the enormous variations in placement experiences by using two approaches. First, we counted all shifts in care following the initial placement, excluding any discharge home or reentry into foster care. We included temporary placements in mental hospitals or the facilities of the Division for Youth if the youngster was there for more than 30 days. We did not, however, include shifts that were voluntary such as when a young person ran away from a group home in order to return to a foster home. Our purpose was to enumerate all distinct environments to which each individual was assigned.

The second approach consisted of classifying each person according to type of placement—whether a foster home, agency-operated boarding home, group home, group residence, or institution—and the number of times a youngster had been in each type. The essential distinction between the two approaches was that one focused on shifts in environments irrespective of their character, the other on the different kinds of placements and their number. As the reader might well imagine, the latter approach resulted in an almost unmanageable variety of placement patterns. It became necessary to combine various types of placements into eleven patterns in subsequent analyses.

Before moving on with this discussion it might be useful to recall that during the 1950s and early 1960s when a majority in the sample were placed, a fair number of infant nurseries and children's shelters existed. These were used rather frequently as the entry point into foster care. Thus, about 50% of the total sample, whether eventually discharged from a foster home or not, began foster care in such group settings. Some entered care through other institutional settings, not called nurseries or shelters. The reliance on group settings while decisions were being made about desirable subsequent placements can clearly be seen if one examines the 201 adults who were discharged from foster homes. Only 34.3% had lived in one or more foster homes. The rest had all lived in a group setting and typically this occurred at the point of entry into foster care.

Placement in these entry institutions was frequently short in duration, but not always. For instance, an infant might remain in a group nursery for well over a year before being placed in a foster home. I was interested in each child's first long-term placement since this might have some bearing on later development. For this purpose any placement was considered long-term if it lasted six months or longer. For somewhat more than 39% of those who were later placed in and discharged from a foster home, the first long-term placement was in an institutional setting. Only two things distinguished them at placement as far as I could tell: their age and the religious affiliation of the agencies responsible for their care. They tended to be about a year older on the average (4.5 years) than those who were moved into a first long-term foster home more quickly, and more of them were placed in Catholic agencies.

Table 3.3 summarizes the total placement history of the young adults. Among those who were eventually discharged from foster homes, only 7.5% were in just one foster home; close to four out of ten (35.8%) were in one or two placements during their stay in foster care. Clearly a majority had a greater variety of placements. At a minimum this consisted of three foster homes or three placements in some combination of foster homes and group settings. At the opposite extreme, the maximum, it consisted of five or six foster homes in addition to some institutional care.

Of the young adults who were discharged from group settings, only about one out of ten resided in just one facility. Table 3.3 indicates a difference in the placement experiences of the males and females. The latter were more likely to have spent some time in a foster home than was true of the males. It is clear from table 3.3 that large differences existed in the ages at placement of those who had never lived in foster homes as opposed to those who did. For males and females alike those who had never been in a foster home were much older at the time of placement than those who were transferred into group settings from foster homes.

The picture, therefore, is not one of placement stability and continuity. Most of the young adults were shifted about as they

Table 3.3
Placements and Age at Entry into Care

	Discharged From:							
	Foster Home				Group Setting			
	M (N = 109)		F (N = 92)		M (N = 52)		F (N = 24)	
	%	mean age	%	mean age	%	mean age	%	mean age
or 2 foster homes only, or 1 foster home with 1 group setting	32.1	3.7	40.2	3.4	3.8	2.6	—	—
or more foster homes or mixed placements	67.9	4.0	59.8	3.6	19.2	3.1	58.3	4.4
or 2 group settings only	—	—	—	—	76.9	10.3	41.7	9.2
	100.0		100.0		99.9		100.0	

were growing up. Following placement the total group was shifted an average of 2.4 times during their stay in foster care, with a few of them shifted as many as eight times. They were shifted more frequently on the average than has been reported by others (Kadushin 1978; Shyne and Schroeder 1978). Most likely this was a function of their having been in care for a longer time.

Shifts sometimes included changes in the child caring agencies that were involved. In fact, in more than 63% of the sample there was at least one change in agency auspices during the time in care. This, among other things, also meant a change in the caseworker assigned to work with that child and family. Such changes often occurred even without an agency shift. Indeed, in reviewing the records, we had the feeling that there was an ever changing stream of caseworkers who left or shifted jobs in an agency, or who were by definition temporary because they were students assigned for an academic year.

There is yet another element in the life of a foster child that can produce a feeling of instability. Before their very eyes children in care watch other children arrive and depart. To make matters worse, it can occur without warning or while they are at school. The ones left behind may well wonder whose turn will be next.

The lack of continuity and consistency, therefore, came in many forms, and most of the young adults were exposed to all of them. But there is a brighter side of the picture. Although there was a lot of shifting about, for many of the children the shifts in care occurred early. For instance, among 183 children who had entered care by age 5, 69% had been shifted at least once before they reached that age and well over one-third of these had been shifted two or three times. So it would seem that for many the early years in care were the most unsettled ones. That is not the bright side, but it is also no surprise because it undoubtedly took some time for children, particularly those who were not infants, to adapt to being in placement; agencies also moved children about in an effort to find an appropriate fit between the children and foster parents or group settings. After a while, however, most of the children remained in one placement over an extended period of time. For the sake of illustration, table 3.2 shows that those who were discharged from foster homes began their longest placement when they averaged about 6 years of age and remained in that foster home an average of 12 years. There were, however, large variations in the length of time in that placement since this time span depended in part on their age at initial placement ($r = -.64$).

It was surprising to find a sex difference in the length of the longest placement among those from foster homes. Females, when compared with males, were about one year younger at the start of their longest placement and remained in that foster home for a longer time. Yet males and females who were discharged from foster homes did not differ in their age at original placement. At first glance it seemed possible that girls might have been thought of as easier to handle and thus were more quickly placed in a foster home and remained there. Perhaps boys were seen as, or were, more problematic at the start of placement and therefore it took longer to find a long-term arrangement for them. The case record information actually indicated that more of the boys exhibited psychological problems quite early in care.

After a review of the placement information, however, one might want to conclude that the sex difference in the length of the longest placement was an artifact. Girls were indeed placed in foster homes more readily than boys, but significantly more of them were also shifted out of such homes over time and placed into group settings when things did not work out. Thus, more of the young women who were discharged from group settings had been in a foster home earlier. When compared with females who remained in foster homes, they were about a year older at placement. Had they remained in foster homes, rather than been transferred to group care, they would have reduced the average length of the longest placement among the women eventually discharged from foster homes, and probably the observed sex difference among those from foster homes would have disappeared. The observed sex difference in age at the start of the longest placement and time in that foster home was therefore, at least in part, a function of who remained in a foster home until young adulthood rather than being transferred into a group setting.

To summarize, most children in our sample were shifted about quite early in their foster care experience. After these initial changes many of them remained in a stable location for an extended period of time. The shifts that occurred early in placement were usually in response to emergency or crisis situations, when there was little or no time to plan, and also a consequence of the way foster care was organized. Less emphasis was placed on planning for permanency than there is today, and foster care departments in agencies tended to be separate entities. These units officially tried to select placements for temporary care, even if this was often not the outcome. Given the assumption that such placements would be temporary, less stringent criteria were used in selecting foster parents than in choosing those who hoped to adopt. The label "short-term" was changed to "long-term" after a period of time, a practice that continues today, and often accompanied geographical shifts in placement. Thus, children were moved about following entry into care as workers planned for the children's future. These efforts often resulted, as Kadushin (1980:338) has pointed out, in "the best plan possible rather than the best possible plan," particularly when there were shortages of some kinds of placements but not of others. Administrative expediency, often a euphemism for filling vacancies, guided many plans that were made, and shifts occurred when a more appropriate placement became available. These factors, in conjunction with the prevalent use of group settings at entry into care, explain to a large extent the amount of shifting that occurred early in care.

But these factors do not explain all of the moves that occurred after these youngsters had been in placement for some time. They were generally of three sorts. The most common moves were due to problems that developed in a placement because of behavior or attitudes exhibited by the child, by kin, by foster parents, or by several of these in combination. For instance, there were foster homes where "the chemistry" no longer worked as the child became older, or the foster parents could not endure the turbulence often experienced with teenagers. Some placements were disrupted because of the behavior of the biological parents which the foster parents could not tolerate. Shifts also occurred sometimes at the insistence of kin if they felt that their child was not being properly treated, or perhaps if they feared competing with the foster parents for their child's allegiance. On occasion shifts were instigated by the foster children themselves. For instance, a small number told us of finding a foster home on their own among friendly neighbors in order to avoid a foster father's sexual advances, which the youngster was afraid to divulge to a caseworker. In such cases the new home was licensed subsequent to the move.

A second sort of move was more deliberately planned. In some situations youngsters were moved in order to be in the same location as their siblings. Other situations concerned children with severe emotional, cognitive, or physical problems who were shifted into a different kind of placement, such as a residential treatment facility, that could provide a specialized form of care that seemed needed at the time.

The third sort of move was a result of agency policies. In some instances a foster family had to leave New York for job-related reasons or because the family simply wanted to resettle elsewhere. Agencies responded differently to such situations. Some allowed a foster child to move with the foster family, whereas others did not, even if no kin were in the picture. Where biological family members were in touch with a child, this usually determined the decision. Agency policies also came into play if a foster parent became seriously ill or died. Single parent foster care was usually not acceptable, and so the child was shifted to another placement.

This brief review does not do justice to the multiplicity of reasons for replacement, factors that sometimes were compounded. I merely have tried to illustrate the kinds of situations that resulted in shifts while these young adults were growing up in care.

Their Reactions to Shifts in Placement

Only those whom we interviewed who recalled such a shift (N = 167) were asked whether they felt they had been moved "too much, about the right amount, or too little." Most (62.3%) felt generally satisfied, while 29.9% felt they had been moved too much, and 4.8% felt there had been too few shifts. These latter had been in generally unsatisfactory foster home situations. There were no sex differences among those discharged from foster homes, but among those from group settings the females were considerably less satisfied than the males, with close to 53% of them feeling they had been moved too much. They had been shifted significantly more than the males, and a larger proportion had earlier been in a foster home. We thought that the women who had been transferred from foster homes to group settings might have been particularly dissatisfied with the number of moves, but the data did not bear this out. About as many females who had been in group care only were dissatisfied with the number of moves they had made as those who had once resided in a foster home.

Their feelings about their own experience differed markedly from their opinions about shifts of foster children in general. This question was asked of the total sample, irrespective of whether they had been moved or not. Children in foster care exchange experiences with others in placement and may witness arrivals and departures of others. Their opinions were therefore colored not only by their own experiences, but also by what they had heard and seen. In any event, the 263 young adults who answered this question were fairly unanimous in believing that children in foster care are moved around too much. Somewhat more than 72% said that in their opinion this was "very" or "pretty true," and only 5% disagreed completely. Thus, while most were satisfied with the amount they themselves had been shifted, they were more critical about what they thought generally occurred. Perhaps this was a reflection of what they had heard from, or had seen happening to, others. Perhaps some of their own moves were from a poor situation to an improved one, and this weighed heavily in their reactions. Perhaps it was a way of gradually coming to terms with their past, similar to the tendency of people to review their own life in more favorable terms in comparison with others. After all, people are rarely inclined to see themselves and their experiences as average; rather, they strive to perceive their own circumstances as positively as possible (Campbell 1981). In this sense our sample may have viewed the grass as greener on their own side of the fence.

Their Use of the Foster Family's Name

Little has been written about this subject, although from a child's perspective it must be important. The matter of names or modes of address can be very confusing early in placement. The dilemma was mentioned by a number of young adults and was vividly portrayed by one: "It was very confusing . . . what do I call that lady . . . Mom? . . . mam? . . . aunt? . . . Mrs. X? . . . I thought about that a lot and wished someone would help me out."

Agencies generally tended to assume a laissez-faire stance, leaving it up to foster parents to provide cues to the children in their homes. So, too, with regard to a child's use of the foster family's last name. I wondered about its prevalence during the last years in care and whether such use was confined to certain situations or was more general. I was curious whether those who maintained their own identity would benefit in the long run, although it seemed equally plausible that benefits could derive from such name use if it signified identification with, and closeness to, a foster family. In any event, 168 from foster homes responded to the questions about this in the interview. Somewhat more than 17% spoke of calling themselves by their foster family's surname, with more than half of them having done this "a lot." Most used the name in social situations, with their friends, and in school. Close to 21% said that they had not used the foster family's name but had wanted to do so. The remaining majority (61.9%) neither used nor wanted to use any name but their own. Those who used or wanted to use the foster family's name were more likely than the rest to state that they felt very close to that family.

Wishes About Adoption

Perhaps feelings about using the foster family's name indicated their wish for adoption. If so, it was an idle wish, for only a few (4%) of the total 277 respondents had ever been surrendered or legally freed, and this occurred mostly when they were teenagers. Fewer yet had ever been placed in an adoptive home, and only three were eventually adopted by their foster families following their discharge in 1975. Perhaps policies against adoption by foster parents, prevalent at that time, had prevented them from adopting these children. Perhaps such policies discouraged others from even moving in that direction. Yet quite a few (40.5%) of these young adults stated that they wished they had been adopted. Four out of five of them expressed this wish vis-à-vis their last foster home, while the others spoke of having wanted to be adopted by a previous foster family. Males and females were alike in this regard. There was also a linkage between foster family name use and the wish for adoption. Those who used or said they had wanted to use that name were particularly likely to wish they had been adopted.

Those who were discharged from group settings were also asked about adoption. Close to 31% stated that they wished they had been adopted. This figure was 45% for those who had been placed at an early age and had once lived with a foster family, and only 24.4% for those who had not.

All in all, close to two out of every five respondents stated

Table 3.4
Discharge Destination

| Destination | Discharged From: | | | |
| | Foster Home | | Group Setting | |
	M (N = 109)	F (N = 92)	M (N = 52)	F (N = 24)
Own responsibility	22%	33.7%	50.0%	70.8%
College	4.6	8.7	3.8	4.2
Armed forces	21.1	1.1	17.3	—
Foster home	37.6	45.7	—	4.2
Biological home	11.0	10.9	28.8	20.8
Institution	3.7	—	—	—
	100.0%	100.1%	99.9%	100.0%

that they had wished to be adopted. This group in particular must have felt a sense of uncertainty about their foster care status, and they tended somewhat more (31.7%) than others (19.4%) to feel very strongly that "children in foster care feel different or set apart from other young people."

At the Time of Discharge

Most of the young adults were discharged from one of the 27 voluntary agencies in our sample. Some 40% came from Catholic auspices, close to 35% from agencies that were Protestant or nonsectarian, and about 11% from Jewish auspices. The remainder (14.8%) had been in care under public auspices, at least during the few years prior to discharge. On leaving care, it was possible to apply to the Bureau of Child Welfare for a grant of up to $500 to help the young adults make the transition to independent living. Such grants could, for instance, be used for various household purchases, including furniture. There appeared to be little consistency among agencies in the use of these grants, and few actually applied for them. Therefore, fewer than one out of five of the young adults received a grant.

According to official records, the vast majority (98.2%) of the young adults were discharged to their own responsibility, while the remaining were either in correctional facilities or were discharged to the care of their biological families. Actually, however, these young adults headed in a number of directions as can be seen in table 3.4. With the exception of those who continued to live with their foster families, most were on their own in the community, had enlisted in the armed forces, or were residing at a college. A small proportion returned to their biological families, those who were discharged from group settings were much more apt to be on their own in the community than living with a family. There was often little in the way of a period of transition. At age 19 many were faced with the sudden necessity of making it on their own. Many young adults recalled their feelings at the time rather vividly.

> It was frightening . . . I didn't know the first thing about living on my own.
>
> > Interview
> > September 1979
>
> It's a hard world out there, and I wasn't at all prepared.
>
> > Interview
> > March 1980
>
> Oh yes, we discussed it in a group, but much too little . . . and too late. The hard reality did not sink in.
>
> > Interview
> > February 1980

The gist of these comments is succinctly summarized by the 273 young adults' replies when we asked them how much "on the whole" agencies had prepared them to go out on their own. Only 24.9% felt they had been prepared "a lot." About 23% felt they had been prepared "some," 9.2% said "a little," and a surprising 42.9% said "very little" or rejected that choice and voluntarily added "not at all." We will return to this subject later on, for we discussed this topic with them in some detail and heard their suggestions.

Table 3.5
Well-Being and Discharge Group

	Discharged From:											
	Foster Home						Group Setting					
	M (N = 109)			F (N = 92)			M (N = 52)			F (N = 24)		
	Mean*	(S.D.)	N	Mean*	(S.D.)	N	Mean*	(S.D.)	N	Mean*	(S.D.)	N
Well-being index	.33	(2.31)	105	.24	(2.36)	91	−.53	(2.43)	50	−1.05	(2.63)	23

*Z-scores: A high positive score signifies a more positive sense of well-being.

Placement Characteristics and Sense of Well-Being

A vital question is whether and to what extent their placement experiences ultimately had any bearing on the young adults' assessments of themselves and their lives. For the group as a whole, those who were discharged from foster homes assessed themselves and their lives more positively than those who were discharged from group settings. This was equally true of males and of females. Within each discharge group, whether foster home or group setting, the sexes did not differ from each other. These data can be seen in table 3.5. Before any conclusions can be drawn, however, these placements and the children's movement while in care must be examined separately. It is important to remember that the number of respondents in each of the subgroups vary somewhat from the original totals because out of the 277 respondents there were 8 for whom some of the data needed for calculating the well-being index were missing. The discussion will therefore include 196 young adults who were discharged from foster homes and 73 who left group settings.

Among the young adults who were discharged from foster homes, neither the number nor type of placements had any bearing on their sense of well-being. For instance, the number of foster homes they lived in was totally unrelated ($r = -.02$) to their assessment of themselves and their lives at the time of our interviews. No matter what the combination of types of placements, there was no connection. I even examined separately all those (N = 61) who had either lived with one foster family for the entire time or who had done so following a brief period in a temporary placement. This group certainly had the most consistent experience. Yet, when compared with the other young adults from foster homes, their sense of well-being on the average did not differ. A separate examination of each component of the index of well-being, such as their self-esteem, yielded similar results. There was no association with the number and type of placements.

A somewhat different picture emerged for the young adults who left foster care from group settings. Here also the number of shifts in placement was unrelated to their sense of well-being at the time of our interviews, but the nature of the placements was related. The 24 males and females who had at one time lived in a foster home, but who had been transferred to group care, had a poorer view of themselves and their lives than those whose placements had been only in group settings. I do not know why these foster home placements had been disrupted. Whatever factors led to the disruption, or whatever the consequences may have been, they eventually made a difference in these young adults' sense of well-being.

It is also noteworthy that the young adults who were placed into group settings from foster homes tended to have less education by the time of our interviews (mean = 11.3 years) than those who remained in a group setting throughout (mean = 12.1 years). A parallel picture existed at the time of discharge. I do not know what caused this, nor whether their lower scholastic functioning was a factor in their removal from the foster homes or a product of it. However, it was no doubt a factor in their poorer view of themselves and their lives.

The observed difference in well-being between the 196 who were discharged from foster homes and the 73 who left care from group settings was in large measure a result of the poorer self-assessments of the 24 who had lived in a foster home for some time prior to their placement in a group setting. In fact, a comparison between the other 49 young adults from group

Table 3.6
Well-Being and Location at Discharge

Discharged From:	Mean*	S.D.	N
Foster home	.29	2.3	196
Group home	−.04	2.5	22
Group residence	−.81	2.7	18
Institution	−1.06	2.3	33

*Z-scores: A high positive score signifies a more positive sense of well-being.

settings who had never been in a foster home and the 196 eventually discharged from foster homes yielded a much reduced difference that was no longer statistically significant.

One further comment is in order. It will be recalled that the young adults from group settings consisted of those who had been discharged from group homes, group residences, or from institutions. By comparison with young adults discharged from foster homes, those from institutions had the poorest sense of well-being while those from group homes or residences fell in between. This can readily be seen in table 3.6. I immediately examined whether those who had been discharged from institutions consisted in large measure of young adults who had been transferred from foster homes, since the latter had the poorest well-being scores. The data showed otherwise since a smaller proportion of those who were discharged from institutions had been transferred from foster homes than those who were discharged from group homes or residences. The data did indicate, however, that those from institutions had completed fewer years of schooling, and varied more in this regard than all others in our sample. Clearly those at the lower range of intelligence and the poorer scholastic achievers were, at discharge, more apt to reside in institutions than in group homes, residences, or foster homes. Unfortunately, we do not know which came first—the placement or the scholastic deficit. We do know that, after full statistical account had been taken of the level of education, the differences in well-being no longer obtained. That is, the well-being scores of those from group homes, group residences, or institutions were similar when education was controlled. This suggested that the link between institutional placement and the young adults' poorer sense of well-being was a result, at least in part, of their lower educational achievement rather than a function of having lived in an institution.

In the group as a whole there were no differences in the sense of well-being among young adults of different ethnicity, nor were there differences in the proportion of each ethnic group that was discharged from foster homes or group settings. But among those from foster homes whites had a better sense of well-being than did black or Hispanic respondents. Precisely the opposite picture emerged among those from group settings, for here whites had a poorer sense of well-being than did the others. The differences in well-being were, therefore, strongly influenced by who was placed where rather than by ethnicity.

One could speculate ad infinitum about what was going on, but the following is at least one plausible guess as to the factors at play. At the time these young adults came into placement relatively more white foster homes were probably available for children than homes for black or Hispanic children. Therefore, it was possible to be more selective when placing a white child in a foster home. This must have affected the quality of the environment for some while growing up, and it could account for the poorer sense of well-being of black and Hispanic children eventually discharged from foster homes.

How to explain the better sense of well-being of blacks and Hispanics, than of whites, who were discharged from group care is less clear but other factors were likely at work. Black and Hispanic children who needed specialized residential care probably had fewer options available to them within the foster care system. They were therefore placed elsewhere, such as in the correctional or mental hygiene system, and never entered the foster care system or did not remain there very long.

What other elements of placement were ultimately linked to the young adults' sense of well-being? It is worth repeating here that shifts in care were not associated with the sense of

Table 3.7
Correlations Between Placement Characteristics and Well-Being

	Discharged From:							
	Foster Home				Group Setting			
	M (N = 105)		F (N = 91)		M (N = 50)		F (N = 23)	
	r*	(p)	r*	(p)	r*	(p)	r*	(p)
Age at initial placement	−.21	(.03)	.19	(.07)	.28	(.05)	.11	(.61)
Age at final placement	−.21	(.03)	.13	(.21)	.30	(.04)	.17	(.44)
Number of shifts in care	−.07	(.45)	.01	(.95)	−.02	(.87)	−.30	(.17)
Age at start of longest location	−.22	(.02)	.13†	(.21)	.19	(.19)	.18	(.42)
Years of longest location	.13	(.19)	−.13†	(.23)	−.24	(.10)	−.30	(.16)

* Pearson product-moment correlation coefficients.
† Based on 90 cases.

well-being of the major subgroups examined. The mere fact of having been moved about was apparently not important in the long run. Perhaps the most startling point that emerges as one reviews table 3.7 is the limited effect of placement factors on the young adults' sense of well-being. Nonetheless, there are some statistically significant relationships here and there that require comment.

The age at placement is one. Males discharged from foster homes who were placed at an early age (for instance, at age three or younger) tended to feel better off in the long run, whereas the opposite tended to be true of all the rest in the sample. Similarly, if such males began their longest tenure in a specific location, as in a particular foster home, at an early age, they were more likely to have a better sense of well-being as young adult men. Again the results for the rest of the sample were in the opposite direction. These associations were not strong, but nevertheless were difficult to understand. If one imagines that males were more seriously affected than females by what had gone on at home prior to their placement, so that an earlier placement had been beneficial, why was this not the case for all males? If one imagines that stronger bonds with foster parents developed if boys were placed early, and that this ultimately had a positive effect on their sense of well-being, why was this not true among the girls? Is it possible that foster parents reacted differently to young boys than to young girls and that this had an effect on their development? For some reason the results concerning males who were discharged from foster homes moved in the opposite direction from the other groups, but it is not clear why.

Other placement factors discussed so far were not linked to their sense of well-being. For instance, the young adults who were discharged from voluntary or public agencies, or who had been in placements of various religious groups, did not differ in their sense of well-being at the time of our contacts. Use of their foster parents' surname, or their wishes about adoption were also not connected. Their destination at the time they were discharged, according to the case records, was also not linked to their sense of well-being. Nor were their assessments of how well the agencies had prepared them for discharge, except in one instance. Among the young adults from group care those with a poorer sense of well-being were less satisfied with the preparation they had received, and vice versa ($r = .29$). Perhaps their ex post facto view on preparation included an element of blame. They may have felt that better preparation would have altered their life events in a positive direction. But why not a similar reaction among those who were discharged from foster homes? This was puzzling. The following speculation offers a possible explanation. For many in the foster home group, discharge from care was not a sudden rupture since they had foster families to fall back on. On the other hand those from group care probably felt the separation more keenly since more had to fend for themselves following their discharge. If things did not work out, who was at fault? In answering this question, those who ended up feeling more poorly may have been more inclined to single out their preparation for discharge and to blame the agencies for having been remiss in this regard.

Our data on shifts in care require comment because much emphasis in the field, and in the community, has been placed on this aspect of continuity of care. It has been assumed that shifts will inevitably have deleterious effects on individuals. Yet we found that the number of replacements during care was quite unrelated to the sense of well-being of these young adults.

This prevalent assumption has many roots. One in particular was revealed in our data. Although the young adults' sense of well-being was unrelated to the number of times they were replaced, their satisfaction with their foster care experience was connected. Among the young adults discharged from foster homes, those who had been shifted the most were the least satisfied and vice versa ($r = -.35$). The tendency was similar for those from group settings, but considerably weaker ($r = -.15$). It is possible that such satisfaction has at times been misconstrued to signify a positive outcome, and thus has influenced assumptions about shifts in care.

But to say that people's satisfaction with an experience on the one hand, and the effect of that experience on the other, have at times been confused did not enable us to understand the results. I was frankly puzzled, for I too had expected to find a linkage between shifts in care and later feelings of well-being. Such broad generalizations about the negative effects of replacement are, however, overly simplistic. They merely single out a symptom rather than searching for what lies beneath. In fact, some shifts in foster care arrangements can be beneficial if they are deliberately planned to ameliorate an untenable situation. Some shifts can result in a better placement for a child, and no doubt that occurred for some. Or perhaps shifts that occur early in placement, as was true for many in the sample, are not so harmful if a stable arrangement ensues.

There is yet another aspect of the situation that needs to be considered. From a psychological standpoint a consistent environment is preferable to one that is not, all other things being equal. That is the ideal world which these children, by virtue of having been placed in foster care, never experienced. But people's reactions to turbulence in their own lives are not of necessity pathological, although they are frequently assumed to be. The therapeutic emphasis in the child welfare field has frequently leaned in that direction. Assumptions about situations are, after all, in part a function of acceptable professional values, but here, as elsewhere, rigid approaches are a poor guide. Flexibility in one's thinking may be preferable. Most young adults in our sample were exposed to turbulence and change, to unanticipated events in their childhood both before and after placement. Children in the midst of upheavals are affected, but the experience can also shape them into survivors. They may even gain strength, for they have to grow up more quickly and confront situations not faced by those who are more protected. Children the world over who have survived as strong people in the aftermath of famine, war, and revolution are surely a testament. Something is at the core of that ability to survive and gain. Perhaps a familiar face, a memory, or a fantasy offers stability. Perhaps social comparisons, or what one uses as a point of reference, can make a difference. If others are also moved, or if a child knows of moves by others then the experience is not unique and can provide a basis for coping. If, on the other hand, a child feels, or is, singled out, it may be more difficult to confront, to gain, and to survive.

In short, attempting to understand the variety of reactions to shifts in care is a complex task. If people are moved about in a haphazard way, they are apt to begin to feel less than human—for example, like a package or a cereal box. If the reasons for moves are understood and accepted, it is quite another matter. Moves are therefore not intrinsically damaging. But to begin to understand these young adults' reactions to the inconsistencies and discontinuities they faced in the past would require more precise knowledge about the range of human adaptability than is now available.

Chapter Four

CONTACT WITH KIN DURING PLACEMENT

There should be family contact if the child wants it and if the family wants it.

Interview
November 1979

There was contact with our family . . . there was no negative feeling on either side . . . the foster family created an environment that let us know we were there due to circumstances beyond our parents' control . . . they never tried to play one against the other.

Interview
January 1980

Over the years studies and other reports in the social work literature have focused increasing attention on the vital subject of contact between foster children and their biological families. This literature will not be summarized here except to note some of the questions addressed. Writers have, for example, examined the connection between biological parent contact and the child's adjustment in the foster home (Sherman, Neuman, and Shyne 1973; Holman 1975), the difficulties of such visits for foster parents and for the families of origin (Littner 1971; McAdams 1972; Jenkins and Norman 1975), possible reasons behind limited visiting by kin (Claburn and Magura 1977; Gruber 1978), placement agreements (Festinger 1974), social worker skill in relation to contact (Shapiro 1975), and the connection between parental visiting and length of care (Fanshel 1975; Vasaly 1976; Fanshel 1977).

The long-range consequences of biological family contact has up to now received scant attention. In fact, we are aware of only two studies that report some data on this issue. Van Der Waals (1960) found that adults whose mothers had maintained regular contact also "tended to speak kindly of their foster parents." The author's interpretation suggested that the devotion conveyed by such regular contact helped the former foster children to develop a positive relationship with their foster parents. Van Der Waals reported no other findings about a connection between biological family contact and adult outcome. The second study (Meier 1962) examined this only in a few instances because so few of the adults had been visited regularly. These instances showed no association with adult adjustment.

We sought to understand this issue by gathering information about contact from the case records. Because so many in our sample had spent long years in care, and because patterns of contact inevitably varied both in amount and in terms of who was in touch during those years, it was not feasible to capture the extent of contact with kin* throughout the entire placement period. Therefore, we concentrated on contact during the first and last few years of placement between the children and their biological mothers, fathers, and adult relatives. For each of these family members contact was classified as high, fairly high, sporadic (which usually meant low), low or minimal, and no contact. For example, consistent contacts of once a month or so were classified as high, whereas one to a few contacts over the span of several years were considered as low. All family members were eventually combined to provide a composite picture of biological family contact. The final picture can only be as good as the information in the records and the sensitivity of the case readers. In full recognition of this fact we routinely conferred on any case that appeared un-

---

*"Kin" here and elsewhere refers to biological mothers, fathers, and relatives other than siblings. The latter will be discussed separately.

clear or ambiguous; in view of the plethora of variations, we conferred almost continuously. Nevertheless some error may have intruded, particularly in adjacent categories such as high and fairly high. In order to minimize the error, I combined these categories as well as sporadic and low contact.

Early Contact

The amount of contact between the children and their kin during the first few years of placement is shown in table 4.1. A majority of the children had such contact at that time. But a difference existed among the groups. There was a tendency for proportionately more of those who were eventually discharged from group settings to have had some contact, and a larger proportion of them had frequent contact, than was true of those who were eventually discharged from foster homes. This difference was especially large among males. Why was the difference between the females from foster homes and group care less pronounced? As it turned out this was an artifact of who was placed where rather than a difference be-

Table 4.1
Contact During Placement, Location, and Sex

	Discharged From:							
	Foster Home				Group Setting			
	Males		Females		Males		Females	
	N	(%)	N	(%)	N	(%)	N	(%)
Early Contact								
High, fairly high	24	(22.0)	35	(38.5)	36	(70.6)	12	(52.2)
Low sporadic	58	(53.2)	38	(41.8)	10	(19.6)	7	(30.4)
None	27	(24.8)	18	(19.8)	5	(9.8)	4	(17.4)
Total	109		91		51		23	
Late Contact								
High, fairly high	28	(25.7)	28	(30.8)	32	(62.7)	9	(39.1)
Low, sporadic	63	(57.8)	52	(57.1)	17	(33.3)	14	(60.9)
None	18	(16.5)	11	(12.1)	2	(3.9)	0	(0.0)
Total	109		91		51		23	

tween the sexes. It will be recalled that a larger proportion of the females from group care, when compared with males from group care, had at an earlier time lived in a foster home. These children were younger at their initial placement than others in group care, and the pattern of contact with their kin was generally similar to others who were later discharged from foster homes. When these cases were excluded from the analysis, there were roughly equivalent differences in contact between the males and females from group care and their counterparts from foster homes. In other words, the difference in early contact between those from foster homes and those who were discharged from group settings was a function of those in group care who had never lived in a foster home. They were older when they entered care and their ties with kin were therefore generally stronger at that time. In view of this, it is not surprising that more of this older group had contact, and more frequent contact, with biological family members than the young adults who were eventually discharged from foster homes.

Among those discharged from group care the level of contact with kin was associated with the children's age at placement. Those with the most frequent contact were on the average 9.2 years old at placement, whereas those with infrequent contact were about 7 years old, and those without early contact were the youngest—somewhat less than 4 years old at the time they entered foster care. In contrast, among those discharged from foster homes there was no link between their average age at placement and the amount of early contact with kin. For instance, those with frequent contact averaged 3.4 years, those with infrequent contact averaged 4.1 years, and those with no contact averaged 3.3 years of age. Age was not associated with early contact among those discharged from foster homes because many were so young that ties with kin were less well established, although there must have also been somewhat older ones who, despite ties, were, for one or another reason, not visited.

What other factors were associated with contact during the

initial years of placement? As a whole, the group who had contact during those early years were somewhat more apt to have mothers and fathers who had been married to each other, and they tended to be shifted somewhat less frequently. Perhaps this occurred because children without contact were moved about more during the early period in an effort to find arrangements that would be permanent. It is also possible that the children who had no contact were shifted more simply as a function of time in placement because they were younger when they entered care.

Among those from foster homes no other background factors distinguished those with different amounts of early contact with kin. However, for those from group care one additional factor—their reason for placement—was connected. Those who entered care because of the mental or physical illness, or the death, of a parent were more likely to have had frequent contact during the early years of placement than children placed for reasons of neglect, abandonment, or because their caretakers could or would no longer cope with their particular situation. This was not a function of the ages of the children. Perhaps it reflected their home situation at entry into care. Apparently some of these parents continued to abandon their children, whereas others were too beset by circumstances to visit regularly, or were discouraged from doing so.

The next chapter will discuss the problems that were observed among the children during placement. Nevertheless, one finding needs to be examined here because it concerned contact during the first years in care. Overall there was no connection between the amount of early contact and the problems the children exhibited later on in their placement. The connection depended on who visited. Among foster home and group care children alike, those who had frequent contact with a relative, such as a grandparent, aunt, or uncle, were less likely to exhibit one or another sort of problem at discharge than all others, including those who had frequent contact with only their biological parents. The reasons for this are not clear. Perhaps contact with relatives during the early years in care provided the children with a broader sense of family than when their contact was only with their biological parents. The interest shown on the part of members of the extended family could have led to fewer problems in the long run.

Earlier in this chapter it was mentioned that a study (Van Der Waals 1960) found a connection between regular contact during placement and acceptance of the foster parents by young adults. Naturally I was eager to determine whether a similar situation existed here. In an attempt to parallel the study from Holland, I singled out those with living mothers who were in touch with their foster parents at the time of our interviews, and examined whether early frequent contact with kin was associated with the young adults' closeness to their foster parents. Among the men there was no connection but among the women there was, although the association was weak. In this subgroup of 43 women from foster homes, there were 20 with frequent contact with kin during the initial years in care. Sixteen of them, or 80%, spoke of feeling very close to their foster parents, compared with 52.2% of those who had had infrequent or no contact with kin during those early years. For these women, therefore, our data lend some support to the notion that early contact, particularly if frequent, can be a beneficial factor in children's relationships with their foster parents. The idea that such early, frequent contact can assist in children's adaptation to placement has been stressed by others (Cowan and Stout 1939; Weinstein 1960). At the same time one should not make too much of this. Our findings were not strong and pertained only to one small subgroup, and even there only to the girls. Numerous other factors besides contact could have influenced the results. Furthermore, for the total group from foster homes there was no association between early contact with kin and the young adults' sense of closeness to their foster parents at the time of our interviews.

Other aspects of the young adults' lives at the time of our contacts were also examined. Among those discharged from foster homes, current life factors such as their closeness to kin, education, employment, and marital status were not related to the level of contact with their biological families during the early years in care. Their satisfaction with foster care was also not connected. The picture was similar for the young adults from group care, with one exception. Those who had frequent early contact with their kin were much more likely to tell us they felt very close to one or more adults from their biological families than those with more limited early contact. For this group frequent contact during the early years following placement was clearly indicative of the bonds that had previously developed, which were generally maintained in young adulthood.

Finally, the most important question. Was early contact with kin related to the young adults' assessment of themselves and their lives at the time of our interviews? These data can be seen in table 4.2. For those from foster homes, neither the fact of contact, when compared with no contact, nor the amount of contact during the first years in care was associated with the young adults' sense of well-being. Among those from group settings, the well-being scores of those with frequent and those with no contact were quite alike, but those who were visited minimally ultimately had the poorest outlook. Perhaps limited

Table 4.2
Contact During Placement and Sense of Well-Being

	Discharged From:					
	Foster Home			Group Setting		
	Mean*	S.D.	N	Mean*	S.D.	N
Early Contact						
High, fairly high	.32	2.6	58	−.30	2.3	47
Low, sporadic	.21	2.3	94	−1.65	2.6	16
None	.36	2.1	43	−.52	2.7	9
Total	.27	2.3	195	−.63	2.4	72
Late Contact						
High, fairly high	−.02	2.3	54	−.03	2.3	41
Low, sporadic	.43	2.4	114	−1.37	2.4	29
None	.21	2.2	27	−2.08	2.9	2
Total	.27	2.3	195	−.63	2.4	72

*Z-scores: A high positive score signifies a more positive sense of well-being.

and sporadic visits communicated ambivalence on the part of adults, so that these children became unsure about what to expect. When this occurred early in placement it may have had a particularly negative and ongoing effect, unlike situations where the message was clearer, even if it meant no contact at all.

Table 4.2 obscures another association that emerged. Among young adults whose biological families were in touch with them during those early years, males and females did not eventually differ in their sense of well-being. But if there was no contact, a sex difference existed, but only among those who were discharged from foster homes. Here females fared significantly worse (mean = −.39) than males (mean = .90), although their ages at placement were virtually identical. One can speculate about a variety of reasons why girls were ultimately more affected than boys by the absence of kin during the early years in placement. But such speculation leads nowhere because we cannot here establish cause. However, the fact of a sex difference is noteworthy in itself. It means that generalizations about contact with kin are not too useful if they do not differentiate among various groups, including males and females.

Late Contact

Not surprisingly, there was a strong connection between contact during the early and last years of placement. Some 77.5% from foster homes and 87.8% of those from group settings had some contact with their kin at both points in time. In fact, there was no one with contact at the start of placement who did not also have contact at the end. There were, however, some with no contact to begin with who were in touch with their kin at the end. This included a few people from foster homes (8%) and a similar proportion from group settings. There were also some who had no contact with their kin at either time: this was so for 14.5% from foster homes but only 2.7% from group settings.

It was impressive that such a large majority of the biological families maintained some contact at both points in time. Although no information was collected on contact during the intervening years in care, and perhaps some kin were in touch only during the early and last years, it seems reasonable to assume that a majority maintained some contact throughout placement. Perhaps this is one reason why these youngsters were never adopted.

Contact with kin was, however, often minimal. For 40% of those discharged from foster homes contact was low or sporadic at both the start and end of placement, and for an additional 13.5% contact between these two time periods had dropped from frequent to low or sporadic. Only 16% had frequent contact at both points in time. Those from group settings had more contact: some 44.6% had frequent contact and 16.2% had low or sporadic contact at both time periods, and for 20.3% contact had dropped from frequent to low by the time the young adults were discharged.

For some 16% of the sample contact with kin increased over time. Shifts in the amount of contact thus occurred in both directions. Some biological families lost interest, while others gained. Some kin had died. Some kin whose whereabouts were unknown reappeared. Some kin who were initially discouraged from visiting were later encouraged to do so. Some teenage foster children initiated contacts themselves, and others avoided or rejected contacts with their biological parents or relatives.

There were many patterns and reasons for them. Yet there was also a consistency in most instances, so that the amount of contact at the start of placement was fairly predictive of the amount of contact at the end. For example, among those from foster homes a majority of those with high, low, or no contact at the start continued to have high (54.2%), low (83.3%), or no (64.4%) contact during the last years of placement. As for those from group settings, close to 69% of those with frequent contact at the beginning had frequent contact at the end, and close to 71% of those with low or sporadic contact at the start continued to have low contact later on. Only a tiny group shifted upward, and in most such instances the shift was from no contact at the start of placement to low contact by the time of discharge.

In sum, while most young adults in the sample had some contact with their kin both at the start and end of placement, for many it was minimal. This was particularly true for those discharged from foster homes. Furthermore, the amount of contact at the start of placement frequently predicted the amount of contact later on in placement. It appeared that the frequency of contact at the start often set the stage for the level of contact during the later years in, and perhaps throughout, placement. This may have been simply a function of the particular families in this study. On the other hand, one cannot help but wonder whether agency expectations, communicated at the start of placement, set a tone that persisted over time.

The data on contact with kin during the last years in placement are shown in table 4.1. What had a bearing on contact at that time? In view of the close relationship between contact at the start and end of placement, it is no surprise that similar factors were related at both times.

For instance, contact during the last years in care was again more prevalent among those who were discharged from group settings. In this group there were only two individuals without contact in the years just prior to their discharge. But whether discharged from foster homes or group settings, older age at placement was associated with the amount of contact during the last years of placement. This factor had not been linked to contact at the start of placement for those who were eventually discharged from foster homes, but during the later years in care it was. Apparently for those who were somewhat older at placement, ties with kin were reestablished over time.

Those discharged from foster homes who were in touch with their kin once again had been shifted less, and more tended to have biological parents who had been married, when compared with those without contact. Furthermore, as was the case with early contact, those who had frequent contact in later years with members of their extended family were less likely to exhibit one or another sort of problem at the time of discharge. No other aspects of their background or current circumstances were related to contact with their biological families during their last years in care. For instance, among those discharged from foster homes who were in touch with kin at the time of our interviews, closeness to kin was unrelated to the frequency of contact during their last years in placement. Contact during those years also had no bearing on their overall satisfaction with foster care.

Among those from group settings, additional factors distinguished those who had frequent contact from those who did not. As was the case with contact during the early years, the reason for placement was related. Those who were placed because of the mental or physical illness of kin, for instance, had more contact than those placed for reasons such as neglect. In addition, those who had frequent contact during their last years of placement were less likely to exhibit serious social or emotional problems around the time of discharge than those who had infrequent or no contact with kin. This was especially so if there was frequent contact with members of their extended family. And again, those who had frequent contact during those last years in care were more likely to feel very close to some member of their biological family by the time of our interviews than those who had more limited contact. Nothing else in their background or current life, including their satisfaction with foster care, was related to contact with kin during the years prior to their discharge from group care.

Was the young adults' contact with kin during their last years in care eventually associated with their sense of well-being? These data are presented in table 4.2. For those discharged from foster homes there was no link between contact and their view of themselves and their lives at the time of our interviews. And unlike the situation at the start of placement, sex differences no longer existed among those who were not in touch with kin.

In contrast, the young adults who were discharged from group settings showed a clear difference. Those who had frequent contact with kin displayed a better sense of well-being than those with less contact during the last years in care. Males and females were quite alike in this regard. Contact with kin was particularly important for those teenagers who lived in group settings, for this was their principal link with a family.

To recapitulate, among those discharged from foster homes, whether male or female, there was no connection between their sense of well-being and contact with their biological families at the start and end of placement. In other words, such contact, whether frequent, infrequent, or nonexistent, ultimately had no impact on their view of themselves and their lives. The only observed difference was sex-linked, but this occurred only among those without any familial contact at the start of placement. Females who had no contact ultimately felt worse than males without such early contact. On the other hand, among those who had such early contact no sex differences in the sense of well-being were observed, nor were any sex differences associated with contact during the last years of foster care. Similar sex-linked differences were not apparent among those who were discharged from group settings. The young adults from group care also did not differ in their sense of well-being if early contact with their kin had been frequent or absent, but there was a tendency to assess their lives somewhat more poorly if contact had been infrequent. Contact with kin during the last years prior to discharge was also associated with the sense of well-being of these young adults from group care: those who had frequent contact ultimately felt better about themselves and their lives than those who had more limited contact.

Thus, while the importance of contact with kin has generally been emphasized in the field, and no doubt it affects discharge rates, such contact seems to have had little bearing on young adults out on their own except among those from group care. They were older when they were placed, and therefore had more ties with their families of origin. Those who came into placement at an earlier age, and who were therefore more apt to live with, and establish ties with, a foster family were less affected by contact with their biological families during placement. It is not that such contact had a negative influence or that it had a positive influence; it simply had no influence in the long run.

Their Recollections of Contact

The young adults' recollections of contact with their kin were no doubt influenced by many things. Accuracy of recall depended on such things as their cognitive abilities and the distorting effects of intervening events. It also depended on what they may have been told by various people, including their kin, particularly if they were very young at the time they were placed. Nevertheless, we wondered about their recollections and therefore asked each young adult, but only those who were interviewed, about the amount of contact they had had with kin during their first and last years in placement. Detailed information was collected ranging from "never" to "once a week or more," and it covered all forms of contact whether by visit, mail, or telephone. These were reclassified for ease of reporting into frequent or high, low, and no contact. For example, contacts of any variety once a month or more often were considered to be frequent or high.

Because of the problems connected with recall, the young adults' responses could not be used as a check on the accuracy of the case record information about level of contact. There was an additional problem. From the young adults' prespective, letters and telephone calls were an aspect of contact, but such communications were sometimes not known by or recorded by caseworkers in the records. For all of these reasons, this subject will not be discussed in detail. In any event, of 133 young adults from foster homes who were interviewed and who had some contact noted in their records during the first years in placement, close to 62% recalled some contact. Infrequent or sporadic contact during those early years was most often not remembered. A few spoke of some contact, although minimal, where none had been recorded, and the recollections of only a handful were more discrepant. Statements about early contact by those who were discharged from group settings paralleled case record notations more frequently. Of the 58 with some contact at that time, more than 86% recalled it, and there were few disagreements on the amount. Once again, nonrecall occurred most often when contact with kin was infrequent.

Memories of contact with biological families during the years close to discharge were only slightly more in line with case record entries. Among those with contact recorded, some 64% from foster homes and 89% from group settings recalled it. Almost all instances that were not recalled had been recorded as infrequent or sporadic. Fewer instances of more serious disagreement existed here than in the recollections of contact during the initial years.

The main point is that nonrecall occurred primarily when contact was infrequent. Although this is not surprising, it is noteworthy. It leaves one with questions about the meaning of infrequent contact, even for the child who is somewhat older at placement. Any tendency to concretize contact, on the assumption that a visit here and there is so perceived, is apparently a mistake. From the child's standpoint such visits may not be perceived as real contact and often may not even be recalled. The atmosphere surrounding visits can also play a role in such perceptions. For instance, some young adults spoke at length and in picturesque detail about "agency visiting day." They described it as confusing, hectic, and noisy, with children running about and so many families present at once that one hardly thought of it as a visit. Some went so far as to say they sometimes felt unsure whether anyone from their biological family had been present. And in the crisp words of one: "Visiting should be more personal. There were too many people in one room . . . and everyone was running around . . . it was like a zoo."

We do not know the prevalence of this attitude. The fact that it existed at all was important, for, in addition to gaps in recall, it raised a more fundamental question about the meaning of infrequent contact for some of these young adults.

Contact with Siblings

This discussion of contact with kin has singled out biological parents and relatives. Yet brothers, sisters, and half siblings also played an important role in the foster care experience of these young adults. At least this was our impression as they spoke of siblings as companions and allies. We asked about each sibling and whether they had lived with that person, or been in touch with him or her, during their time in placement. Only 28 of the 241 young adults who were interviewed said they had no sibling or were unaware of any. The rest knew of one or more brothers and sisters. A majority of these young adults had either lived together with a sibling at some time during their placement (71.8%) or had been in touch with a brother or sister (91.5%) while in foster care. But only 44.1% were in touch with all the siblings they knew of, and 8.5% had contact with none at all. The rest saw one or more but did not see all their siblings. The data suggested that the siblings not seen were either younger or older than those they did see; those seen tended to be close to their own age.

One aspect of such sibling contact was associated with the young adults' sense of well-being some years later, but only among those who had been discharged from group settings. Whether contact was with all or only some of their siblings, those from group care who saw more of them eventually tended to have a better sense of well-being ($r = .24$). It was not a question of contact as opposed to no contact, but of the actual number of siblings with whom they had been in touch, irrespective of whether they had lived together in placement. But was this simply a function of their contact with biological parents or relatives? That is, it seemed possible that the number of siblings with whom these young adults had contact was associated with the frequency of their contact with kin during the last years before their discharge. Since those who had more frequent contact with kin tended to be in touch with more of their brothers and sisters ($r = .22$), and since, as reported earlier, those from group care who saw their kin more often during the last years in placement assessed themselves and their lives more positively, it seemed useful to examine this more closely.

As both the frequency of contact with kin and the number of siblings they saw were associated with the young adults' sense of well-being, and the more they were in touch with kin the more siblings they saw, the question was whether contact with a number of siblings was connected with their sense of well-being irrespective of the frequency of contact with kin. It was possible to address this question statistically by means of a partial correlation. The number of siblings seen by those from group care contributed independently to their sense of well-being ($r = .20$). That is, it was a factor in their sense of well-being irrespective of the frequency of contact with kin. This latter was also independently associated with their sense of well-being ($r = .20$), and for the statistically minded, the two together accounted for 9.3% of the variance of their well-being scores.

It should be stressed that the number of siblings seen was eventually more important than whether or not they had been in touch with any sibling. Perhaps this was so because those who were in touch with many siblings had such contact more frequently or for a longer span of time, or perhaps the "safety in numbers" notion ws applicable here. In any event, like frequency of contact with parents or relatives, contact with a number of siblings carried a special meaning for the young adults who were discharged from group settings. It provided them with a sense of family, or strengthened it, and this had a long-range bearing on their sense of well-being. For those living in foster homes, who therefore had a substitute or supplementary family, the number of siblings seen ultimately carried less weight.

Their Satisfaction with Contact

Only one out of three (32.8%) young adults who knew of a sibling were satisfied with the amount of contact they had. The rest were dissatisfied, with complaints more prevalent among those from group care (78.0%), than among those from foster homes (62.8%). Dissatisfaction could mean that they felt there was too little contact or too much. Most (62.7%) complained of too little contact, but a small group (4.4%), all discharged from foster homes, felt there was too much. One young man who felt this way stated:

> I was always told to watch my younger sister and take her along. She was awfully messed up. It spoiled a lot of fun I could have had.

But much more frequently the complaint was about too little contact:

> There should be more visiting with brothers and sisters from the start.

> The social worker made it difficult to keep in touch with sibs . . . appointments had to be made to see them.

> The agency should let him know if he have some brothers and sisters . . . you know how much better that will make a person feel for their brothers and sisters to visit him.

> It's better if you can be kept with your own brothers and sisters . . . able to talk with each other . . . knowing that they're your family . . . you're at ease.

> I felt good that some of us were kept together. I think it helped a lot . . . I think we could have had more contact with other brothers and sisters though.

On the whole the young adults were less satisfied with the amount of contact they had with brothers and sisters than with their biological parents and other relatives. We inquired about this only of those who remembered some contact with a biological mother (N = 156), father (N = 98), or relative (N = 129). On the whole, close to 54% stated that they felt generally satisfied with the amount they saw their biological mothers during their total placement. The proportions for biological fathers and relatives were 49% and 58.9%, respectively. Here, too, in each instance a fair number were not satisfied with the amount of contact they recalled, and most often the complaint was on the side of too little contact. But there were inevitably some who complained about too much contact. For example, when asked about the last years in placement, 10.2% felt they had too much contact with their biological mothers, 19.4% felt this about their fathers, and 4.3% thought they had seen adult relatives too frequently. Those from foster homes and group care were quite alike in this regard, but in each group the young women complained more than the young men about too much contact. Perhaps the most interesting aspect of these findings was the fact that complaints about too much contact were leveled more often against biological parents than against members of the extended family. In sum, most of those who were not satisfied wanted more contact, but not all viewed the contact they had in such a positive vein, and wished there had been less.

So much for the group that had contact. There were also some who recalled no contact with anyone in their family of origin who wished there had been some. For instance, they may have been in touch with their biological mothers but wished they also had had contact with a relative. All together there were 167 individuals who spoke of no contact with someone whom they thought was alive. About 30% of them were quite satisfied with the situation; the other 70% wished there had been some contact. Forty young adults wished there had been some contact with their biological mothers, 82 stated that they wanted contact with their biological fathers, and 54 spoke of wishing they had seen certain relatives.

To sum up, these young adults were least satisfied with the amount of contact they had with their siblings. The message was unambiguous. However, their satisfaction with the amount of contact with kin was more mixed. One cannot make a summary statement about it. Some wanted more frequent contact, while others wanted less. Some wanted contact with people who were not in touch, while others were quite satisfied. If one could make a generalization on the basis of the young adults' statements, it would be in the direction of a desire for more contact. But the picture was too complex for such a sweeping statement. Perhaps the real message from these young adults was different, for in a sense they were saying they wished their own perspective on contact had been given greater weight. Some in fact raised this point quite directly; in the words of one: "It was always the grownups who were making the decisions . . . I was treated like a child . . . never consulted even in my teens."

Of course, in the world of foster care it is often impossible to satisfy the wishes of all, for too many factors and different interests are involved. The very fact of visiting, let alone its frequency, is often determined by factors beyond an agency's control. The young adults were quite aware of this. At the same time some of them, in looking back, advocated more opportunities for direct discussion about all of this with the children themselves. Perhaps such discussions would have led to greater satisfaction on their part in the long run.

Kin, Foster Parents, and House Parents

The biological families were in touch not only with their children but with the foster families, and with house or cottage parents in group settings. In the interviews the young adults were asked about this. Close to 69% of those from foster homes, but only about 47% of those from group settings recalled such contacts. In most instances (83.4%) such contacts were "occasional" or "rare," rather than more frequent. In all, 77 young adults from foster homes spoke of their biological mothers having had some contact, while 45 spoke of fathers and 45 mentioned a relative. These numbers are not additive, for in about half of the cases more than one family member was involved. On the whole, the young adults felt that the contacts were positive. Accordingly, about 70% of the biological mothers, about 65% of the biological fathers, and about 73% of the relatives got along very well or fairly well with the foster parents. Only some 16% of the biological mothers and fathers, and about 9% of the relatives were thought to get along fairly or very poorly with the foster parents, and the remainder were assessed as neither positive nor negative. In contrast, almost all of those who were discharged from group settings recalled contact between kin and house or cottage parents in positive terms, with but a handful describing such contact as neither positive nor negative.

Given the potential for conflict between kin and foster parents, it is perhaps surprising that so few were described in such terms. It is, of course, possible that those who were in contact were a select group. Caseworkers may have intervened and discouraged contacts in situations that they felt to be explosive. It is also possible that with the passage of time the young adults recalled these contacts in rosier terms than had prevailed at the time. Whatever the case, ultimately their recollections were of prime importance to them, and these memories were decidedly in a positive vein. Yet the young adults' sense of well-being and their satisfaction with foster care were not in any way connected with whether or not there was contact between kin and foster, house or cottage parents, nor with the quality of the contacts recalled by these young adults.

Contact During Placement and After

Was there a connection between contact during placement and contact with kin at the time of our interviews some years later? Was contact with kin maintained once the young adults were on their own, and to what extent was it established where none had existed? These data can be seen in table 4.3. The total numbers on contact during placement refer to information from the case records. They vary somewhat from figures presented earlier since only those who were interviewed are included. Mail questionnaires did not include questions about contact with kin.

Those who were discharged from group settings will be discussed first. If kin were in touch during the early years in

Table 4.3
Contact with Kin During Placement and at Interview

	Discharged From:					
	Foster Home			Group Setting		
	CONTACT: EARLY YEARS					
	High (N = 53)	Low (N = 81)	None (N = 38)	High (N = 44)	Low (N = 15)	None (N = 8)
Contact: Interview						
High	43.4%	29.6%	21.1%	72.7%	53.3%	37.5%
Low	17.0	19.8	10.5	22.7	26.7	12.5
None	39.6	50.6	68.4	4.5	20.0	50.0
Total	100.0%	100.0%	100.0%	99.9%	100.0%	100.0%
	CONTACT: LAST YEARS					
	High (N = 51)	Low (N = 98)	None (N = 23)	High (N = 36)	Low (N = 29)	None (N = 2)
Contact: Interview						
High	64.7%	20.4%	8.7%	72.2%	58.6%	—
Low	17.6	17.3	13.0	19.4	27.6	—
None	17.6	62.2	78.3	8.3	13.8	100.0
Total	99.9%	99.9%	100.0%	99.9%	100.0%	100.0%

placement, whether frequently or minimally, a majority of the young adults maintained frequent contact at the time of our interviews. This was particularly true of those with frequent contact during the early years of placement. At the time of our interviews 72.7% of these maintained frequent contact with kin, while 53.3% of those with infrequent contact during the early years were now frequently in touch. Essentially, the same pattern prevailed with regard to contact during the last years in placement. Clearly those who had minimal contact while in placement increased the amount of contact following discharge. This was not surprising since their kin were in most instances the only link that they had to a family.

The picture was somewhat different for those who were discharged from foster homes, but there were also similarities. If contact during the last years in foster care was frequent, most often that frequency was maintained four or five years after discharge. Only a small number were in touch with kin where there had been no contact during the last years in placement. For this small group there had also been no contact with kin at the start of placement. They apparently had established contact following their discharge.

The young adults from foster homes differed most sharply from those discharged from group settings in the converse of this—the number of instances where contact had been dropped altogether. This occurred most often where contact during the last years had been infrequent. Of these 98 young adults, some 62% were no longer in touch with their biological families at the time of our interviews. Could the death of family members be a possible explanation for this drop? Our analysis indicated that this was the case for some, but for only a few. In most instances, contact had simply ceased. Unfortunately, we do not know what took place in the interim, or on whose initiative this occurred. Some young adults spoke of pressure from their workers about visits with kin, said that such contact had not been their choice, but went along in order "not to rock the boat" while in foster care. As mentioned earlier, some felt they had too much contact. Furthermore, some did not recall any contact during their last years in care. One can also imagine that some foster parents discouraged contact with kin once the young adults had been discharged from foster care. It is also possible that some biological families were encouraged to visit but no longer did so when their caseworkers were not in the picture. Whatever the reasons, over the years following discharge family members who had been minimally in touch gradually receded into the background as these young adults began living more independently, carving out their own lives.

Final Comments

This chapter has dealt with biological family contact during placement from a number of perspectives. Most of the children did have contact, although for many it was minimal. Our review of background and placement factors suggested that the age of the children at placement was a central link. Biological families were more apt to maintain contact with children who were older at placement. Since those who were discharged from group settings tended to be older at placement, a larger proportion of them had contact with their kin than was true of those discharged from foster homes. Familial circumstances that led to the children's placement were also associated with contact for some. Furthermore, the data lent some support to the notion that contact with kin can ease a youngster's transition into foster care. However, support for this idea was quite weak and applied only to females.

Most important, among those discharged from foster homes contact with kin during the early years of placement had no bearing on their view of themselves and their lives at the time of our interviews. This was so among males and females irrespective of their age at placement. The only sex difference was observed among those from foster homes who had no contact with kin. In this group the young women eventually assessed themselves and their lives more poorly than the young men. As for the young adults from group care, those with infrequent or sporadic contact during the early years ultimately felt most poorly about themselves and their lives.

Contact with kin during the last years before discharge also had no bearing on the sense of well-being of those who were discharged from foster homes. But among those who were discharged from group settings, frequent contact was associated with a more positive appraisal of themselves and their lives at the time of our interviews. Furthermore, the more siblings they saw, the better their outlook. Links with biological family members were clearly more important for those who left group care.

Our review of the young adults' recollections of contact showed that infrequent contact was often not remembered. The young adults had mixed reactions to the amount of contact with their kin. Many felt there had been too little contact, but some thought there was too much. Contact with their own siblings, on the other hand, was generally regarded as too limited. Contacts between biological families and foster parents or group care staff were on the whole positively remembered.

Finally, the matter of whether contact with kin during placement had been maintained some years following discharge was examined. While those from group settings generally continued to be in touch with their kin, infrequent contact among those discharged from foster homes tended to be dropped by the time of our interviews, in part because such limited contact was not recalled or recognized.

As these young adults looked back on their stay in foster care, one was often left with the impression that they believed they should have had more say about a number of things, including contact. They had opinions about the atmosphere surrounding visits, about timing, and about whom they saw or did not see. They felt that their thoughts about these matters could have been sought more often and taken into account, particularly as they grew older.

There was a wistful tone in their voices, and perhaps some wishful thinking, as they spoke of fathers and mothers whom they wished they had known better, and of deceased grandparents whom they never met. By and large, however, they took a matter-of-fact approach to the past. There were suggestions for youths now in foster care, but few regrets about their own experience. Bygone was bygone. What happens now, rather than some time ago, seemed most important. Perhaps it was this attitude more than anything else that carried weight in what has been reported, and so for most there was no connection between visiting patterns in the past and their current happiness, their sense about themselves, and their lives.

Chapter Five

PROBLEMS THEY HAD

Sometimes when you're separated from your family you can't really expect love from others . . . or you can expect it, but you must realize that it may not come. The burden rests on the foster child to adapt to the situation. I was able to roll with the punches.

Interview
January 1980

There is a common assumption that youngsters who grow up in foster care are a problem-ridden group. Neither adopted nor discharged home, they must perforce develop social or emotional problems, and eventually constitute a group among whom such problems are legion. It was, therefore, important to learn about the actual prevalence of problems exhibited by the sample children during their placement. Information about such problems might also shed light on aspects of the young adults' lives following their discharge from placement.

Our review of case records focused on three problem areas: the state of each child's physical health, problems of a social or emotional nature, and difficulties in the intellective and learning spheres. In each area we gleaned whatever information was available, using reports of physical examinations, psychological and psychiatric evaluations, school achievement, and teachers' appraisals, in addition to the caseworkers' descriptions and assessments of the children. Because of the size of the records two time periods were again singled out—the early and last years in care. Problems were rated as absent, slight, moderate, or severe according to a set of criteria that will be described as each area is reviewed. Once again those who read the case records conferred routinely on any situations that were ambiguous.

Unfortunately, case records are a limited instrument for such assessments. One must be concerned about information that may be missing, and about relying too heavily on the perceptions and recordings of numerous caseworkers, teachers, and house parents who are not apt to be using identical criteria. Heavy weight was therefore placed on corroborated reports and on descriptions of repetitive rather than episodic behavior. Nevertheless, some errors were bound to occur when fine distinctions had to be made, particularly when using the adjacent categories at each end of the scale. Therefore, in much of the analysis I combined individuals who exhibited no problems with those whose problems were thought to be minimal or slight, and also combined those whose difficulties were assessed as moderate with the severe problem group.

When one examines everyone—respondents, nonrespondents, and those who were excluded from the study because of the severity of their problems—complete information about social and emotional problems was available on 378 individuals. Some 21% exhibited such problems to a moderate or severe degree at the time they were discharged from foster care. It is unfortunate that equivalent information about young adults in the general population is not available for comparison. Nevertheless, to think of those from foster care as problem-ridden psychologically is clearly unwarranted.

Let us then turn to the respondents, and to table 5.1 and review the three problem areas during the earliest and last years in care. It is well to remember that each area is not independent. That is, health problems could also generate emotional problems, and the latter could lead to learning difficulties. However, each area will be examined separately, before a more composite picture is presented.

Table 5.1
Moderate or Serious Problems at Placement and at Discharge

	Discharged From:							
	Foster Home				Group Setting			
	M (N = 103)		F (N = 91)		M (N = 42)		F (N = 18)	
	N	(%)	N	(%)	N	(%)	N	(%)
Problems at Placement								
Health	10	(9.7)	4	(4.4)*	5	(11.9)	3	(16.7)
Learning	8	(7.9)*	7	(7.8)†	17	(42.5)*	1	(5.6)
Social/Emotional	22	(21.4)	8	(8.8)	22	(53.6)†	4	(22.2)
Problems at Discharge								
Health	3	(2.9)	5	(5.5)*	6	(14.3)	1	(5.6)
Learning	33	(32.4)*	18	(20.2)†	11	(27.5)*	1	(5.6)
Social/Emotional	21	(20.4)	8	(8.8)	9	(22.0)†	4	(22.2)
Problems at Placement and Discharge								
Health	1	(1.0)	3	(3.3)*	4	(9.5)	1	(5.6)
Learning	7	(6.9)*	2	(2.2)†	6	(15.0)*	0	(0.0)
Social/Emotional	7	(6.8)	0	(0.0)	4	(9.8)†	2	(11.1)

*Based on one less case than total.
†Based on two less cases than total.

Health Problems

Our classification of moderate or severe problems in this area included such impairments as serious deformities, chronic ailments of various sorts, serious allergies, severe circulatory problems, and substantial visual or hearing disabilities. As can be seen in table 5.1, our sample on the whole did not exhibit such problems in large proportions either at the time of placement or at discharge. Young adults who were discharged from group settings were somewhat more likely to be discharged with a health problem than those who were discharged from foster homes. Among all respondents it can be seen that for some, problems that existed at an earlier period were no longer in evidence at discharge, while others had developed such problems by the time of discharge. A few had such problems at both times and probably throughout their stay in foster care.

Intellective and Learning Difficulties

Before we began reviewing the case records we hoped to find information on the intelligence test scores of each of the children. Although arguments have raged about the precise meaning of such scores, we felt they could provide a useful, even if imperfect, indicator of the children's intellectual functioning. Our initial optimism waned quickly. It was not so much a case of missing information, for we found IQ scores in 84.1% of the records, but the test results were for children at different ages. We looked for the last score in each record, but this may have been at age 9 for one child and at age 16 for another. In addition, the use of different tests made for questionable comparability. For whatever it is worth, the sample mean fell in the lower part of the normal range, with an average score of 93.6. The respondents' scores varied from a low of 58 to a high of 128, with no differences between males and females, or between those discharged from foster homes and from group settings.

Because of our doubts about these scores, more weight was attached to psychological assessments of intellective development and to the youngsters' functioning in school. For instance, any child whose schoolwork fell clearly below par for his or her age, or who was in a class for very slow children, was considered to have moderate or severe learning problems.

The proportion of children whose records indicated some intellective or learning problems early in placement is clearly linked to their age when they entered care, since such problems were rarely identified until they entered school. Thus, few respondents who were discharged from foster homes were thought to have moderate or severe learning problems at the time of admission. However, by the time of discharge, the proportion with such learning difficulties had risen. In fact, about one out of every four young adults discharged from foster homes, and somewhat more males than females, were then considered to have a problem with work at school. The reasons for this increase among the foster home group are of great interest. Was it merely that such problems were increasingly identified as children became older, or was it a result of entering and being in foster care? The young adults might have developed these problems no matter where they lived. Two findings fail to resolve the role of placement. For one, those with learning problems at discharge tended to have been shifted more often than those without problems. But I could not establish which came first—the shifts or the problems. Second, more of those with learning problems at discharge, when compared with those without, had their first long-term placement in an institutional setting, and this was so irrespective of the age at placement. For instance, among infants who were 11 months or younger at the time they were placed, some 43% of those who later exhibited learning difficulties, as compared with some 24% of those who did not, had remained in an institutional setting (usually a baby nursery) for an extended period in their early life. Was such lengthy group care at a young age deleterious? Or was their nursery stay extended because they appeared to be less alert and slower in their development at the time they were placed? We are left with an unexplained concern about the effects of initial lengthy group care on the intellective development of those who were discharged from foster homes.

Those who were discharged from group settings presented a different picture. More males than females exhibited educational problems, particularly at placement. More than one-third of these males continued to show such problems over the span of their foster care experience; eleven males no longer exhibited these problems at discharge, but five other males had developed them by that time. Why did a larger proportion of males than females from group care exhibit learning problems during the early years of placement? In part their somewhat older age at the time was a factor, since more males were of school age when they were placed. We do not know whether their learning problems had already developed before entering foster care, or whether the turmoil surrounding placement, which often included a change of schools, affected their educational functioning at the start of placement. Intellective and learning problems diminished for some during the course of placement, so that the proportion of males with such problems at discharge had dropped. On the other hand, for those who were discharged from foster homes, the proportion with learning problems, whether male or female, had increased by the time of their discharge.

Social and Emotional Problems

Problems in this area were rated as moderate or severe if, for instance, a child tended to withdraw from personal relationships, exhibited eating or sleep problems, had frequent nightmares or enuresis, often displayed depressive moods, was hyperactive, or was frequently in one or another sort of difficulty with adults or peers.

About 22% of the respondents exhibited moderate or severe social or emotional problems at the time they were placed, and nearly 17% were considered to have such serious problems when they were discharged. This included about 5% who exhibited such problems at both points in time. In other words, the problems of some 17% of the young adults diminished over time in care, while for a smaller proportion (12%) problems arose where none had been noticed during the early years. Males who were discharged from group settings were the only subgroup among whom the proportion with such problems dropped between entry into and discharge from care.

A sex difference in prevalence of social and emotional problems can readily be seen in table 5.1. A larger proportion of males than females exhibited problems during the early years of placement. What could account for this? Perhaps such problems were more noticeable among males since they, as a group, tended to be older at placement. Yet, the sex difference in the proportion with problems at placement also existed among those who were eventually discharged from foster homes, and these males and females did not differ in their age at placement. Since age was, therefore, not a factor in the observed sex difference, and other background characteristics were similar as far as we knew, the explanation had to lie elsewhere. Perhaps, as conjectured in another context, males reacted more than females to disturbances in their families which had led to their placement, or to being separated from their biological families. Perhaps boys were less flexible than girls with respect to making peace with a new environment. It is also possible that for whatever reason boys were more rambunctious and lashed out more than girls so that their behavior was simply described as more problematic during the early years of placement, although it did not in fact mean that more had problems at placement.

By the time of discharge, a different picture emerged. Here a sex difference in the proportion of young adults with serious problems existed only among those from foster homes. At first blush this might suggest that males fared worse than females in foster homes. Such an interpretation might make sense were it not for the fact that one-third of the males had also exhibited such problems at the time they were placed, and therefore they started out with these problems and did not develop them later on. In fact, when only those who had developed problems in the course of placement were singled out, there were no longer any sex differences among those who were discharged from foster homes. Thus, the males did not fare worse in foster homes, but a larger proportion of males with serious problems at the start continued to have them at the end of placement than was true of females who were discharged from foster homes.

Only two other factors were found to be clearly associated with the presence or absence of social and emotional problems at placement. Those who exhibited such problems at placement were on the whole older (mean = 7.8 years) at placement than those who did not (mean = 4.0 years); and if discharged from a foster home they had a larger variety, but not a greater number, of placements. This suggested that during the course of their stay in a particular foster home, they had also spent interim periods of a month or more in diagnostic and treatment facilities.

Social and emotional problems at the time of discharge were associated with three elements in placement. Among those eventually discharged from foster homes, the nature of their first long-term placement was an issue. If that placement was in an institutional setting rather than a foster home, there was a modest trend toward more problems by the time of discharge, both among males and females, and irrespective of their age at placement. The connection was not strong but worth a passing comment, particularly since this finding was similar to what has been presented on learning difficulties at the time of discharge. Once again there is the matter of what produced the connection. Perhaps, as already mentioned, such early group placements augur poorly for youngsters in the long run. On the other hand, it is possible that they remained in such institutional placements longer because of questions about their responsiveness and development at an earlier period. This conjecture is made even though there was no connection at all between the severity of their social or emotional problems at placement and the nature of their first long-term placement. However, many were so young at the time that incipient problems were not easy to detect, and when noted they were apt to be seen as relatively minor. Hence, the chicken and egg conundrum cannot be solved here.

The second factor that was associated with the presence of serious social or emotional problems at the time of discharge concerned the young adults' contact with members of their biological families, but a connection existed only among those who were discharged from group settings. More young people exhibited such problems if their contacts during the last years of care were minimal or nonexistent. For this group, ties with the biological parents and extended family played a very important role. Not so for those who were discharged from foster homes, where neither contact early in placement nor during the final years was associated with psychological problems at the time of discharge. This was clearly indicated in our data. About 85% of those with frequent contact, 87% of those with

low contact, and 82% of those with no contact with their biological families during the last years in care exhibited no psychological problems at the time they were discharged. In other
words, for the foster home group the proportions remained
alike irrespective of the amount of family visiting. The picture
with respect to family contact during the early years was quite
similar. Although in an earlier chapter it was noted that extended family members played a special role in connection with
the absence of one or another sort of problem in this group,
such extended family contact was not as important when we
singled out social and emotional problems.

The third and final element from placement that was connected with social and emotional difficulties at the time of discharge was education. Only 30% of the respondents who were
discharged with serious social and emotional problems had
completed or gone beyond high school by the time of discharge, compared with more than 84% of those who were discharged without such serious problems. The link between level
of education and social and emotional problems is not surprising. What is not clear is which preceded which, for while serious social and emotional problems can lead to difficulties with
schoolwork, it is also possible to imagine that problems with
schoolwork can generate anxieties and doubts about one's capacities and lead to social and emotional problems. In any
event, the link was not a perfect one, for some with serious
social and emotional problems had moved ahead in school,
while others who were not viewed as having social and emotional difficulties had fallen behind in school.

The Hierarchy of Problems

In describing each problem area separately, an important
consideration has been omitted—the prevalence of each of the
areas both at the time of placement and at discharge. This
hierarchy can also be seen in table 5.1.

At the time of placement, problems of a social and emotional nature predominated. Among those who were eventu-

ally discharged from foster homes 15.5% exhibited such a problem, while for 7.9% the problem was intellective or educational, and 7.3% entered care with a serious health problem. The hierarchy for those eventually discharged from group settings was similar. Close to 45% exhibited a social or emotional difficulty, whereas 30.5% manifested an educational and 13.3% a serious health problem.

Findings on the nature of their problems at discharge were especially interesting and perhaps surprising. We had expected psychological problems to predominate, as was the case for the time of placement, but found otherwise. Among those discharged from group settings 22.4% exhibited social or emotional problems, 20.3% had fairly serious educational problems, and close to 12% had problems in the area of health. The difference in types of problems was most dramatic for those discharged from foster homes. Some 4.1% were discharged with a health problem, and 14.9% exhibited social or emotional problems. But 26.7% left care with an educational deficit which, in most instances, had either developed or come to light during the course of placement, following their entry into school.

At both these time periods the proportions with problems in each area were not additive, for as mentioned earlier some individuals had problems in more than one area. This will be discussed shortly. The important point here is that by the time these young adults were discharged, problems connected with learning had risen in the hierarchy. Such problems had apparently not been effectively dealt with during their time in foster care. They were therefore discharged into the community with deficits that would have serious consequences in the years ahead.

Problems and Their Sense of Well-Being

On the whole, the absence or presence of serious problems at placement in each of the areas discussed was not associated with the young adults' assessments of themselves and their lives at the time of our interviews. These data are presented in table 5.2. The differences move in various directions with no consistency throughout. There is only one suggestive finding. Among the young people who were eventually discharged from foster homes, those who quite early showed intellective or learning problems tended eventually to have a poorer sense of well-being. However, the association was very weak. The limited effect of early problems on the young adults' sense of well-being was undoubtedly in part a function of problems that diminished among some of the respondents between the time they entered and were discharged from placement.

Table 5.2

Health, Social/Emotional, Learning Problems and Sense of Well-Being

| | Discharged From: | | | | | |
| | Foster Home | | | Group Setting | | |
	Mean*	S.D.	(N)	Mean*	S.D.	(N)
Health Problems						
At Placement:						
None/slight	.21	2.37	(176)	−.36	2.37	(51)
Moderate/severe	1.45	1.96	(12)	−1.66	2.57	(7)
At Discharge:						
None/slight	.29	2.36	(180)	−.26	2.27	(52)
Moderate/severe	.10	2.50	(8)	−2.80	2.51	(6)
Social/Emotional Problems						
At Placement:						
None/slight	.34	2.40	(161)	−.64	2.59	(32)
Moderate/severe	.06	2.04	(28)	−.32	2.23	(25)
At Discharge:						
None/slight	.29	2.42	(160)	−.18	2.43	(45)
Moderate/severe	.35	1.97	(29)	−1.72	2.06	(12)
Learning Problems						
At Placement:						
None/slight	.35	2.32	(171)	−.84	2.33	(39)
Moderate/severe	−.69	2.54	(15)	−.04	2.31	(17)
At Discharge:						
None/slight	.56	2.27	(137)	−.43	2.43	(45)
Moderate/severe	−.56	2.41	(49)	−1.31	1.80	(11)

*Z-scores: A high positive score signifies a more positive sense of well-being.

The picture at the time of discharge was somewhat differ-ent, although uniform differences are not apparent in each problem area shown in table 5.2. For instance, with respect to health there was a link to the sense of well-being, but only among those who were discharged from group settings. In this group, those who were discharged with serious health prob-lems had a poorer outlook at the time of our contacts with them. The results on social and emotional problems late in placement are quite similar, since a connection existed only among those who were discharged from group settings. Those who were thought to have serious social or emotional prob-lems late in placement felt worse about themselves and their lives as young adults.

The most consistent connection between a problem area and the young adults' sense of well-being is evident when one ex-amines learning difficulties during the last years in placement. Among those who were discharged from foster homes there was a strong link. Those who exhibited difficulties in learning, who had fallen behind in school, felt worse about themselves and their lives than those without such problems. The data on learning problems at discharge among respondents from group settings were very similar to the data on those from foster homes, although the latter differences were not statistically significant. On the whole, problems in the educational sphere augured poorly for the young adults in our sample.

Problems in Combination

Our examination of separate problem areas has provided an incomplete picture. Problems may overlap since any given in-dividual may have exhibited problems in more than one area. In order to arrive at a full picture, we looked at how many of the young adults had a serious problem in one or more areas. We had complete information on this for 249 respondents at the time of placement and for 247 at the point of discharge.

During the early years of placement 32.1% of the sample

exhibited a serious health, social and emotional, or educational problem, or some combination of these. These 80 respondents were, on the average, older (mean = 7.0 years) at the time they were placed than those who exhibited no serious problems during the first years in foster care (mean = 3.9 years). We do not know to what extent the onset of problems preceded placement or were precipitated by placement. Second, those who early in placement displayed one or more problems constituted a larger proportion of those who were eventually discharged from group settings. In this group 54.2% had entered care with a problem, as compared with 25.3% of those who were eventually discharged from foster homes. This is not surprising since some were placed directly into group care because of their age and because of the problems they exhibited. In fact, those who displayed one or more problems at placement were less apt to have ever lived in a foster home at all. Third, in the group as a whole, boys were more apt to have one or more problems (40.8%) at placement than girls (20.6%). This was true for both those who were eventually discharged from foster homes and from group settings but the difference was larger for the latter.

Nothing else that we examined, whether from the young adults' background, their placement experience, or major aspects of their lives at the time of our interviews, was associated with the problems they exhibited during the early years of placement. Their sense of well-being as young adults was also not at all related. No doubt this was in part so because somewhat more than 56% of those who had entered foster care with one or more problems no longer exhibited such problems when they were discharged. On the other hand, 29.6% of those who displayed no noticeable problems around the time of entry had developed problems by the time of discharge.

All together 34% of the young adults in the sample were discharged from foster care with a fairly serious health, social and emotional, or educational problem, or a combination of these. This was equally true of those who were discharged from foster homes (32.8%) and from group settings (37.9%), and was not associated with their age at placement. Among the 62 who were discharged from foster homes with one or more problems, 66.1% exhibited a problem at discharge where none had been noticeable when they entered foster care. This was true of only 40.9% of the 22 young adults who were discharged from group settings with problems. A majority of the latter had therefore entered with problems that were still present at discharge, while for the foster home group most of the problems seen at discharge had emerged during their stay in placement. Their younger age at placement was no doubt a factor here.

What elements from their background or placement were associated with the presence of one or another sort of problem during the last years of placement? For one, the young adults' sex was linked. Somewhat more than 39% of the young men, in contrast to about 27% of the young women, were discharged with a problem of some sort. This was so regardless of whether they were discharged from foster homes or group settings. Beyond these sex differences, background and placement characteristics were generally unrelated. For instance, neither the respondents' race nor their reasons for placement were associated; such factors as shifts in care or the variety of placements were also unrelated. Agency characteristics of various sorts, such as their religious or nonsectarian affiliation, likewise had no bearing. But among the young adults who were discharged from foster homes, somewhat more (40%) of those whose first long-term placement was in an institutional setting displayed one or more problems at the time of discharge than those whose first long-term placement was in a foster home (28.1%). However, the association was quite weak. The amount of contact with their kin during the early and later years of placement also had no bearing except in one instance, which was already examined in an earlier chapter. Those who had frequent contacts with a member of their extended biological families (such as a grandparent, aunt, or uncle) at the beginning or end of placement were less likely to exhibit one or another sort of problem at discharge than all the others, including those who had frequent contact with only their biological parents.

Problems of various kinds were, however, linked to certain areas of life that were explored during the course of our interviews. As these linkages will be reported in subsequent chapters, the focus here will be limited to those aspects of our interviews that touched on the educational deficits already reported. For one, those who were discharged with one or more problems had, by the time of our interviews, completed fewer years in school. For instance, respondents from foster homes who were discharged with problems had on the average completed somewhat less than 11 years of school; in other words, they had not graduated from high school. In contrast, those without serious problems at discharge had on the average completed somewhat more than 13 years of school. They therefore had continued with their education following high school graduation. Parallel differences existed among those who were discharged from group settings. Other areas in life were affected by these educational differences. For instance, the young adults who were discharged with one or more problems were much more likely to be unemployed at the time of our contacts with them. Among those with problems at discharge more than 36% were unemployed and looking for work, whereas among those who did not display problems 13% were unemployed at the time of our contacts. Lack of employment was clearly not a temporary happenstance, for those who were discharged with one or more problems were also more apt to be receiving public assistance at the time we heard from them. This was true of somewhat more than 32% of those who were discharged with problems. In contast, 13.5% of those without problems at discharge were receiving such aid at the time of our contacts.

Finally, the young adults' sense of well-being was seriously affected. Those who exhibited one or more problems at discharge assessed themselves and their lives considerably more poorly at the time of our contacts with them than those who left foster care without noticeable problems.

Final Comments

In reflecting on the aforegoing, several important issues stand out that require attention. At the start of this chapter the question was posed whether those who left foster care were psychologically problem-ridden. Such a generalization, however, seems quite unwarranted. Even when all kinds of problems were considered—psychological, educational, or physical—all together a minority of the young adults in our sample, exactly 34%, left care with such problems.

Whether one considers the proportion with problems at discharge high or not is left as a matter of opinion, for there is no absolute standard and no proper comparison can be made with the general population. In any event, a majority of the young adults were discharged from foster care without any particular problems whatsoever. But the important question is still a different one: to what extent did problems develop or come to light during the course of the young adults' stay in foster care? All together some 20% of the young adults were discharged with one or more problems when none had been in evidence at the time of placement, whereas about 14% exhibited moderately serious problems at both points in time. In thinking about foster care the opposite side of the coin, if you will, must also be considered. That is, some young people came into placement with problems that were no longer noticeable when they were discharged. This was the case for 17.8% of the 247 respondents. The largest group of all, however, both entered and left foster care without any problems. This group constituted 48.2% of our sample: 53.4% of those from foster homes, but only 31% of those who were discharged from group settings.

But the central point concerns those who exhibited problems at the time of their discharge. Whenever these problems have been discussed, the tendency in the child welfare field, as well as among others, has been to emphasize those of a psychological nature. Yet our data clearly showed the predominance of educational and learning problems at the time of discharge, particularly among those from foster homes. In large measure these became apparent during the course of placement as children entered the school system.

We do not know what precisely caused these educational deficits. No doubt, some youngsters were intellectually impaired. Perhaps for others psychological problems lay beneath. Factors connected with placement may also have contributed. Perhaps learning problems were allowed to simmer while caseworkers and foster parents attached greater weight to the psychological aspects of development and did not place equal emphasis on the youngsters' functioning in school. Expectations about schoolwork may have been lowered as part and parcel of a protective stance, or not clearly spelled out or emphasized to the youngsters by foster parents, house parents, or caseworkers.

Whatever the cause or causes, ultimately there were serious consequences for these young adults, for learning problems at discharge were so clearly associated with the young adults' poorer sense of well-being. Perhaps it was not these problems as such that led to a more negative view of their lives. Rather, such problems meant less achievement in school, which in turn limited their options for finding employment, which in turn influenced their assessments of themselves and their lives.

We cannot disentangle the variety of factors that underlay the development of educational problems. Nor do we know if a similar situation exists at this writing, although there is little reason to think otherwise. Whatever the case, our results clearly argue in favor of greater concern about the education of youngsters who are in foster care. Educational demands and expectations need to be communicated clearly to foster parents, house parents, and to the children themselves. Some of the young adults even singled out this issue:

> They should have demanded more of me . . . I was capable of doing much better in school, but no one seemed to care much about that.
>
> Interview
> October 1979

If learning problems arise they need to be identified and accurately assessed as early as possible, and then addressed quickly. It is well established that once a youngster falls behind, a vicious cycle develops all too easily. Clear lines of communication with school personnel are therefore a necessity.

It seems plausible that if tutors had been available, some of the youngsters would have benefited. The picture also might have been different had the agencies devoted more time to consultation with educational psychologists and others specifically trained to deal with existing and incipient learning problems with skill and sensitivity.

Professionals in the child welfare field have long stressed the importance of developing each individual's potential. Although we had no way of assessing the potential of those in our sample, it seems reasonable to assume that some, at least, did not reach it. Educational functioning has been emphasized because the findings were troubling. In view of the important ramifications of this subject for young adults following their discharge from foster care, it is urgent that more stress be given to this area than seems to have been done in the past. Only in this way can one truly address the goal of developing individual potential, not only in the psychological realm but in the educational realm as well.

PART TWO

THE YOUNG ADULTS IN
THE COMMUNITY

Chapter Six

CURRENT CIRCUMSTANCES

Four or five years had passed since the young adults had been discharged from foster care. Many had moved about, and by the time we made contact a fair number were living some distance away from New York City. In the interim, they had worked out a variety of living arrangements.

Some had ventured forth on their own, while others chose to remain with biological or foster families. At the time that we spoke with them, some seemed quite transient, while others were firmly situated in the communities where they lived. Some had many friends, others but a few; some maintained neighborly contacts, while others knew no neighbors; and some were active members of social organizations, while others kept their distance.

This chapter will briefly review these circumstances at the time that we gathered our data and, in addition, will examine the connection between factors in the young adults' current lives and their view of themselves and of life as a whole.

Place of Residence, Mobility, and Living Arrangements

At the time of our contacts a majority of the 277 young adults were residing in New York City (55.6%), Westchester County (5.1%), or a community on Long Island (8.7%). Close to 12% were living elsewhere in New York State or in a neighboring state. The remainder were much farther away. Somewhat more than 16% had taken up residence in distant states such as Oklahoma or California, and a small group (2.5%), primarily men in the armed forces, were overseas. More of those who had been discharged from group settings (67.1%), whether male or female, than those from foster homes (51.5%) were living in one of the five boroughs of New York City rather than farther away. Those from foster homes who were residents of Westchester and Long Island accounted for part of the difference. Some foster families lived in these suburbs and perhaps more of their former wards chose to remain in those areas than was the case for those discharged from group settings in those same suburbs. In some instances, foster families moved to other regions along with the young adults. In addition, since those from group settings had more contact with their kin during the last years of placement, their ties with their biological families probably played a role in keeping more of them in New York City. Ethnicity also played a role in where they resided, but this was so regardless of whether they were discharged from foster homes or group settings. More black respondents (68.4%) than others (45.6%) were living in New York City than elsewhere at the time of our contacts. It is unclear why this was so.

All in all, since the time of discharge more than one out of four of the young adults had moved a fair distance away from where they had been reared. Even if they remained in the same city or town where they were discharged, most had changed residences and neighborhoods. Only some 13% remained at the same address where they were living at the time of discharge. This was indeed a mobile group of young adults. On the average, excluding moves while in the armed forces, they had lived at four different addresses since they left foster care. Still, there was much variation in the group because some had never moved, while others commented that "there were too many addresses to count . . . I've lived in over 30 places." No doubt, the search for better, more convenient, or more permanent housing, for living quarters in proximity to work, to shopping areas, to schools, or in more congenial surround-

ings accounted for many of the moves. Those who were discharged from group settings, whether male or female, had
lived at more addresses since discharge (mean = 5.1) than those
from foster homes (mean = 3.6). This was so whether they resided in New York City or elsewhere. It was so whether they
had exhibited psychological problems at discharge or not. What
could account for the difference? Most likely the young adults
from foster homes moved less because, at discharge, they were
under less immediate pressure to begin to search for a separate residence. They therefore had more time to explore suitable housing than was true for those from group settings.

The information on the number of addresses allowed me to
reexamine Meier's (1965) earlier finding of a strong relationship between the number of residences in adulthood and the
frequency of foster care moves in childhood. Meier had speculated about the long-range negative impact upon the individual of shifts in foster care. In our study shifts in childhood
were associated with the presence of psychological problems
at the time of discharge, but such problems were totally unrelated to the amount of movement once out of foster care.
There was absolutely no connection between the number of
moves while in foster care and mobility in young adulthood.

As might have been expected, at the time of our contacts
the young men and women lived in a variety of kinds of dwell-
ings. The majority were living in rented apartments, but some
were residing in houses with former foster parents, spouses,
sexual partners, or friends. A few lived in trailers. Only a minority were living in rooms they had rented from strangers,
and a small number were renting a room from their former
foster families.

We probed for feelings about their places of residence, their
neighborhoods, and the availability of municipal services by
asking them to respond on a seven-point scale, using response
categories that had been developed over time and tested extensively (Andrews and Withey 1976). These data can be seen
in table 6.1. On the whole, the young adults felt more positively than negatively about the places they called home and

Table 6.1
Feelings About Living Conditions and Social Participation

	Discharged From:					
	Foster Home			Group Setting		
Feelings About	Mean*	S.D.	N	Mean*	S.D.	N
Apartment, room etc.	2.8	1.6	172	3.6	1.8	65
Neighborhood	3.4	1.8	171	3.8	2.0	65
Municipal services	3.3	1.6	165	3.6	1.7	63
Safety	2.9	1.5	170	3.3	1.8	66
Privacy	2.7	1.7	173	2.9	1.7	66
Neighbors	3.2	1.5	146	3.7	1.5	54
Friends	2.4	1.1	168	2.5	1.2	62
Organizations	2.1	1.1	72	2.4	1.2	32

*Seven-point scale: 1 = delighted, 2 = pleased, 3 = mostly satisfied, 4 = about equally satisfied and dissatisfied, 5 = mostly dissatisfied, 6 = unhappy, 7 = terrible.

the neighborhoods in which they were living, but their satisfaction was generally moderate. There was a suggestion that those who rented or owned a house were more satisfied with their home than those who lived in an apartment, a room, or a trailer. Those discharged from group settings were appreciably less happy about their living quarters than those from foster homes, although they did not differ much in their assessments of their neighborhoods as places to live, or in their satisfaction with municipal services such as garbage collection, street maintenance, and police protection. Women respondents, whether from foster homes or group settings, felt less safe in their neighborhoods than the men, a finding that has also been reported for the general population (Campbell 1981). Beyond this there were no sex differences in their reactions. Nor were there any differences in their sense of privacy, their feelings about being alone when they wanted to be. This feeling was unrelated to the number of other people in their immediate households, excluding those in service or college facilities. This household number ranged from none to eight, and on the average included between one and two adults or children.

The variety of living arrangements at the time of our contacts were considerable, ranging from those who lived totally alone (23.9%) or only with their offspring (4.7%) to those who were living with friends, siblings, spouses or partners, in-laws, biological or foster families, or some combination of these. Most (39.9%) were living with a spouse or someone whom they considered an established partner. Close to 12% remained with their foster families; a smaller proportion (5.4%) lived with their biological parents or relatives; an additional 3.3% lived with siblings. The remainder (11.2%) resided with friends or in an armed forces or other congregate facility.

Thus, a minority were living alone and most were no longer with either their biological or foster families. They had worked out various styles and arrangements for living in the communities where they resided. More of those discharged from group settings (46.9%) than those from foster homes (23%) were living alone or only with their offspring.

Neighbors, Organizations, and Friends

Generally, the young adults felt they belonged to the neighborhoods they called home. For instance, most (72.3%), whether from a foster home or a group setting, spoke of knowing some neighbors well enough to visit or call on, and more than one-fourth of these felt they knew many neighbors. On the whole, the young adults felt reasonably satisfied with their neighbors. Close to 45% spoke of getting together with a neighbor at least once a week, 16% socialized with a neighbor a few times a month, and 11.5% spoke of less frequent contact. Only about one out of four of the respondents said they never called on a neighbor or vice versa. The place of residence, whether New York City or elsewhere, was totally unrelated to the amount of neighborly contact.

In addition to neighborhood socializing, some relied on more formal organizations for social activities. Roughly 45% of the young adults said they belonged to such an organization, most often a club or group connected with a church or temple, or a community group engaged in athletics. Those who belonged felt quite pleased with their experience in these organizations.

Membership in clubs and groups provided an avenue for meeting people and served as a source, though not by any means the only source, of friendships. At the time of our contacts, the young adults were hardly devoid of friends whom they considered close. Of the 273 who answered a question about friendships, only 7%—fewer from foster homes than from group settings—felt they had no close friends. On the average they spoke of having four to five close friends, with those from foster homes and group settings quite alike. We had wondered to what extent children from foster care "stick together," but most (74%) said that to their knowledge none of their close friends had ever been in foster care. It was also clear that many of the friendships were not of recent origin, for nearly 65% spoke of having met at least some of their close friends during the time they, the young adults, were still in foster care. In any event, they were on the whole fairly pleased with the sort of friends they had, maintained regular and generally frequent contact with them, and most felt they had as many friends as they wanted. Only 36.5% stated that they would like to have more friends, and one out of four said that they often wished that people would like them "more than they do." This was equally true of males and females, and of those from foster homes and group care.

Psychological Support

Sheer numbers of friends, are of course, less important than knowing that someone else is available with whom one feels free to talk and on whom one can count for advice or help if one has worries or problems. This could have been a friend or neighbor, someone from the agency, or a member of the biological or foster family. The vast majority (96%) of the young adults felt there was someone to whom they could turn for advice or help, and nearly 22%—more of the young women than the men—felt there were many such people. Yet, while so many spoke of having someone to count on for advice, about three out of ten were uncertain about whom they could count on for help. This was particularly so among those who felt there were only a few people to whom they could turn.

Feeling that there are people one can count on is related to, yet somewhat different from, feeling that people really care. Thus, while only 4% felt they had no one to count on for advice or help, 10.5% felt that the statement "no one cares much what happens to me" was "very true" or "pretty true" for them. More males (13.7%) than females (6.1%), whether from foster homes or group settings, agreed with the latter statement, just as more of the males had also spoken of having no one or only a few people on whom they could count for advice or help.

Spiritual Support

Participation in a community, having social contacts with neighbors and friends, and reliance on others for support are important aspects of the social and psychological dimensions of life. A description of the young adults' circumstances, however, would not be complete without touching on the spiritual aspects, usually associated with religious beliefs.

In an earlier chapter it was mentioned that a majority of the young adults designated a religious preference, but that 15.3% considered themselves as having "no religion" in a formal sense. One out of three said that they never attended religious services and another 42.4% attended anywhere from "less than once a year" to, at most, "several times a year." Only about one out of ten said that they went to services at least every week. Yet a majority expressed a sense of satisfaction from their religion. Clearly, for many their "spiritual values" had an importance regardless of the frequency of their attendance at religious services. Nearly 26% said that they felt "some" and an additional 36% felt "much" or "very much" satisfaction from religion at the time of our contacts. There were no sex differences or foster home or group setting differences in any of this, and those who designated a Catholic, Jewish, or Protestant preference were quite similar with respect to attendance and satisfaction. On the whole, those who belonged to smaller religious groups, such as Jehovah's Witnesses, said that they attended services more frequently and expressed a greater sense of satisfaction with their particular faith.

Connections with Their Sense of Well-Being

In earlier chapters it was noted that, on the whole, with some clear exceptions here and there, background and placement factors were less important predictors of the young adults' sense of well-being than might have been expected. When their current circumstances are considered, however, a very different picture emerges. The conditions in which they lived at the time of our contacts, their assessments of that environment, and the support they felt they received were more clearly related to their happiness, their feelings of well-being, and their sense of self. The here and now of their existence was a strong force in their sense of well-being. That is not to deny that developmental predispositions and past experiences undoubtedly played a role in shaping the young adults as individuals, and, in turn, influencing their approaches and reactions to current circumstances. It is simply to point out that in most instances no direct links were discerned between factors in the past and their sense of well-being as young adults, whereas there were such direct connections with their present experiences.

In order to assess the contribution of various aspects of life experience to the young adults' sense of well-being, some of the discussion will draw on factual items, such as organizational membership, and some will be based on the young adults' reactions to, or satisfaction with, various aspects of their existence, such as their feelings about the place they called home.

Among the things discussed in this chapter, three general areas stand out: community involvement; reactions to physical surroundings; and social, psychological, and spiritual supports.

The first of these, the extent to which these young adults were settled and involved in their communities, was measured indirectly by the number of addresses they had since discharge, by their relationships with neighbors, and by their participation in community organizations. There was only a modest inverse connection between the number of addresses and the young adults' sense of well-being $(r = -.19)$. This, therefore, accounted for very little of the variation in their assessments of their lives. Apparently, in addition to those who had many addresses and felt poorly, there must have been a number who had moved a lot but had positive feelings or who moved little but still had a poor sense of well-being. Nevertheless, the relationship was statistically significant and was stronger among males than among females. Psychological problems at discharge had no bearing on this relationship. The connection between moves and the sense of well-being existed regardless of whether or not they were discharged with psychological problems.

The young adults who were more rooted in their immediate communities, who knew many or at least several neighbors well enough to call on, exhibited a better sense of well-being $(r = .29)$ than those who spoke of only a few or of no neighbors. This was particularly true for those who were discharged from foster homes, perhaps because of those who continued to live in the very areas where they had been raised. Organizational membership was also, although weakly, connected with the young adults' sense of well-being. Those who were members felt on the average more positively (mean = .34) than those who were not (mean = −.24).

Physical surroundings also played a role in the young adults' sense of well-being. Those who resided in one of the five boroughs of New York City felt more poorly (mean = −.24) than those who lived elsewhere (mean = .35). This suggests that in New York City various preconditions for a more comfortable life, such as employment and adequate living quarters, were more difficult to attain by young adults attempting to make their own way. Perhaps the sheer size of this metropolis, and its associated impersonality, was also a factor in their poorer outlook. Whatever the reasons, the feelings of the young adults in New York City reflect those of the general population, which is less satisfied with life in urban centers (Campbell 1981). Other reactions to physical surroundings were also important. For instance, as can be seen in table 6.2, their ratings of their neighborhoods "as a place to live" and their reaction to their immediate surroundings—for example, their room or apartment—were both connected with their sense of well-being.

Finally, various aspects of support were associated with their sense of well-being. For instance, the number of close friends they claimed had a bearing ($r = .28$) as did their satisfaction with their friends (table 6.2). The young adults' responses to statements about people who care and can be counted on were perhaps the most direct measures of their feelings of support. Those who disagreed with "no one cares much what happens to me" and "these days I really don't know who I can count on for help" had a better sense of well-being, as can be seen in table 6.2. So, also, those with a more positive outlook spoke of more people they felt free to talk with and count on for advice or help if worries or problems arose ($r = .33$).

Table 6.2
Areas of Satisfaction and Sense of Well-Being

	Discharged From:					
	Foster Home			Group Setting		
	r*	r^2	N	r*	r^2	N
Positive Feelings About						
Who cares what happens to me	.42	.18	196	.32	.10	73
Who can be counted on for help	.38	.14	195	.43	.18	73
Home (apartment, room, etc.)	.37	.14	170	.28	.08	64
Friends	.36	.13	166	.30	.09	62
Neighborhood	.33	.11	169	.29	.08	64
Amount I am liked	.32	.10	193	.34	.12	73

*Pearson product-moment correlation coefficients.

The spiritual aspect was also a factor in their assessment of themselves and their lives. In a previous chapter it was reported that those who claimed to have a religious preference exhibited a better sense of well-being than those who had none. Furthermore, those who attended religious services more frequently had a more positive outlook on life ($r = .20$). Perhaps spiritual values provided some stability and sense of support in an ever changing world. What is less clear is whether such values or somewhat more social considerations were responsible for the connection between religious practices and well-being. Perhaps it was some of each, for those who gave a religious preference also had more close friends, and the more they attended services the more friends they claimed ($r = .13$). Since the organizations they joined were often sponsored by a church or temple, there was also a connection between such membership and the degree of attendance at religious services ($r = .35$).

In summary, community involvement; reactions to the physical surroundings of life; and the social, psychological, and spiritual supports all contributed to the sense of well-being of these young adults. These were not, however, independent of each other; rather, they were intertwined. For instance, those who knew more neighbors well enough to visit were also apt to report more people with whom they felt free to talk or on whom they could count for advice or help. Statistically it was possible to assess the combined contribution of the various factors by means of an ordinary multiple correlation. We did this by selecting ten major items* as indicators of the areas discussed.

The results of the multiple correlation are based on a reduced number of individuals, for anyone who was not asked a question (as was sometimes true of those who responded by questionnaire) or who did not answer a question that was asked

*The ten variables were: number of addresses, acquaintance with neighbors, place of residence (recorded in dummy form), number of close friends, frequency of attendance at religious services, feeling about living quarters, feeling about neighborhood, number of people one can count on for advice or help, feeling that no one cares, knowing whom one can count on for help.

was dropped from the analysis. Therefore, we were dealing with only 228 respondents. Since the multiple correlation coefficients were virtually identical for those who were discharged from foster homes and from group settings, the group as a whole will be considered. In combination these ten indicators contributed a fair amount to the young adults' sense of well-being. In more statistical language, there was a multiple correlation coefficient equal to .643 and thus the combined factors accounted for 41% of the variance in well-being scores.

The full sample needs to be considered for a comment on the contribution of individual items to the young adults' sense of well-being. On the whole the strongest connections were with items that signified social or psychological supports, and with items concerned with their view of their immediate environment, such as their apartment. Aspects of community involvement, such as the number of times they had moved and organizational membership, contributed less to their sense of well-being.

Subjective reactions—the young adults' feelings about the physical, social, and psychological environment—contributed more strongly to their assessments of themselves and their lives than the more objective indicators of their current circumstances discussed so far. This does not imply that the objective characteristics of their various environments were unimportant in the young adults' satisfaction with their lives. But they provided only a partial explanation. In part this was so because of flaws in our objective measures and because we had no actual behavioral indicators of important affective domains. In part it was so because the correspondence between objective conditions and subjective experience is generally far from perfect. Such things as one's happiness, one's assessment of oneself, and how one feels about one's life as a whole inevitably involve very personal and subjective judgments that hinge on factors beyond the more objective conditions of life.

The disucssion of current circumstances and the sense of well-being avoided any references to cause. Instead, connections and contributing factors were mentioned. In a study of this sort it is rarely possible to deal with the question of cause unless one is, at the very least, certain about the sequence of events in time. In all of this discussion, it is not at all clear what came first. For instance, one could argue that the number of close friends did not result in a better sense of well-being, but that those who were more satisfied with their lives in the first place were more apt to develop close friendships, or were simply more likely to say they had more close friends. The fact that such friendships were often of long standing, having developed many years earlier, lends some support to the notion that close friendships did influence their sense of well-being at the time of our contacts. But what about the other factors? Perhaps those with a better outlook were more apt to become members of various organizations in their communities, to reach out to neighbors, to move away from New York City, to attend religious services, to feel positively about their living quarters and neighborhood, and perhaps to feel that people cared about them and to say they knew whom they could count on for help. Perhaps those who were more satisfied with their lives were simply less critical about everything and portrayed the present in more optimistic terms. They were, for instance, more apt to say that they always felt pretty sure their life would work out the way they wanted ($r = .29$), felt generally less alienated from the society at large ($r = .32$), felt they were having more fun ($r = .54$), worried less often ($r = .41$), and were more optimistic about achieving their personal hopes and goals in the future ($r = .26$).

Connections with the Past

Although it is not totally possible to disentangle the cause-effect web of the young adults' current circumstances and their sense of well-being, some ideas can be obtained by examining links between their prior experiences, such as their background in placement, and their circumstances at the time of our contacts with them. Several instances where those discharged from group settings differed from those discharged from foster homes have already been discussed. The former were more apt to be living in New York City; they had resided at more addresses since their discharge in 1975; and they were less satisfied with their living quarters. Beyond this, however, past experiences in foster care, such as the length of time in placement or the number of times they were shifted, were not related to the young adults' current circumstances that have been reviewed up to now.

However, one aspect of the past—the problems they exhibited—was connected with their current circumstances, but not in a consistent way. For instance, if they had been discharged with a problem of some kind, the young adults, whether from foster homes or group care, were less apt to belong to an organization at the time of our contacts, but other aspects of their community involvement were not connected. Furthermore, one link existed for those who were discharged from foster homes, but not for those from group settings. Those who were discharged with a problem claimed to have fewer people to talk with and count on for advice or help when worries arose than those from foster homes without such problems. This was so even though they expressed as much closeness to their foster parents as those who displayed no problems at the time of discharge. Perhaps those with a problem were more sensitive about the amount of support they received, and thus felt there were fewer people to lean on, or perhaps they felt more distant from people. Whatever the case, one should not make too much of this since it was an isolated finding that did not pertain to those who were discharged from group settings.

Final Comments

On the whole, then, how were the young adults doing and feeling? The general thrust of this chapter reflects their resourcefulness. Since their discharge from foster care in their late teens or early twenties, they had moved about a fair amount but had worked out living arrangements that on the whole satisfied them. How settled they were in their communities was less clear. Some, at least, appeared to be in a temporary holding pattern. Whatever the case, most were outgoing people who looked to their neighbors, in addition to their friends, as a source of social activities and support. They had close friends and felt more than satisfied with their friendships, with how they tended to get along with other people, and with the number of people with whom they could really feel comfortable. Most felt there was someone who cared what happened to them and knew whom they could count on for help, although most could think of only a few such people.

The young adults were generally satisfied with the amount of fun they were having, but felt their day-to-day lives were not too interesting. They tended not to be overly worried about things; a majority felt that their life would work out the way they wanted; and most felt very or fairly optimistic about achieving their personal hopes and goals in the future. In this context a separate examination is warranted of the three components of the index of well-being: their happiness, their self-esteem, and their feelings about their "life as a whole." Somewhat more than two out of ten said that, taken all together, they felt very happy "these days," and another 55% spoke of feeling pretty happy. The young adults' self-assessment on Rosenberg's (1965) 10-item self-esteem scale could have ranged from an average high score of four to a low of one. Their average score was 3.2, and when asked how they felt about themselves, they were, on the average, mostly satisfied. So, it is not surprising that, as a group, they were mostly satisfied with their "life as a whole."

Generally, then, these young adults were managing their lives adequately and feeling quite satisfied with their physical, social, and psychological environments. Yet, in reporting this, one is left with an uneasy feeling since the most important question has not been dealt with. For, to give full meaning to such descriptive material, one has to confront the most difficult question: how did their circumstances and their feelings about various aspects of life compare with those of other young adults their age? Unfortunately, such comparison data are sparse. In a later chapter what we found will be reported. But first it is necessary to complete the portrait of these young adults and examine other vital areas of life.

Chapter Seven

MARRIAGE, PARTNERSHIP, AND CHILDREN

During the period when the young adults were growing up, the 1960s and 1970s, attitudes toward the institution of marriage were shifting. In comparison with earlier years, more young adults were postponing decisions about marriage since they felt less urgency to take the legal plunge. The need for a relationship that would provide affection and support was often fulfilled by another sort of pairing, living with another person to whom one was not married. Young adults also delayed having children while they sought more education, moved into the labor market, or continued to further their career. The number of divorces rose.

The young adults in our sample were naturally influenced by these trends. A later chapter that examines a small group of older adults from foster care will provide some evidence to support this point. But I do not know the full extent of these influences on our sample; no comparable data from any earlier study exist.

Marriage and Partnership

Since their discharge from foster care, 83—close to 30%—had married. Twenty-one of these initial marriages ended in divorce or separation, but by the time of our contacts a few had remarried. Thus at that time, 66—or 23.8% of the 277 young adults—were married. Young women who were discharged from foster homes were more likely to be currently married, or to have ever married, than any of the other groups. This can be seen in table 7.1. Among the young women marriage was most prevalent among whites, least among blacks, with the Hispanics in between. On the average, the women first married when they were 20.7 years old, while the men were 21.5 years old. On the surface this might appear to be quite young, but since most of them had remained single their average age at first marriage will ultimately be much higher.

In view of the trends of the time, it is perhaps no surprise that 21 of the initial marriages had dissolved. Well over half of these were in a state of separation, rather than final divorce, at the time of our contacts. These terminated marriages were of necessity all rather shortlived; they could not have lasted long since only five years had elapsed from the time of their discharge to the time of our contacts. In fact, only three had lasted as long as three or four years.

Conventional marriage was not the only kind of sexual partnership for these young adults. Nearly as many (17.5%)—more women than men—were living with others whom they considered "a partner," but to whom they were not married. All together, 42% of the 269 young adults who answered a question about partnership were either married or living with a sexual partner at the time of our contacts. This was more true

Table 7.1
Marriage, Partnership, and Children

| | Discharged From: | | | |
| | Foster Home | | Group Setting | |
	M (N = 109)	F (N = 92)	M (N = 52)	F (N = 24)
Ever married	25.7%	41.3%	26.9%	12.5%
Currently married	22.0	32.6	19.2	8.3
Currently with partner	12.3*	23.3*	14.3*	25.0
One or more children	26.9*	45.7	34.6	54.2
Lives with one or more children	15.6	41.3	15.4	54.2

*These percentages are based on one to three fewer cases.

of women than of men, but only among those who had been discharged from foster homes. No sex difference was apparent among those who were discharged from group settings in the total percentage who were living with a spouse or partner.

What might account for the difference in the foster home group? Earlier it was reported that a larger proportion of men than women were discharged with one or more problems. I thought this might have had a bearing on their motivation or capacity to establish ongoing sexual unions. The data, however, do not lend support to any notion about the impact of such problems. A smaller proportion of males than females from foster homes were married or living with a sexual partner whether or not they had been discharged with a problem.

Perhaps the men from foster homes were simply more inclined to bide their time, to "play the field" if you will, before settling down and were not expected to do otherwise by those in their environment. On the other hand, the women from foster homes were perhaps more inclined, whether because of internal or societal expectations, to settle into a partnership more quickly. It also seemed plausible that foster parents might have had different expectations about acceptable roles for the young women than for the young men in their homes. On this point it was interesting to note that the women who were married said they felt closer to their foster families at the time of our contacts than all the other women from foster homes. The men, on the other hand, felt equally close whether they were married or not. Perhaps women became more trustful about entering marriage if they had had close relationships with their foster families. On the other hand, perhaps women who married came closer to fulfilling the foster parents' expectations, thus earning their approval and, in turn, greater expressions of closeness.

There was an additional difference that is noteworthy. A larger proportion of women who were discharged from foster homes, compared with those from group care, were married or living with a sexual partner at the time of our contacts. It seems likely that the women from foster homes had more opportunities over time to meet suitable partners in the communities where they resided. More of those from group care, on the other hand, lived in sexually segregated environments with less flexible rules, and inevitably they had to resettle once they were discharged from care. All these factors could have interfered with their social life and the opportunities for meeting potential mates.

In an earlier chapter the issue of settling down from the standpoint of geographical movement and community participation was discussed. Settling down will now be considered with respect to their marriages and partnerships. These had, on the average, lasted more than two years by the time of our contacts. The relationships these young adults had established, whether by marriage or otherwise, were therefore not hasty or temporary arrangements. Yet ultimately, the test of a relationship is not its duration, but the partners' happiness with it. The two are of course related, although most people can cite exceptions. We asked all who were married or living with a partner to describe their relationship. Close to 46% rated it "very happy," about 44% said "pretty happy," and somewhat less than 10% felt it was "not too happy." Males and females were quite alike in this regard, as were those discharged from foster homes and group settings. Since we did not interview the young adults' partners, this was a one-sided rating; in a sense it was biased because the most disgruntled had probably separated in earlier years. Yet some had persisted in relationships they considered unhappy. Perhaps some maintained unhappy unions because children were involved. Our data did show that young mothers were more likely to rate their relationships with husbands or partners as "pretty happy" (54.5%) or "not too happy" (12.1%) than the young women who had no children. Somewhat under 31% of the latter felt their relationships were "pretty happy," and none rated it as "not too happy." In other words, a clear majority of the childless women felt very happy with their marriages or partnerships, whereas young mothers were on the whole less positive in their ratings.

This difference was not a function of the duration of those relationships.

Among the men such happiness was not connected with fatherhood. Of course, the men's situation differed from the women's in several important respects. Their children were less likely to be living with them, but even if they were, the major responsibilities for child care no doubt rested with the mothers. Among the young mothers, on the other hand, child care responsibilities and the psychological and economic burdens of parenthood perhaps helped to reduce the glow of their relationships with husbands or partners. Some may have even entered such relationships because they became pregnant, and others may have maintained less than happy marriages or partnerships because there were children.

Children

Although there were children among those who were married or living with a partner, others had given birth to children as well. We asked everyone how many living children they had who were born to them, their children's ages, their weights at birth, where the children were living, and whether any had ever been placed in foster care or relinquished for adoption. All in all, of the 276 who answered the question about the number of children born to them, nearly 37% spoke of one or more children, including a few who were about to become parents. A larger proportion of the 116 women (47.4%) than of the 160 men (29.4%) had had children, and more of the women (44.0%) than the men (15.6%) were living with all, or at least some, of their children at the time of our contacts. Stated somewhat differently, about 57% of the young fathers but 96.2% of the mothers were living with their children. A further difference stood out. Fathers who were living with their children were all either married or living with sexual partners, whereas among the mothers who were living with their children close to 31% had never married nor were they living with a partner by the time of our contacts.

Unfortunately, the information about children given by the men is flawed, since some of them were not sure about pregnancies or births among previous partners. Even when they knew of children, they were not always sure about their ages or their whereabouts. In order not to give a false picture of these young men, it should be pointed out that many did know their children, either lived with them and their mothers or visited them, and obviously cared about them. The concern here is with accuracy, and the fact is that unmarried males sometimes were not, or perhaps could not be, as certain as females about such basic facts as birth. For these reasons, the focus will be on the young women in much of what follows.

To repeat, there were 55 (or 47.4%) young women who were, or were about to become, mothers. There were only two of the latter, both in their final months of their first pregnancies. Most, or 37, had given birth to only one child, 12 had two children, and 4 had given birth to three children. Women who were discharged from foster homes and from group settings were quite alike in this regard. Of the 51 mothers who recalled their children's birth weight, 8 had given birth to children of low weight, or less than 5½ pounds. Perhaps this was an indication of inadequate prenatal care.

The young mothers were on the average 20.5 years old when their first child was born, and by the time of our contacts, the children ranged in age from 1 month to 8 years, but most, not surprisingly, were quite young. Only five mothers had a school-aged child. Most were taking care of children well below the age of nursery school and, as will be seen, the young mothers were largely responsible for that care. Although a majority were married or living with a partner, a few were divorced or separated and, as already mentioned, nearly 31% were on their own. One could imagine that those without husbands or partners had the most difficult time managing. Almost four out of five of these partnerless mothers were homemakers, and most were receiving public welfare. More of them had been discharged from group settings than from foster homes. It is not that the women from group settings were more likely to give birth to a child, but if they had done so, they were more apt not to have married and not to have a partner by the time of our contacts.

What else can be said about the women in this predicament? Unfortunately very little because there were so few that an intensive analysis is precluded. But a few points did stand out when the 16 mothers who were on their own were compared with the 37 mothers who were married or had a partner when we met them. Although there were no ethnic differences in the proportion of black, Hispanic, and white women who were mothers, a disproportionate number of those who were on their own were black, irrespective of whether they had been discharged from foster homes or group settings. Perhaps black women were more choosy about their mates or perhaps they were left in the lurch more frequently by those they chose.

Mothers who were on their own also felt generally less happy and tended to be less positive in assessing themselves as parents compared with mothers who had married or had partners. Perhaps this was so because they felt most burdened by parenthood. The only other observable differences were found among mothers who were discharged from foster homes. In this group more of the 9 mothers who were on their own had displayed educational problems during their last years in foster care than was true of the mothers with mates; by the time of our contacts those without mates had on the average completed 10.8 years of school compared with 12.8 years completed by the mothers with mates. Perhaps such deficits, or what lay behind them, interfered with the choice of mates or the ability to establish more lasting relationships.

Educational differences were, however, not at all apparent among the young mothers who left group care. They had completed 10.7 years, on the average, whether they had married, had partners, or were on their own. One must therefore look elsewhere in order to conjecture about the reason why more of the mothers from group settings were left with chil-

dren on their own. Perhaps, as previously mentioned, life following discharge was generally more unsettled for those from
group care, and fewer of them had adults available as sources
of support. They may have entered relationships for the sake
of the support they missed and gave birth to a child before
realizing that the partnership would founder. They may have
had fewer opportunities to meet a suitable mate. They may
have wanted a child as a way of filling a void. Finally, it is
possible that those from group settings were less well prepared on how to avoid pregnancy, if they wished, and thus
more ended up without partners, fending for themselves.

Factors Associated with Marriage, Partnership, and Children

Earlier it was reported that the women from foster homes
were more likely than the women from group settings to be
married or living with a partner by the time of our contacts.
Beyond this, however, placement and background factors, such
as their age at placement, contact with biological family, and
shifts in placement were not associated with marriage or partnership. The problems they had or did not have at the time
of their discharge and their level of education were also unrelated to whether or not they were married or living with a
partner. Women who were married or living with a partner*
were, however, generally happier "these days" $(r = .28)$
than those who were not, and those who described their relationships with their mates more positively felt generally happier $(r = .54)$.

Background and placement factors were also not linked to
the advent of children. But a larger proportion (50%) of the
women who were discharged from care with a serious educational problem than those who were not so discharged (36.8%)

*Here, and in other parts of the book, Pearson product-moment correlation coeffi-
cients will sometimes be reported for nominal variables that were dichotomized and
treated as "dummy variables." Doing this provides an easy way to convey the magnitude of various relationships.

had given birth to one or more children by the time of our contacts. By that time those who were mothers had completed fewer years of school—11.6 years on the average—than the 13.3 years completed by the women who had not given birth. The difference between the mothers and the other women existed irrespective of whether or not they had mates. One could imagine several influences at work. No doubt, some women opted for motherhood since they had little interest in furthering their education, whereas for others childbirth interfered with plans to move ahead in school. Conversely, some no doubt postponed having children in order to seek further education. Then there were those who had fallen behind in school, had more difficulty competing in the labor market, and thus settled into motherhood as their principal occupation. Perhaps those with limited education were least informed about ways to avoid pregnancy, and therefore more of them were mothers. Clearly, for some women motherhood was a factor in limiting education while for others the direction of causation was the opposite.

But, one must ask, were those who had children particularly happy? The answer was no. For instance, among women with mates, those with or without children were similar in their general happiness. But children were not a positive asset in these women's assessment of their relationships with their mates; as already noted, but repeated here, those without children described their relationships with husbands or partners as happier than did those with children. Whatever the reason for this, the presence of offspring was not an unalloyed blessing for these young women.

Child Care

It is sometimes asserted that foster care repeats itself. Since we also wondered about that, we asked several questions. All but four of the 53 mothers were living with all of their children, and two of these four had at least one child with them.

All four had been discharged from foster homes themselves. In the main the "placements" were with grandparents or with the young mother's foster mother. Two of the "placements" followed separations from husbands, and were perhaps temporary while the young mother worked or attended school. Only one of the mothers had offspring in a foster home at the time of our contacts, although a few others had in previous years used foster care temporarily. We do not know about the future, but the situation at the time of our contacts does not warrant the conclusion foster care will inevitably be repeated.

Not only were most of the young mothers living with their children, but nine out of ten of them were also principally responsible for their care. Only a few spoke of others—foster mothers, grandmothers, or sitters—who had such primary responsibility. Mates were never mentioned in this regard, and very few spoke of husbands or partners as sharing any of the responsibilities for child care. So much for changes in roles in a period of women's liberation!

Attitudes About Parenthood

The young mothers were also asked to rate themselves as parents. A large majority, about 81%, felt they were "excellent" or "good" mothers. The remainder evaluated themselves as "fair" and one said "poor." It will be recalled that mothers without mates were less positive about themselves as parents than the rest.

At the same time most of the young women viewed motherhood as desirable. With the exception of those who already had two or three children, most wanted to have children or wanted to have more children. Only 4.3% of the young women said they wanted no children at all. In fact, when asked what they thought was the ideal number of children for a person or family, their answers ranged from 1 to 6, and averaged 2.8, somewhat above the prevailing concept of ideal family size in the population at large. But their response was quite in line with that given by others of their age.

Finally, we inquired about the timing of their children, and whether they would have children again if they could step back in time. If they "had it to do over again," a majority—close to 69%—said they would have children again, although more than one out of ten did not feel strongly about this. Conversely, about 31% of the young mothers regretted that they had children at this time, although again some one in ten did not feel strongly about it. The question we posed was, of course, difficult to answer in the negative since it is usually more comfortable to justify one's past decisions or acts. It was therefore surprising that so many answered negatively, but not surprising that such answers came primarily from those who were not legally married at the time of our contacts.

It is quite evident that the responsibilities of rearing children weighed quite heavily upon a number of these young mothers. This became especially clear in what they said about the timing of their first child. Some 51% felt that if they could do it all again, they would have had that child when they were older, and one asserted that she wished she had no offspring at all. Women without husbands were again in the majority in expressing such feelings. Therefore, both here and in the earlier question about regrets, mothers with partners joined those who were on their own in being most dissatisfied, although there were some who were married who wished their first child had been born later. We do not know how much information about family planning these young women had acquired or the extent to which they took steps to avoid pregnancies or to control the timing and spacing of children. It is significant that only a small minority, or about one out of ten women in our sample, felt that the agencies had prepared them well in this regard prior to their discharge. Our data even suggested that many did not gain such information after they left foster care.

Pregnancies

Two-thirds of the 108 young women who were interviewed had been pregnant at least once, including a small proportion

(18.5%) who had been pregnant at least three times. While most first pregnancies among those from foster homes occurred following their twentieth birthday, those from group settings were more apt to become pregnant for the first time in their late teens. Although officially discharged at about the same age, the young women from group settings had to fend for themselves at a somewhat younger age since they did not have the ongoing support of a foster home. They were therefore more at risk of an early pregnancy than those from foster homes.

Most women had been pregnant, and most of these were either married or living with a partner at the time of our contacts. But the picture was complicated since their pregnancies were not necessarily carried to term. About 17% of the women who had been pregnant spoke of one or two miscarriages, and close to 46% of those who had been pregnant reported one or more abortions, including 20% who had aborted two or more times. In fact, of a total of 144 pregnancies, we were told of 51 that had been aborted. Married women as well as others spoke of abortions, but they were more prevalent among the women who had no mate at the time of our contacts.

These young women had rather frequently turned to abortion as a way to avoid or defer childbirth. This raised several concerns. First, there is always an element of risk attached to any medical procedure, even if the risk is slight. If abortions are performed outside the regular channels, as may have been true in some of these cases, the risks are even greater. For some, the psychological risks may also have to be considered. A further serious concern derives from the fact that these abortions were performed mostly at a time when policies on abortions in some states, for example, New York, were relatively flexible and available to those of limited means. But policies can and do change. For all of these reasons, the extent of these young women's reliance on abortion as a means of birth control was of concern. It was clear that agencies would do well to give much greater emphasis to family planning in preparing young people in foster care to live on their own.

The Young Men

Although some of the information the young men gave about children was flawed, a few additional comments are necessary. To repeat, 34.8% of the men were married or living with a partner at the time of our contacts. About 29% spoke of having sired children, but only about half of these fathers were living with all of their children. Unlike the women, their level of education was totally unrelated to fatherhood. About 17% of the fathers felt that if they could relive the past they would have avoided having children, and close to 40% of the fathers said they would have preferred to have their first child when they were older. At the same time more than 88% considered themselves to be excellent or good parents. Most males wanted children or wanted more children. Only about 6% said they wanted no children at all. Their ideal number of children was precisely the same as mentioned by the young women— 2.8 on the average. The young men were also quite similar to the women in that the vast majority felt they had not been well prepared with information on sexual matters and family planning prior to their discharge from foster care.

There was one fundamental difference between the women and the men. Unlike the women, the men who were married or living with a partner did not feel generally happier than those who were not. Involvement in an on-going relationship at this point in their lives played a less important role among the men than among the women. As in the case of the women their positive assessment of their relationship with a mate contributed substantially ($r = .41$) to the young men's general sense of happiness. They were also similar to the women in that the fathers were neither more nor less happy than the other men. But they differed from the women in that the presence or absence of their children in the home had no bearing on the young men's assessments of their relationships with their wives or partners.

In a few instances in this chapter the young adults' general happiness has been reported; it is one component in the index

of well-being. Nevertheless, here, as in other chapters, data on
the full index will also be presented. This seems worthwhile,
even at the risk of some repetition.

Marriage, Partnership, Children, and the Sense of Well-Being

Marriage, partnership, or fatherhood were not linked to the
sense of well-being of the young men in our sample. In contrast, the women who were married or living with partners
had a better sense of well-being (mean = .51) than those who
were not (mean = −.56). Women differed in other ways as well,
for women who were living with mates tended to have a better
sense of well-being if they had no children (mean = 1.05) than
if they did (mean = .11). Mothers without mates had the most
negative outlook on life (mean = −1.22).

The young men and women were similar in one respect.
Among people who were living with mates, those who assessed
their relationships more positively had a better sense of well-
being than those who gave a less positive portrayal. This connection was, however, more substantial for the women ($r = .61$)
than for the men ($r = .38$). Earlier it was reported that when
the women and men rated their happiness with their marriages or partnerships, the distributions were quite similar, yet
here it can be seen that positive feelings about such relationships were more closely tied to the women's sense of well-being
than to the men's. In addition, involvement in such relationships was an important factor in the women's, but not the
men's, outlook on life. Thus, although concepts of women's
roles have been changing, there was little evidence for it here,
at least in this regard. This was, however, no peculiarity of
those who were in foster care. Rather, it mirrored what has
been reported by others (Campbell 1981) who have found
happiness in marriage and happiness in life to be more closely
associated among women than they are among men.

Final Thoughts

More of the young women than the young men had established relationships with mates at the time of our contacts, and such relationships were more important for their sense of well-being. Women without mates apparently missed the support that such relationships provided, and their outlook on life suffered. Partnerless mothers were most severely affected, since they had to fend on their own. Children were generally not a positive addition at this stage in the lives of the young adults. This is not to imply that parenthood was inevitably a negative experience, for some certainly blossomed in that experience. But on the whole the presence of children was not linked to the young adults' sense of well-being, and among women it was a dampening factor in their happiness with their mates. Perhaps the burdens of parenthood contributed, or possibly some young adults maintained less than happy relationships because of children. Whatever the reasons, these young women were facing the responsibilities of parenthood, but at some cost to themselves.

By and large the young adults conveyed a feeling of satisfaction with the relationships they had established, with their children, and with themselves as parents. Their main bone of contention concerned their preparation for all these roles. In the years since their discharge from foster care, they had been faced with, and made, many choices. They felt that their ability to choose had at times been hindered by their lack of preparation. They felt that better preparation on family planning, for instance, would have permitted a greater freedom of choice.

Chapter Eight

EDUCATION AND EMPLOYMENT

Americans in general attach considerable value to formal education; therefore, the fewer years of schooling they have, the greater their sense of deprivation and the lower their feelings of satisfaction and happiness (Campbell 1981; Veroff, Douvan, and Kulka 1981). This, as will be demonstrated, is an apt description of the young adults from foster care. Many had left care with limited schooling, having fallen behind in the years before their discharge. Some had received further training following their discharge, a few were attending school at the time of our contacts, and most hoped for further training in subsequent years.

In much of what follows grades completed will be used as a measure of formal schooling or education. These are not strictly synonymous in view of the school system's tendency to use lax standards in promoting students. It will be assumed that this occured across the board, that various groups in our sample (for instance, males and females) were not differentially affected, and that comparisons between such groups are therefore possible.

Level of Education at Discharge and Later

At the time they were discharged in 1975, more than one-third (34.6%) of the young adults had not completed high school, although most of them had finished the tenth or eleventh grade. Nearly 40% were high school graduates and 25.7% had completed some college. None of them were college graduates. There are, however, differences within our sample, one of which is shown in table 8.1. On the average, those who were discharged from foster homes tended to have completed more years of school than those who left group settings. It is also noteworthy that the women had received more education (mean = 12 years) than the men (mean = 11.5 years). This was so whether they were discharged from foster homes or group settings.

The men also had a more checkered history in school than the women. For instance, nearly 43% of the men told us that they had at one time or another been suspended from school. A smaller proportion of the women (27.4%) said this had occurred to them. Perhaps the women were more tractable than the men, or possibly the schools were more prone to use suspension as a disciplinary device for males than females. Since suspensions could have interfered with progress in school, it was important to examine whether those who had been suspended had also completed less schooling by the time of their discharge from foster care. This, however, was true only among the women. Males who had been suspended had completed as many grades on the average as males who had never been suspended. Perhaps their suspensions were quite temporary.

Table 8.1
Grades Completed at Discharge and at Interview

	At Discharge From:		At Interview, Discharged From:	
	Foster Home (N = 199)	Group Setting (N = 70)	Foster Home (N = 201)	Group Setting (N = 76)
Less than high school	34.7%	34.3%	22.4%	28.9%
High school completed	34.2	55.7	35.3	40.8
Some college	31.2	10.0	36.3	26.3
College completed	—	—	6.0	3.9
Total	100.1%	100.0%	100.0%	99.9%
Mean	11.83	11.49*	12.46	11.82
S.D.	1.56	1.22	1.82	1.99

*Based on 68 cases because 2 cases could not be precisely classified.

In any event, both for the women and the men earlier suspensions had no bearing on their level of education by the time of our contacts. By that time, both among the women and the men those suspended and not suspended had, on the average, completed the same amount of schooling. Women who had been suspended had made up for lost time in the interim.

If one looks only at grades completed during the period between their discharge and the time of our contacts, close to one out of three of the young adults had moved further ahead with their schooling. This was equally true of males and females, of those discharged from group care and from foster homes. Most of this additional schooling was at the college level, so that by the time of our contacts 39% had completed one or more years of college, including about 5% who by that time had earned a college degree or had gone beyond. The earlier educational differences between those from foster homes and group settings persisted, as can be seen in table 8.1. The sex difference in education at the time of discharge had, however, diminished and was no longer statistically significant. Although the young men and women had pursued further schooling in equal proportions, the men had done more catching up so that by the time of our contacts the gap between them and the young women had narrowed.

The picture presented here is incomplete. Many of the young adults spoke of receiving additional training, usually of a vocational nature. Some of this training occurred before discharge: sometimes agencies sought out special training opportunities to prepare the young adults for discharge; in other instances they heard about such programs themselves from teachers, friends, or others. However, it was our impression that most such additional training occurred after the young adults' discharge from care. They frequently spoke of special training on a job or in preparation for a job, of specialized training received in the armed forces, and of attending various classes on their own while working. All together 58.7% of the young adults spoke of some training beyond whatever grades they had completed. For 21.4% this consisted of additional high school, college, or graduate credits, while 37.3% spoke of some training in a particular field. Technical and electronic fields were most often cited, followed by business and secretarial training. The rest were scattered over a dozen fields such as nursing and human services, fashion and design, police, security, and the building trades. Such additional training was most often pursued by those whose education had not gone beyond high school, by males somewhat more (63.4%) than by females (52.2%), and particularly by males from group settings. About 73% of them spoke of receiving additional training as compared with roughly 59% of the males from foster homes.

Factors Connected with Educational Achievement

People have sometimes wondered whether there are differences in educational achievement for those whose schooling is on the grounds of an institutional setting rather than at a school in a nearby community. Of those who were discharged from institutions or group residences, 28% said they attended school on the grounds, 38% went to school in the community, and 34% spoke of attending both. Those who went to school on the grounds had completed fewer grades by discharge than those who either went to school in the community or attended both. Since those who remained on the grounds may have been a selected group, it is not possible to draw any final conclusions about the relative merits of such education vis-à-vis integration into the community school system.

For the respondents as a whole, their educational levels at the time of their discharge and at the time of our contacts were, of course, strongly related. The connections between each of these education measures and other elements in the young adults' past or present were therefore similar. In order to avoid repetition in what follows, only the links with scholastic achievement at the time of our contacts will be reported. A review of many background factors yielded few consistent connections. We had not expected any link with parental characteristics since so many children came into placement quite young, and therefore parental influences on educational achievement, beyond genetic endowment, were probably limited. For instance, the biological mothers' education was not related. But in a small group of 83 cases where information on the biological fathers' education had been recorded, there was a positive relationship ($r = .27$) with the young adults' level of education. Factors such as ethnicity, biological family contact during placement, shifts in care, and the number of foster homes were either unrelated or internally inconsistent. Age at placement was connected, but only for those discharged from group settings ($r = .23$); those who were younger at placement ultimately received less education. The group who were transferred from foster homes into group settings accounted for this connection since they were both younger at placement and educationally more limited.

In an earlier chapter the connection between problems noted during placement and scholastic achievement was examined. Aside from the obvious connection with learning problems, those who exhibited social and emotional problems around the time of discharge had less education by the time of our contacts than those without such problems. Those who entered and also left care with such problems had completed 10.4 years of school on the average. Those whose problems emerged while in placement had completed 11.2 years of school, whereas those without such problems at discharge had completed an average of 12.6 years of school by the time of our contacts. For some, such problems had probably interfered with their progress in school, whereas others may have developed social and emotional problems as a consequence of difficulties with moving ahead in school. No other background factors were found to have had an effect.

Various aspects of their life at the time of our contacts were also related to education. Some of these are presented in table 8.2. Those with more education appeared to be more involved in their communities, more content, and less alienated from

Table 8.2
Correlations Between Grades Completed and Various Aspects of Life at Time of Contact

| | Discharged From: | | | |
| | Foster Home | | Group Setting | |
	r*	(N)†	r*	(N)†
Organizational membership	.35	(200)	.29	(76)
People to count on for help	.22	(200)	.47	(75)
Chance of employment	.20	(170)	.17	(66)
Is employed	.22	(195)	.40	(74)
Does not feel alienated	.30	(201)	.38	(74)
Own happiness	.22	(199)	.24	(76)
Self-esteem	.11	(198)	.22	(74)
Well-being index	.19	(196)	.25	(73)
Satisfaction with usefulness of total education	.22	(167)	.46	(64)
Satisfaction with amount of education in care	.30	(173)	.36	(67)
Satisfaction with quality of education in care	.23	(172)	.25	(67)

*Pearson product-moment correlation coefficients.
†Largest variations in totals because some questions were not included in the mail questionnaire.

society. For instance, they were more apt to be members of organizations and were more apt to feel they had people to count on for help, although they felt no closer to their biological or foster families than those with less education. Those with more education were more apt to be employed and felt positively about their chances of getting a good job if they went looking for one. They generally felt happier, assessed themselves more positively, and had a better sense of well-being.

On the whole these relationships were modest. Yet the number of grades they had completed had a partial bearing on how they felt as young adults. It is interesting that the relationships in table 8.2 are almost always somewhat stronger for those from group settings than for the young adults discharged from foster homes. The differences were small but fairly consistent. Those from group care had on the average completed less education, but in some ways it counted more.

Although this is a slight digression, there were also some

differences here and there when the young men and women were separately examined. For instance, in an earlier chapter it was noted that the women with more education were less apt to have given birth to a child ($r = -.41$). Although having a child was not linked to the women's sense of well-being, the schooling they had completed was, but not significantly more strongly ($r = .30$) than was the case for the men ($r = .17$).

Their Assessments of Their Education and Preparation

In this area it may be at least as helpful to know the young adults' evaluation of their education as it is to know the objective facts about their scholastic achievements. Since people apply different standards, an individual with a tenth-grade education could be more satisfied with his or her educational achievement than another individual who had completed high school or college. The young adults' satisfaction with the usefulness of their education was not very strongly, although positively, related to their scholastic achievement ($r = .28$). Apparently some were quite satisfied with their lower education and vice versa, yet on the whole those with less education were least satisfied with its usefulness to them.

Satisfaction with one's achievements no doubt has a bearing on how one views oneself and one's life, and it may have more of a bearing than the objective facts about the years of schooling one has completed. The young adults' satisfaction with the usefulness of their education was indeed connected with their sense of well-being ($r = .37$) and affected such feelings more than the objective measure of grades completed at the time of our contacts.

More than four out of ten young adults wished they had gone further in school. At the time they were interviewed only about a third, somewhat more females than males, said they felt they were better off educationally than they had expected to be, nearly 44% said they felt they were worse off, and the rest were in between. Thus, about 56% had met or bettered their expectations, at least in retrospect. Those who felt worse off than expected had completed fewer years of schooling than the rest. But regardless of how much school they had completed, nearly nine out of ten of the young adults thought they would want more schooling in the five years to come.

In addition to their satisfaction with their scholastic achievements up to the time of our contacts, different questions elicited their satisfaction with the amount and quality of education they had received while in foster care. About 37% were very, and 38% were somewhat satisfied, while 25% were dissatisfied with the amount of education they had received. Their ratings of quality were roughly similar. Nearly 40% very satisfied, slightly more than 26% dissatisfied, and the rest were in between. Once again those with more education were on the whole more satisfied with the amount ($r = .33$) and quality ($r = .25$) of the education received. There were no overall sex differences in satisfaction, nor differences between those who were discharged from foster homes and group care, except in one instance. The young women who left group settings were more disgruntled about the amount and quality of the education they had received in care than was true for the young women from foster homes. Oddly enough, both the males and females from group care tended to have less education than those from foster homes but only the females differed in satisfaction. The women felt more strongly, or expressed themselves in more extreme ways, than the men.

Finally, we asked all the young adults about predischarge preparation for getting further training or schooling if they wished it. The responses of males and females, and of those discharged from foster homes and group care, were roughly similar. Fewer than two out of five (36.8%) felt they had been well prepared in this regard. At the same time, when asked to choose the three most important areas for agencies to stress in preparing young adults for discharge, about 51% selected this area. Although a minority felt the agencies had prepared them well, a small majority thought it was vital for agencies to do so. No wonder, for once out on their own many sought fur-

ther training of various sorts, and a large majority still hoped
for more education in the future.

Final Comment

In sum, education was quite important to these young adults.
After their discharge from foster care, they sought out and
pursued a variety of further training opportunities. Although
at the point of discharge the women had completed more
schooling than the men, the difference no longer prevailed by
the time we spoke with them. The difference between those
who had been discharged from foster homes and group settings, although diminished, still presisted. On the whole, those
who fell behind in school while in care still lagged behind years
later despite general educational gains. The young adults'
scholastic achievements were an aspect of their sense of well-
being, but only a small part of it. Their evaluations of their
achievements played a somewhat larger role. Their sense of
well-being was naturally influenced by many facets of their circumstances. Their work and progress in the labor market also
contributed to their view of themselves and their lives.

Employment

A word is in order about those designated as "employed."
In a study like this the particular timing of interviews can inevitably have a bearing. It is difficult to assess such influences
unless one can interview the same individuals at several points
in time. In most instances one could reasonably assume that
although there were some individual variations, the overall
picture would be quite similar. But we had a peculiar situation
with respect to employment, for there were a few instances
where we waited for the young adult to become unemployed,
in a sense, in order to schedule an interview. This occurred in
the case of five men who were in the armed forces. They had

Table 8.3
Employment of the Young Adults

	Discharged From:			
	Foster Home		Group Setting	
	M (N = 106)	F (N = 92)	M (N = 50)	F (N = 24)
Employed full time	74.5%	44.6%	52.0%	29.2%
Employed part time	2.8	12.0	8.0	8.3
School full time	2.8	4.3	6.0	—
Homemaker	—	20.7	—	41.7
Unemployed	18.9	17.4	34.0	20.8
Disabled	1.0	1.0	—	—
Total	100.0%	100.0%	100.0%	100.0%

agreed to be interviewed while they were serving full time, but convenience dictated that we talk with them immediately after their discharge from the service. Some of these five had jobs awaiting them and others were going to look for a job or for further training opportunities. In what follows this small group will be treated as employed—as though we had interviewed them at the time they agreed to participate.

Despite this, the proportion of unemployed in our sample may be exaggerated. There are two reasons for this. First, some may have been too busy and therefore did not agree to participate until they were no longer employed. I do not know precisely how many young adults were in this situation. Secondly, the fee we provided per interview may have been a greater inducement for some who were jobless.

At the time of our study unemployment in the United States, and particularly in this age group, was high and must have affected the proportion of jobless in our sample at the time of our contacts. The detailed figures are shown in table 8.3. Excluding five men who were in jail, 71.8% of the young men were employed full or part time, 3.8% were in school full time, and 23.7% were unemployed. As for the women, 52.6% were employed on a full- or part-time basis, 3.4% were in school full time, 25% stated that they were homemakers, and 18.1% said they were unemployed and looking for a job. The distinction between the last two categories is somewhat cloudy since some in the unemployed group were homemakers but looking for work, while some who had been looking for employment designated themselves as homemakers. When we exclude those who were disabled and those who were in school full time, 75.2% of the men and nearly 55% of the young women were gainfully employed at the time of our contacts. Thus, more males than females, and in each case more of those discharged from foster homes than from group settings, were employed when we spoke with them. Before discussing this, a rough picture will be given of the young adults' employment prior to their discharge and of what they were doing at the time of their discharge, including the intervening years up to the time of our contacts.

Employment During Placement

During the years before their discharge many of the young adults had held a job (60.4%), received some special work training (5.6%), or both (13.8%). This information came from the case records but often did not provide the sort of detail we had hoped for concerning the nature of training programs, the number of jobs, and their length. Our impression was that employment was usually temporary, often consisting of summertime jobs, and that a variety of community programs provided training in such areas as automotive mechanics, beautician skills, and secretarial work. One could imagine that such jobs and training were useful preparation for these young adults. It was therefore puzzling to discover that more of the men (83.1%) tended to have such preparation than the women (73.7%) regardless of whether they were discharged from foster homes or group settings. It is not known to what extent agencies were instrumental in helping youths find such work or training, or in encouraging them to explore this themselves. Perhaps the young men were more prone to venture forth on their own. Whatever the case, it is clear that encouragement in this direction is important for both the young men and women. Not only is work experience useful preparation for the world of work, but such encouragement also conveys an expectation to the young person which can have long-range effects. In fact, those who had held a job during placement were more apt to be employed or in school shortly after discharge, as well as years later, than those who had not worked during the time they were in placement. There was even a suggestion that work experience was more important for entry into the labor market than participation in a training program without actually holding a job.

The Period Between Discharge and Our Contacts

What were they doing in 1975, shortly after their discharge from foster care? Some 63% of the males were employed full or part time, including roughly 18% who had enlisted in the armed forces; 20.3% were in school full time; and 16.7% were unemployed. Four males who were in jail at that time are excluded from these figures. Among females, roughly 38% were employed full or part time, 29% were in school full time, 19.6% considered themselves to be homemakers, 1.8% said they were disabled, and 11.2% said they were unemployed and looking for work. Male and female respondents who were discharged from foster homes and group care were in school in roughly equal proportions, but there was a tendency for more of the females from foster homes (42.4%) than from group settings (25%) to be employed. The picture for males was similar.

I wondered to what extent their situations shortly after their discharge predicted what they would be doing at the time of our contacts some four or five years later. Such a link existed for all the men and for the women from foster homes. Those who were employed or in school in 1975 were more likely to be gainfully employed or in school (76.6%) at the time of our contacts than those who were not employed or in school (45.5%) shortly after their discharge. This was not the case for the young women from group settings, most of whom were unemployed or homemakers by the time of our interviews irrespective of what they were doing shortly after their discharge from foster care.

Almost all the young adults (98.6%) held a job at one time or another, although for a small group (2.2%), primarily women, the only job was prior to their discharge in 1975. After they were discharged about 6%, again mostly women, held part-time jobs only. The rest had held full-time jobs, usually more than one; one person had held as many as twenty full-time jobs. Many had held part-time jobs as well, particularly during periods when they were looking for full-time work. Thus, the average number of full-time jobs of those who had ever been employed since their discharge was considerably smaller (mean = 2.8) than the total number of jobs (mean = 4.3) they had held up to the time of our contacts. One faces an inherent ambiguity in attempting to interpret the meaning of the number of full-time jobs held by people. If that number is low it could imply job stability; on the other hand, it might mean that full-time jobs were difficult to find. A clear interpretation is possible only when the number of full-time jobs is reviewed in conjunction with the total number of jobs held and the frequency of unemployment.

On the whole, the men had held more full-time jobs (mean = 3.2) than the women (mean = 2.3), and also more total jobs. This was hardly surprising since some women became full-time homemakers following a period of employment and vice versa. While there were no differences in the number of jobs held by the women who were discharged from foster homes and from group care, the differences for the men were striking. Males from foster homes had held fewer full-time jobs on the average (mean = 2.8) than males from group settings (mean = 4.0). The latter had also held more total jobs (mean = 5.4) than males from foster homes (mean = 4.2). There was much less job stability for the males from group settings. Most likely their lower level of education played a significant role here.

The respondents' ethnicity was a factor in the number of jobs held. Although there were no educational differences among black, white, and Hispanic young adults, the black respondents had held the fewest full-time and total number of jobs since their discharge from care, while Hispanic young adults had held the most. The blacks apparently had more difficulty obtaining jobs, while for the Hispanics there was less job stability, and both groups had been unemployed more often than was the case among the white respondents.

Unemployment was not uncommon for the group as a whole. When asked whether they had ever been unemployed and looking for work for as long as a month since their discharge from care, 58.5% of the young men and 52.2% of the women said yes. On the average this had occurred 1.5 times since 1975, with no differences between those from foster homes and group care, or between males and females. A maximum of eight periods of unemployment was mentioned. The young adults' level of education was connected with unemployment. Males with less education had been unemployed more often ($r = -.20$) and the relationship, although weaker, was similar for females.

When asked about the longest period they had ever been unemployed and looking for work since their discharge from care, there were no differences in the average number of months mentioned by the males and females. The longest period of unemployment had lasted about seven months on the average. The duration of unemployment was linked to their education. For instance, males with less education had been unemployed for more extensive periods of time since 1975 ($r = -.34$) than those with more education. The connection for women was similar ($r = -.25$). For males there was also a relationship ($r = .43$) between the duration of unemployment and the number of times they had been unemployed. Those who had been unemployed more frequently spoke of longer single periods of unemployment. This was not so among the women.

Other factors were also related to the number of times the

young males were unemployed since their discharge from foster care. For instance, the problems they exhibited at discharge were connected. Those with social and emotional ($r = .18$) or educational problems ($r = .32$) were unemployed more frequently than those without such problems at the time of discharge. Males with more periods of unemployment since their discharge from care were also less apt to be employed at the time of our contacts ($r = -.19$); if employed, they had held their jobs for a shorter time ($r = -.28$). They were more apt to be receiving welfare at the time of our contacts, their own incomes during the year prior to our contacts were lower ($r = -.39$), they were less satisfied with their financial situations ($r = -.29$), and they said they generally worried more ($r = .23$). They were also more apt to be living in New York City than elsewhere ($r = .23$) at the time of our contacts. Finding and keeping a job in the metropolis was apparently more diffiuclt than for those in the suburbs or for those who had moved to more distant places. Finally, young men who were unemployed more frequently felt more alienated ($r = .16$) and their sense of well-being was poorer ($r = -.25$) than in the case of those who were unemployed less frequently in the years between their discharge and our contacts.

Among the young women fewer factors were connected. Those who were unemployed more frequently were also more likely to be living in New York City than elsewhere ($r = .23$), were more apt to be receiving welfare at the time of our contacts, had less income during the preceding year ($r = -.30$), and were less satisfied with their financial situation ($r = -.22$). Other areas that were important for the young men—such as their education, their employment status at the time of our interview, their worries, and their sense of well-being—were, however, totally unrelated to the women's history of unemployment. For women as a whole the amount of past unemployment was less important since it was a function of who sought jobs, which in turn depended on who was a homemaker and when that occurred.

Employment at the Time of Our Contacts

To repeat, a larger proportion of men than women, and more of those from foster homes than group settings, were employed at the time of our contacts with them. As one could imagine, they were employed in a large variety of jobs: the men were spread across a full range of positions, including 27 in the armed forces, while the young women predominated in clerical and service jobs. Only a handful of young adults were self-employed. Some had been working at the same place since their discharge while others had fairly new jobs. On the whole they had been with their "current" employers 1.8 years, and were on the average moderately satisfied with the work they were doing.

We asked each young adult to estimate the gross annual income of his or her household for the preceding year, taking all sources into consideration. Some 233 were able to provide at least a rough figure. These household incomes ranged from less than $4,000 to above $20,000, with a median figure of about $8,800. Males and females were quite alike in this regard but differed considerably when asked about their own incomes during the preceding year. The 156 males who responded had a median income of $6,800 while the 111 females had about $3,700. This difference was due mainly to the larger proportion of women who were employed on a part-time basis while their mates were fully employed, and to women who were dependent on public assistance as their only source of income. Poorer remuneration may also have contributed to the women's lower income.

On the whole the young adults felt neither satisfied nor dissatisfied with their financial situation. When asked to rate their satisfaction with the amount of money they had for basic things such as food, housing, and clothing, their average (mean = 3.8) was near the midpoint of the seven-point scale that was used. Their satisfaction with their own financial situation was similar (mean = 4.1). In each instance those who had been discharged from foster homes were more satisfied than those from group settings. The latter were less apt to be employed so that their incomes at the time we spoke with them were lower. On the whole, many of the young adults considered themselves to be on the lower edge of the income scale, for when asked to compare their incomes with those of Americans in general, some 52.6%—more from group settings (68%) than from foster homes (46.7%)—rated their incomes "below" or "far below" the average, and only 10.9% thought their incomes were above the average. At the same time somewhat more than 50%, more from foster homes (56.2%) than from group settings (34.2%), felt that during the past few years their financial situation had improved, while a much smaller proportion (18.8%) felt their situation had become worse. Yet, on the whole, the young adults were optimistic about the future, for when asked to think about the next five years, close to 93%, again more from foster homes (94.9%) than from group care (88%), thought their financial situation would improve. They also expressed strong hopes of improving their own position on the occupational ladder.

Public Assistance

All together 20.6% of our total sample, 10.6% of the young men and 34.4% of the young women, were receiving public assistance at the time of our contacts. An equal proportion (20.6%) had received welfare at a previous time but were no longer receiving such aid when we spoke with them. They had received such aid temporarily, often around the time of their discharge in order to help make ends meet until they could support themselves. This latter group had received public assistance for about 13 months on the average. In contrast, those who were receiving public assistance at the time of our contacts had been getting such aid for close to 36 months on the average. Most of the 57 who were receiving public assistance at the time of our contacts were unemployed or, in the case of women, homemakers. There were also 10 who had some part-time employment, 2 who were disabled, and 5 who were full-time students.

The proportion of women who were receiving public assistance outweighed the proportion of men whether they had been discharged from foster homes or group settings. Furthermore, among the women nearly 63% of those who had been discharged from group settings, in contrast to about 27% of women from foster homes, depended on public assistance at the time of our contacts. No such difference existed among the young men. The women obviously differed from the men in that they bore the children and then were more apt to be left to fend for themselves and their offspring, and this was especially so among women who were discharged from group settings.

What other factors distinguished those who received public assistance at the time of our contacts? For one, they were more apt to have been discharged with a problem of some sort ($r = .22$). They also had completed fewer years of school (mean = 11.0) than those not receiving such aid (mean = 12.6). They had been unemployed more frequently (mean = 4.4) since their discharge from foster care than those not receiving public assistance (mean = 1.6). At the time of our contacts 85.7% of those receiving public assistance lived in New York City; in contrast, 49.3% of those not receiving such aid lived in New York City. Those who resided in New York City tended to have had fewer years of education than those who lived elsewhere, and therefore their job prospects were poorer.

A larger proportion of the black respondents (26.8%) than of the Hispanics (15.7%) or whites (13.5%) were receiving public assistance at the time of our contacts. The differences were particularly sharp among the women, while the differences among the men were slight. There were no educational differences among these three ethnic groups. In order to understand the factors responsible for the larger proportion of black respondents receiving assistance, one must look separately at the black men and women. While Hispanic and white

males were employed in about equal proportions (81.7%),
fewer black males (67.1%) were employed at the time of our
contacts, and they had held fewer full-time jobs since their
discharge from foster care. They clearly had more difficulty
in obtaining jobs. The black women, on the other hand, were
employed no less than the other women. But in an earlier
chapter it was reported that if they had children more of the
black mothers were living without a mate than was the case
among the other women in our sample. In order to survive
they turned to public assistance.

Special attention has been given here to those who received
public assistance at the time of our contacts in order to stress
that limited education (sometimes but not always combined
with social and emotional problems), limited employment opportunities, and mateless motherhood interwoven with such
limited opportunities became a basis for dependency on public
support. There were others, also unemployed, who seemed to
be struggling against such dependency, relying instead on
friends, or biological or foster families to tide them over for a
time.

Factors Connected with Employment

Since the receipt of public assistance and unemployment
were intimately connected, factors that distinguished those who
received such aid also generally described those who were not
employed. The converse was also true. Factors that were tied
to the absence of public assistance also described those who
were employed at the time of our contacts. At the risk of some
repetition, but to round out the picture of the young adults,
these will be reviewed. Those who were employed at the time
we spoke with them will be compared with the nonemployed
including, in the case of the women, those who designated
themselves as homemakers. Those who were disabled and those
who were full-time students were excluded.

Beyond the sex difference in employment, and the difference connected to whether they had been discharged from foster homes or group care, nothing in their placement experience, such as their age at placement, the shifts in care they experienced, or the amount of contact with their biological families, was a factor in distinguishing who was or who was not employed at the time of our contacts. But the employed were less apt to have been discharged from care with a noticeable social and emotional $(r = -.13)$ or educational $(r = -.24)$ problem, and they had completed more years of schooling $(r = .30)$. The employed males, but not females, had been unemployed less frequently $(r = -.31)$ since their discharge from foster care and were more apt to be living outside of New York City $(r = .35)$ at the time of our contacts. Most likely some young men moved a distance in search of employment. Ethnicity also played a role in male employment, for a larger proportion of the Hispanic and white men were employed when compared to those who were black.

One other factor was important for males. If married, they were more apt to be employed than if not married; close to 94% of the married, as compared with 69.6% of the nonmarried men, were employed at the time of our interviews. Among the women there was no such connection since some of the married women chose to be homemakers. On the whole mothers were less likely to be employed $(r = -.48)$ than were women without children. However, employment made little difference in their, and for that matter in the young men's, assessments of their relationships with their spouses or partners. The employed were as satisfied as those who were not gainfully employed.

On the whole the picture of the employed was one of greater stability. They appeared to be more settled and happy. For instance, these young adults were more likely to belong to organizations in their communities $(r = .13)$, spoke of a larger number of close friendships $(r = .16)$, were more satisfied with the amount of fun they were having $(r = .16)$, felt their day-to-day lives were more interesting $(r = .26)$, and felt less alienated from the society at large $(r = -.26)$. Not surprisingly, they felt more satisfied with their financial situation ($r = .42$), were more optimistic about their chances of getting a good job if they looked for one ($r = .24$), and felt more satisfied with the extent to which they were achieving success and getting ahead ($r = .33$). They felt more certain that their lives would work out in a way they wanted ($r = .14$). Finally, their sense of well-being was better ($r = .27$) than that of the young men or women who were unemployed or homemakers. On the whole, the well-being scores of the women who were unemployed and who were homemakers did not differ from each other, but in each instance were poorer than the outlook of women who were employed or who were in school.

Earlier it was pointed out that scholastic achievement was important in determining who was employed, and that both education and employment were linked to the young adults' sense of well-being. Which was ultimately more important for their sense of well-being—education or employment? By an analysis of covariance it was possible to answer this question. For both males and females employment was related to their sense of well-being irrespective of their level of education, that is, when level of education was controlled. But the importance of education differed for the young men and women. Among the latter education was linked to their sense of well-being whether or not they were employed, whereas this was not so among the young men. Apparently education had a special significance in how the women felt about themselves and their lives, while for the men employment was more important than scholastic achievements in their assessments of themselves and their lives.

While education and employment were important in different ways, there is no question that both were important. The young adults attached considerable value to each. At a minimum, education provided an avenue toward employment, and employment provided a means for economic independence. Given the importance of these two areas, the need for predischarge preparation in both areas requires little comment. Before they are discharged young men and women must learn where to turn in order to find employment, how to complete job applications, and what to do in a job interview. Also, extensive efforts must be made to help them to find steady employment, and information must be provided about a variety of educational and training opportunities.

The case records were quite spotty about the specifics of such preparation. They contained more information on counseling efforts, particularly those addressing the young adults' feelings about separation, than on factual training sessions. Although some preparation was reported, it was our impression that it was probably too limited and frequently started too late. In looking back, many young adults were critical, and a majority did not feel well prepared; in the words of one young adult: "I was cut off with no education and no job—they just sweep you away. Who are you supposed to turn to?" (Interview, March 1980).

Chapter Nine

CONTACT WITH BIOLOGICAL AND FOSTER FAMILIES

In our interviews with the young adults it was possible to explore the subject of their contacts with biological family members in some detail. This material was not included on the mail questionnaires because of its complexity. The subject was complicated for a number of reasons. First, we were interested in contacts of various sorts since people can stay in touch by mail and telephone, as well as by visits. Second, people can keep in touch with many different members of their biological families—parents, siblings, and other relatives. To complicate matters further, the amount of contact with different members of a family can, and does, vary. We attempted to capture these three dimensions of contact by asking each individual who, if anyone, he or she was in touch with, the nature of those contacts, and the amount.

At the time of our interviews more than eight out of ten (82.9%) of the young adults were in touch with at least one member of their biological families. About one-half, or 48.3%, were in touch with their mothers, fathers, or both. A large majority of these were also in touch with at least one sibling or another relative. For close to one-fourth (23.3%), contacts were confined to their siblings or half siblings; 2.1% were in touch solely with another relative such as a grandparent, aunt, or uncle; and contacts for another 9.2% were limited to both siblings and relatives.

For greater clarity the number of young adults who maintained contact with specific people will be examined. All together 22.1% were in touch with their fathers, 35.8% with their mothers, 41.7% with another relative, and more than 3 out of 4 with at least one sibling.

Clearly siblings represented the most frequent tie to their families of origin. It will be recalled there were only 28 young adults in the whole sample who said they had no brother or sister or were unaware of any. Most of the rest either lived with or saw a sibling during their time in placement. In most instances these relationships continued following discharge. Their attachments to their brothers and sisters were striking. A majority of those who knew of a sibling stated that they felt either very (62.9%) or moderately (18.3%) close to at least one sibling, and those who felt very close expressed such closeness toward two siblings on the average. Not surprisingly, those who saw some siblings but not others while in placement, said they felt closer to those they had seen. But neither closeness nor the amount of contact was linked to their current circumstances or their sense of well-being.

Factors Linked to Contact with Biological Parents and Relatives

In this discussion of the biological family other than siblings, such terms as "biological family," "kin," and "relatives" do not include siblings. It is clear from table 9.1 that a larger proportion, or 88%, of those who were discharged from group settings, whether males or females, maintained contact with their biological parents or relatives, while this was the case for only 48.6% of those discharged from foster homes. Those from foster homes were much less likely to be in touch with kin. The reason was not because those from foster homes knew fewer family members, for close scrutiny of only those who knew their mothers, fathers, or relatives and reported them to be alive still revealed a difference in contact between those who left group settings and those from foster homes. Rather, the two groups differed because biological parents and relatives represented the main link to a family for those who left

Table 9.1
Current Contacts with Biological Family

	Discharged From:				Total	
	Foster Home (N = 173)		Group Setting (N = 67)			
	N	(%)	N	(%)	N	(%)
Mother and/or father*	28	(16.2)	15	(22.4)	43	(17.9)
Parent(s) and relative*	36	(20.8)	37	(55.2)	73	(30.4)
Relative,* but no parent	20	(11.6)	7	(10.4)	27	(11.3)
Siblings only	51	(29.5)	5	(7.5)	56	(23.3)
No one	38	(22.0)	3	(4.5)	41	(17.1)
Total	173	(100.1)	67	(100.0)	240†	(100.0)

*Includes some who were in touch with siblings as well.
†Although 241 persons were interviewed, one individual did not complete this material.

group settings, whereas those from foster homes also had foster families to whom they could turn.

Those who had had stronger ties to their biological parents or relatives were more apt to maintain contact. One indicator was the children's age at placement. Those who were in touch with their kin were on the average older when they were placed than those who maintained no contact. This was so whether they were discharged from foster homes or group care. Since a larger proportion of the latter were older when placed, a larger proportion also maintained contact. Biological family contacts during the last years of placement were an even more important indicator of ties with kin. In an earlier chapter it was reported that contacts with kin during those years led to ongoing contacts. This was especially so for those who were discharged from group settings, a large majority of whom were in touch at the time of our interviews regardless of whether the amount of contact with kin during the latter part of placement was high or low. The connection was less pronounced among those from foster homes since a majority of those whose earlier contacts with kin were low were no longer in touch by the time of our interviews.

Among those discharged from foster homes, only two other factors distinguished between those who maintained contact with their biological parents or relatives and those who did not: the ethnicity of the respondents and the principal reason for their placement. These two factors made no difference for those discharged from group settings.

Among those from foster homes, 56.5% of the black, 50% of the white, but only 28.6% of the Hispanic respondents were in touch with their kin at the time of our interviews, although there had been no ethnic differences in contact during the last years of placement. The death of kin did not account for the observed difference since this difference persisted when we separately examined only those who had living parents or relatives whom they knew. Perhaps more of the Hispanics' biological families had moved farther away, as would be the case if they had returned to Puerto Rico. It also seemed possible that foster families occupied a more central place for Hispanic respondents, comparable to the importance ascribed to godmothers in the Hispanic community (Mizio 1974). If so, biological families may have receded more into the background among these respondents than among either black or white young adults.

The principal reason for placement also distinguished between those from foster homes who were or were not in touch with kin. Young adults who were placed for reasons of neglect, abandonment, abuse, or the caretakers' inability to cope with their situations were more apt to be in touch with kin, particularly their parents, than those placed because of the mental illness of the primary caretaker. Those who were placed for more concrete, and perhaps to them more understandable, reasons such as the physical illness or death of a caretaker, or that person's inability to assume the care of an infant, were in between. The association persisted for all ethnic groups as well as when I singled out only those whose biological mothers, fathers, or relatives were alive at the time of our interviews, and who said they knew their kin. For the sake of simplicity contact with the biological mothers will be discussed, focusing only on those who were reported to be alive and who were known by the respondents. Of the 52 who were placed for reasons such as neglect, 65.4% were in touch with their biological mothers in contrast to 29.4% of the 17 who were placed because of mental illness of the primary caretaker, and 46.7% of the 15 who came into placement for such reasons as the physical illness of the caretaker. The association between the reason for placement and the young adults' contacts with their biological fathers and relatives was in the identical direction. Other factors such as age at placement, sex, and ethnicity did not shed any light on this relationship. Why were young adults from foster homes who were placed because of a caretaker's mental illness least likely to be in touch with their kin? The reason is not altogether clear. It is possible that some kin were in mental institutions and therefore less available. Or, if it is assumed that the mental illness reason for placement usually referred to the biological mothers, perhaps these young adults were less inclined to maintain contact with mothers who were or had been disturbed.

The Frequency of Contact

Each individual was asked to select which of seven levels of contact, ranging from "less than once a year" to "every day," best described the frequency of contacts with each member of the biological family. A respondent was judged to have frequent contact with kin if he or she reported having contact with any of them once a month or more often. Otherwise they were considered to have infrequent contact with kin. This included contact by telephone and mail because this seemed conceptually reasonable, and because a number of the young adults resided a large distance away from their families of origin.

It has already been pointed out that about 40% of the young adults were in touch with none of their kin. Most of the rest—somewhat more than 41%—maintained frequent contact with their families of origin, while about 18% were in touch less often. I compared those with high and those with low contact on many aspects of their background, their placement, and their lives at the time of our interviews. Nothing clearly distinguished those who maintained frequent contact from those with low contact, except that the former group felt closer to their kin than the latter group.

Closeness to Biological Parents and Relatives

Contact was by no means synonymous with the young adults' feeling of closeness to their biological parents or relatives. In fact, of the 143 who kept in touch, only 37.8% said they felt "very close" to their biological parents or relatives. Another 32.9% said they felt "somewhat close." The remainder felt "not very close" or "not close at all." Those who were in touch with their parents or relatives were examined in order to determine what distinguished those who felt very close to their kin from those who did not.

It quickly became clear that among those who maintained contact with their kin the young men and women who were discharged from group settings were more likely to feel very close to their biological families than those who were discharged from foster homes. This can readily be seen in table 9.2. I reasoned that since those from group settings had been placed an average of 4.3 years later than those from foster homes, they had spent more time with their kin which might have led to greater attachment. The data did not bear this out.

Table 9.2

Closeness to Biological Family Among Those in Touch with Kin

	Discharged From:					
	Foster Home		Group Setting		Total	
	N	(%)	N	(%)	N	(%)
Very close	24	(28.6)	30	(50.8)	54	(37.8)
Somewhat close	25	(29.8)	22	(37.3)	47	(32.9)
Not close	35	(41.7)	7	(11.9)	42	(29.4)
Total	84	(100.1)	59	(100.0)	143	(100.1)

For those from group settings as well as for those from foster homes age at placement was unrelated to their feelings of closeness. Of course, the group that maintained contact was, to begin with, older at placement so that it is perhaps not so surprising that within this older group placement age played no role in their expressed closeness toward kin.

What else distinguished those who felt very close to their biological parents or relatives from those who did not? Oddly enough their sex made a difference regardless of whether they were discharged from foster homes or group settings. Among those who were in touch with kin at the time of our interviews, 44.7% of the males, in contrast to 27.6% of the females, said that they felt very close to their biological mothers, fathers, or relatives, or some combination of these. I do not know why this was so.

The primary reason for placement was also an element in their sense of attachment, but the connection existed only with respect to closeness to their biological parents, not other relatives. Among the young adults who maintained contact with their kin, 9.2% of those who had been placed for such reasons as neglect or abandonment felt very close to one or both biological parents at the time of our interviews. In contrast, 37.7% of those who entered placement because of such factors as the mental or physical illness of their primary caretaker expressed such close feelings toward a parent. Males and females were alike in this regard, as were those who had been discharged from foster homes and group settings. It has already been reported that those from foster homes were less apt to be in touch with their kin if placed for such reasons as the mental or physical illness of a caretaker than if placed for such reasons as neglect. Thus, fewer of the former were in contact but if they were they felt closer. Perhaps only those who felt very close kept in touch. On the other hand, what might account for the more limited closeness, but proportionately greater contact, of those who were placed for such reasons as abandonment or neglect, or because the family could no longer cope with child care?

The answer to this question is fairly obvious with regard to those who were discharged from group settings since their biological families were their prime source, or potential source, of family support. With regard to those who were discharged from foster homes the issue is less clear. There are several reasons why they may have felt less close. Some might suggest that those who had been neglected or abandoned were, for psychological reasons, less able to express closeness. Such an argument tends to fade away in view of the fact that they expressed as much closeness toward other relatives as did those who were placed for what have been called the more concrete reasons. In addition, the reason for the young adults' placement was not associated with their closeness to their foster families. All of this leads to the conclusion that they were able to feel close but were less inclined to do so.

Perhaps they felt less close because the parents of children who had been placed because of abandonment or neglect were generally less accepting of their children and continued to communicate this as the children became young adults. The fact that fewer of those who were placed for these reasons felt very close to their parents irrespective of whether they were discharged from foster homes or group settings suggested that the young adults' relationships with their foster parents were not a salient issue.

It also seemed plausible that they expressed less closeness because they felt more rejected by their biological parents than those who came into placement because of a more concrete reason such as the mental or physical illness of their caretakers. Further contacts with their parents during placement that did not lead to a return home may have reinforced the initial rejection message. On this point it was reported in an earlier chapter that more of them felt that their placement had not been necessary. Having said all of this, one can speculate why so many of those who were placed for such reasons as neglect were nevertheless in touch with their biological parents. In order to cope with their anger at having been placed, individuals may distance themselves psychologically from their biological parents and even come to feel that they do not exist. If this occurred, contact for some young adults could have served the purpose of assuring themselves about the condition and circumstances of their biological parents. In any event, those who maintained contact were reaching out, perhaps in an attempt to develop greater closeness with their parents of origin. By staying in touch they were perhaps also trying to assure themselves that despite past experiences their parents did, and do, love them.

The only other element that was linked to their sense of closeness was their contact with kin during placement. But this connection existed only among those who were discharged from group settings. Among these young adults particularly, it will be recalled, contact with kin at the start and end of placement was linked to ongoing contact. If they remained in touch, 64.3% of those with early frequent contact expressed great closeness toward their kin, in contrast to 17.6% of those who had less contact during the early years. Frequency of contact during the last years of placement was not nearly as strongly linked to closeness. Nearly 59% of those with frequent, in comparison with 40% of those with more limited, contact late in placement said they felt very close to a biological parent or relative at the time of our interviews.

Summary

To recapitulate, a large majority of those who were discharged from group settings, but less than one-half of those from foster homes, maintained contact with their biological parents or relatives at the time of our interviews. The young adults' age at placement and contacts with kin during the later years of placement were important links. If they maintained contact it was apt to be frequent, irrespective of their sex or whether they had been discharged from foster homes or group settings. A minority of those who maintained contact said they felt very close to their kin, although such closeness was more often expressed by those from group settings, by those who maintained frequent contact, and by males. Finally, a smaller proportion of those who were placed for such reasons as the mental or physical illness of their caretakers were in touch, but if so, they were more apt to feel very close to their biological parents than if they entered care for such reasons as neglect or abandonment. The latter, it appears, felt more rejected and the emotional distance between them and their biological parents persisted over time.

Over and over again there were differences between those from foster homes and those who left group settings. The latter were in foster care for a shorter time and their ties to their biological families were stronger than the ties of those who spent many years in foster homes. Such a general statement does not, however, tell the full story. Rather the picture of those from foster homes ranges across many levels of attachment to kin, and many reasons lie at the root. Although a minority, some from foster homes maintained strong ties with their biological families, others maintained ties that appeared more tenuous, and most maintained minimal or no ties at all. They had another family with which they could develop ties. This was not the end result for all, but regardless of their ties to kin, it was an outcome for many.

Contact with Foster Parents

About one-third of those who were discharged from group settings had lived at one time in a foster home. Most of them maintained no contact with that family and only a few expressed any closeness toward its members. This discussion will, therefore, be limited to those who were discharged from foster homes. At the time of our interviews 86.9% of the young adults maintained contact with their last foster family. An additional 1.8% who were not in touch with their last foster parents maintained contact with a previous foster family. Thus, all together 88.7% were in contact with a foster family. Furthermore, among those who were in touch, nearly 89% maintained frequent contact. In other words, more of these young adults were in touch, and more frequently, with their foster than with their biological families.

Factors Associated with Contact with Foster Parents

What distinguished those who were and those who were not in touch with their foster parents? Most aspects of the young adults' background, placement experiences, and circumstances at the time of our interviews had no bearing. However, two related issues—the duration of their longest placement in one situation (for example, a particular foster home) and the number of times they had been shifted during placement—made a difference. Those who maintained contact with a foster family were in their longest placement an average of 12.5 years, whereas the average longest placement of those who were not in touch was 9.7 years. In the vast majority of cases the longest placement was with the foster family with whom they maintained contact. The number of times they were shifted was, of course, related to the duration of their longest placement; fewer shifts make longer placement more likely. Hence the number of shifts was also linked to contact, but less strongly. Those who maintained contact tended to have been shifted somewhat less (mean = 2.2) than those who were no longer in touch with a foster family (mean = 2.9). Clearly, the ties to foster parents developed and grew over the years in a placement, and if allowed to develop over time they were maintained after discharge.

Aspects of placement that distinguished between those who had no contact and those who maintained some contact with their foster parents were also at play in separating those who were frequently in touch from those with more limited contact at the time of our interviews. The latter consisted of a small group of 17 respondents who fell in between those with frequent and those with no contact on such things as the duration of their longest single placement and the average number of times they were shifted.

Closeness to Foster Parents

As was true of contact, their feelings of closeness toward their foster families stood in sharp contrast to what was observed about their closeness to their kin. Among those who maintained contact with their last foster family, 64.4% said they felt very close, and 24.7% felt somewhat close, to their foster parents. An additional few who were not in touch or who did not feel very close to their last foster family felt very close to a previous foster family. Thus, all together 65.1% of the young adults who left foster homes spoke of feeling very close to a foster family. This was equally true of males and females.

Expressions of closeness toward the foster parents and the amount of contact with them were, of course, strongly related. Therefore, factors that distinguished between those with varying amounts of contact also distinguished between those who said they felt very close and those who expressed less closeness. Thus, a longer duration of the longest placement and fewer shifts were linked to expressions of greater closeness to the foster parents.

Males who said they felt very close to their foster parents entered foster care at a younger age (mean = 3.0 years) than those who felt less close (mean = 5.1 years). Among females there was no such connection between age at placement and their expressed closeness to the foster parents. Perhaps in contrast to females, the males needed a longer separation from their biological families in order to express strong closeness to another family.

Two additional factors were linked to the young adults' expressed closeness. Females who were married were more likely to feel very close to their foster parents than those who were not. This was mentioned in an earlier chapter and it was suggested that perhaps their close relationship to the foster parents resulted in a greater willingness to make such a commitment. It is also possible that foster parents expressed greater approval of women who had settled with a legally sanctioned mate. If so, a greater closeness may have developed.

Finally, there was a substantial link ($r = .56$) between the young adults' closeness to their foster parents and their overall satisfaction with foster care. Although this point was omitted from an earlier discussion, such satisfaction was also connected with contact and frequency of contact with their foster families. Clearly, these young adults' feelings about their foster care experience were heavily influenced by their relationships with their foster families, but these feelings were not at all related to their relationships with their kin.

Contact and Closeness Vis-à-Vis Both Families

Although more of those who left foster homes maintained contact, and more frequent contact, with their foster families and expressed greater closeness toward them than toward their biological parents or relatives, there was nevertheless a fair amount of overlap.

Of the 168 young men and women on whom we had both sets of information, 43.5% maintained contact with both their biological and foster families, including 25% who spoke of frequent contact with each. These data are presented in table 9.3. But of those who maintained contact with both families, only 16.4% felt simultaneously very close to one or more members in both families. An additional 8.2% felt somewhat close to members of both.

A number of questions concerning both sets of families arose. For example, did those who maintained frequent contact with one family have less contact with the other? Or, was the expressed closeness toward one family associated with less closeness toward the other family, and did this make a difference in who was in touch with whom? In each instance the answer

Table 9.3
Contacts with Biological Parents, Relatives, and Foster Families
(Respondents Discharged from Foster Homes)

Contacts with Kin	Contacts with Foster Families			
	Frequent	Infrequent	None	Total N
Frequent	42	6	5	53
Infrequent	22	3	4	29
None	68	8	10	86
Total N	132	17	19	168

was no; contact and closeness with one family were quite independent of contact and closeness with members of the other family.

A few illustrations can help to clarify this issue. Were those who had frequent contact with their foster family less in touch with biological family members? One can see in table 9.3 that of the 132 young adults who maintained frequent contact with their foster family, 68.2% maintained infrequent or no contact with their biological parents or a relative. But this was also true of those who maintained infrequent or no contact with their foster family: an almost identical proportion—69.4%—maintained infrequent or no contact with their kin.

Was closeness vis-à-vis foster families linked to similar or diminished closeness toward the biological family? Of those who felt very close to their foster families, 13.4% felt very close to members of their biological family. But this was also true of those who did not feel very close to a foster family; of these, 16.9% felt very close to their kin. In other words, approximately the same proportions felt very close to kin irrespective of their expressed closeness to the foster parents. The proportions were also quite alike when one singled out only those who maintained contact with both families. For males and females alike, contact and closeness to the foster families, therefore, had no bearing on contact and closeness to the biological family.

Contact and Closeness to the Biological Family and Their Sense of Well-Being

Among those who were discharged from group settings, males and females who maintained contact with their biological parents or relatives had a more positive sense of well-being than those who were not in touch at the time of our interviews. However, the amount of contact, whether frequent or infrequent, had no bearing on their feelings about themselves and their lives. These data are shown in table 9.4. Furthermore, if they maintained contact, those who felt very close to their biological parents or relatives tended to have a more positive outlook (mean = .16) than those who did not express such closeness toward their kin (mean = − 1.04). Thus, for those who left group settings, both contact and closeness were linked to their sense of well-being. It is, however, not clear which came first since it is possible that a more positive outlook was instrumental in their keeping in touch and in describing their feelings of closeness in more positive terms.

In contrast, among males and females who were discharged from foster homes there was no connection between their sense of well-being and whether or not they maintained contact with their biological families, nor did the amount of contact,

Table 9.4
Amount of Contact with Kin and Sense of Well-Being

	Discharged From:					
	Foster Home			Group Setting		
	Mean*	S.D.	N	Mean*	S.D.	N
Contact with Kin						
Parents frequent	− 1.06	2.1	22	− .58	2.5	22
Relatives frequent†	1.21	2.1	31	− .37	2.3	22
Parents low	.72	2.2	15	− .40	2.9	5
Relatives low†	.24	1.9	14	− .29	3.1	9
None	.42	2.3	89	− 2.65	1.6	8
Total	.39	2.8	171	− .71	2.5	66

*Z-scores: A high positive score signifies a more positive sense of well-being.
†Includes some who also maintained contact with biological parents.

whether frequent or infrequent, or their expression of closeness, have a bearing. However, I was puzzled by what the data showed about 53 respondents who maintained frequent contact with their families of origin. Twenty-two of them were frequently in touch with only their biological mothers, fathers, or both. If they maintained contact with a relative, it was infrequent. Another 20 maintained frequent contact with a relative and were also in touch with at least one parent. In most instances their contacts with their parents were also frequent. The remaining 11 were frequently in touch with only a relative; in most of these instances their biological parents had died. It was puzzling that the outlook of the 22 males and females who were frequently in touch with only their biological mothers, fathers, or both was much poorer than that of the 31 young adults who maintained frequent contact with at least one relative. This can readily be seen in table 9.4.

What could account for this difference? I tested various hypotheses in search of an explanation. For instance, it was plausible that a conflict of allegiances between two sets of parents might have led to a poorer outlook, If so, one might expect a particularly poor sense of well-being among those who maintained frequent contact with both their biological and their foster parents. But there was no support for this idea in our data.

Other factors that were examined, such as the reason for placement or the problems exhibited at discharge, also shed no light on the observed difference. Before a speculation is made about an explanation, the data will be repeated in somewhat more detailed form. The 22 men and women who maintained frequent contact with only their biological mothers, fathers, or both had the poorest sense of well-being (mean = −1.06). The 20 who maintained frequent contact with a relative, most of whom also maintained frequent contact with a biological parent had a better outlook (mean = .80), and the 11 who were frequently in touch with only a relative were particularly positive in their outlook (mean = 1.95). Two things appeared to be at play.

For one, it is plausible that there were tensions in the relationships between the young adults and their biological parents that were heightened by frequent contact with them alone. These were after all the very parents who had not been able to care for them as children. This line of reasoning gained some support from the fact that those who maintained infrequent contact with only their parents had a more positive outlook. In other words, it was not contact in and of itself, but frequent contact with only their parents, that made the difference.

Second, the more positive outlook of those who simultaneously maintained frequent contact with relatives and biological parents suggested that an extended family support system was important in bolstering the outlook of those who were also frequently in touch with their biological parents. Possibly the relatives served as a buffer or in other ways helped to smoothe over some of the kinks in the relationships between the young adults and their biological parents.

Contact and Closeness to the Foster Family and Their Sense of Well-Being

Very little can be said about those who were discharged from foster homes and their contacts with their foster parents since a large majority remained in touch. Males and females who maintained contact did not differ in their average sense of well-being from those who were no longer in touch. But the picture was complicated because of a considerable difference in the outlook of those who maintained frequent and those with only limited contact. Those who were frequently in touch, and this was a large majority, had a more positive sense of well-being (mean = .54) than those with infrequent contact (mean = −.69), which suggested that tenuous ties with their foster families was an element in their outlook. But the outlook of those who had no contact whatsoever, and who had no strong ties to their foster families, was in between (mean = .19). Close scrutiny of this group showed that a much larger proportion (63.2%) of this small group was living with a mate at the time of our interviews than was the case with those who maintained infrequent contact (29.4%). In the absence of ties to their foster families, they had in a sense established their own families and this played a role in their outlook. In contrast, most of those who maintained infrequent contact had neither strong ties to a foster family nor to a mate, and their sense of well-being suffered.

The link between their sense of well-being and their expressed closeness toward their foster parents differed for males and females. Women who felt very close had a better outlook (mean = .74) than those who felt less close (mean = −.79). In contrast, among the men there was no connection between their expressed closeness and their sense of well-being. Apparently for the women, the sense of closeness vis-á-vis their foster families was a particularly important element in their outlook, whereas the men's sense of well-being was influenced more heavily by other elements in their lives.

Final Comment

The desire to be part of a family is deep within all human beings. We turn to the family for nurture and to learn who we are. But who is that family? The answer is not so simple when one thinks about those who spent many years in foster care. For those from group settings there was generally no family other than their biological kin. But for the rest there was also a foster family. Siblings became their main link to their family of origin. Other ties of blood existed, but they became more tenuous. Reattachments could, and did, occur. And they persisted over time.

Chapter Ten

TROUBLES

Personal troubles come in many shapes. Whether physical, psychological, or of another form, one can expect such troubles to have serious ramifications and to influence people's views of their lives. In order to secure a general picture, we inquired about the young adults' physical health, and also asked them to answer 33 questions concerning a variety of symptoms and other troubles commonly indicative of physical and psychological discomforts. These were answered by the young adults on their own in the hope that privacy would make them less self-conscious and thereby increase the likelihood of honest answers. All respondents were also asked to rate the amount they worried and to describe their use of alcoholic beverages and drugs. Finally, they were asked about any difficulties with the law. Information on this was also obtained independently.

Health and Symptoms

Close to 79% of the young adults stated that they had no particular physical or health troubles of any kind. Problems that did exist ranged from serious disabilities to relatively minor problems. When asked to characterize their own overall health as excellent, good, fair, or poor, only 1.8% stated that their health was poor, while 84.7% rated their health as either excellent or good. On such general levels there were no sex differences and no differences connected with having been discharged from foster homes or group settings. But when asked to rate their satisfaction with their own health and physical condition, males and females differed. The women were on the average less satisfied than the men. There were also sex differences on a number of symptoms.

Using a format developed at the University of Michigan (Veroff, Douvan, and Kulka 1981), the young adults were asked about the frequency of twelve common symptoms. For example, they were asked about problems of getting to sleep or staying asleep, feeling fidgety and tense, headaches, loss of appetite, stomach upsets, dizziness, and nightmares. These data are shown in table 10.1. In each instance the young adults rated the frequency of the symptom on a four-point scale where 4 signified "nearly all the time" or "many times" and 1 denoted "never." On four of the symptoms the women com-

Table 10.1
Frequency of Symptoms

	Males (N = 159)		Females (N = 115)		Males vs. Females
	Mean*	S.D.	Mean*	S.D.	*p*
1. Trouble getting to sleep or staying asleep	1.96	.80	2.03	.75	—
2. Feeling fidgety and tense	2.04	.83	2.42	.79	.0002
3. Headaches or pains in the head	1.70†	.68	1.94	.72	.006
4. Loss of appetite	1.76†	.78	1.97	.86	.04
5. Upset stomach	1.77	.62	1.91	.72	.07
6. Difficulty getting up in the morning	2.18	.88	2.22	.93	—
7. Shortness of breath	1.64	.82	1.70	.92	—
8. Heart beating hard	1.56†	.86	1.55	.81	—
9. Spells of dizziness	1.55†	.74	1.74	.91	.06
10. Nightmares	1.64†	.82	1.92	.95	.01
11. Hands trembling	1.55†	.80	1.47†	.82	—
12. Hands sweating, damp and clammy	1.65†	.95	1.50	.80	—

*Four-point scale: A score of 1 signifies never; a score of 4 signifies high frequency.
†Based on one or two fewer respondents.

plained with reliably greater frequency than the young men, and on two others they tended in the same direction. The women also tended to speak of feeling sad and blue more often. The respondents were also asked to rate the amount they worried on a five-point scale. Once again this was, on the average, more common among women (mean = 3.3) than among men (mean = 2.9). Nearly 41% of the women said they worried "a lot" or "all the time" in contrast to 25.1% of the young men. By and large these sex differences applied equally to those discharged from foster homes and those from group care.

Only two areas distinguished between respondents from foster homes and those from group settings. The latter complained somewhat more of problems with getting to sleep and staying asleep, and spoke of feeling sad or blue more often, than did young adults from foster homes. Apart from these two areas, what stood out were the differences connected with their sex.

Most of the troubles were not independent of one another; there were interconnections throughout. For instance, those who reported better health were less likely to complain about feeling fidgety and tense ($r = -.21$), about upset stomachs ($r = -.24$), about dizziness ($r = -.31$), or about sleep problems ($r = -.18$). Those who complained less about upset stomachs also complained less about feeling fidgety and tense ($r = .32$), about spells of dizziness ($r = .32$), or about sleep problems ($r = .28$). The intercorrelations among other combinations were similar. Furthermore, these troubles were by and large also linked to the young adults' ratings of how much they worried about things. The linkage between frequency of symptoms and the amount they worried existed for the men and women alike. Therefore, their ratings of the frequency of worries will be used as an indicator of this worry cluster in order to describe the connections with selected aspects of their lives. The young men and women will be viewed separately in order to highlight those differences that did exist between them, although there were areas of overlap.

Among the women, feelings of success and achievement, closeness to others and social support, feelings about effectiveness in planning their lives, and economic security distinguished those who worried less. For instance, women who were employed or attending school said they worried less than women who were unemployed or homemakers $(r = -.21)$. Employed women and those who were students were more apt to feel they were achieving success and moving ahead $(r = .42)$, and women who felt they were achieving success said they worried less $(r = -.30)$. Those at the low end of the worry scale felt more effective in planning their lives $(r = -.29)$, were more satisfied about the way they handled problems that arose $(r = -.40)$, had a higher self-esteem $(r = -.33)$, and were more satisfied with the amount of fun they were having $(r = -.40)$. Being married or living with a partner had no bearing on the level of worry, but among those who had a mate the happier ones worried less $(r = -.35)$. The more that women felt they had people to count on for help $(r = -.27)$ and the closer they felt to their siblings $(r = -.20)$, the less they worried. And among those from foster homes, those who felt closer to their foster families worried less $(r = -.26)$. Closeness to biological parents or relatives was, however, not connected. Economic security also played a role, for women who were more satisfied with the amount of money they had for basic things described themselves as less frequent worriers $(r = -.28)$. Finally, and not surprisingly, those who worried less were more satisfied with their health $(r = -.29)$ and had a more positive sense of well-being $(r = -.45)$.

The men's sense of well-being was similarly related $(r = -.38)$. But beyond this there were far fewer connections with the amount they said they worried. For instance, employment had no bearing; those with jobs said they worried as much on the average as the unemployed. For the young men employment had less of a bearing on their sense of achievement than was the case for the women. Perhaps the nature of their jobs caused some of the employed men to worry as much as the unemployed. This issue could be examined only indirectly.

Those who spoke of fewer worries tended to be more satisfied with their jobs ($r = -.16$) and had been unemployed less frequently ($r = .23$) since their discharge from foster care. The frequency of unemployment was connected with their level of education, which also had some bearing on worries. Those who expressed fewer worries were less apt to have left care with a moderately serious educational problem ($r = .18$) and they also tended to have completed more grades ($r = -.13$) by the time of our interviews. They were more apt to feel satisfied with their health and physical condition ($r = -.18$), and were more satisfied with the amount of fun they were having ($r = -.28$) and with the way they handled problems ($r = -.29$). Their self-esteem was higher ($r = -.28$). As with the women they were more positive about having people to count on for help ($r = -.22$), but other aspects of their relationships with people, such as their happiness with their mates or their feeling of closeness toward their foster parents, were not connected as they were for the women. Again like the women, economic factors played a role since those men who were more satisfied with the amount of money they had for basic things said they worried less ($r = -.34$).

Despite similarities here and there, I was left with the impression that various aspects of social support and a sense of achievement vis-à-vis the outside world were more important for the women than for the men in the extent to which they spoke of worries. A multiple correlation using two factors—their sense of achievement and their feelings about having people to count on—illustrates this. These two predicted the extent that women worried ($R^2 = .12$) better than for the men ($R^2 = .05$).

The Use of Alcohol and Drugs

Sex differences were found when I examined the young adults' reports on their consumption of alcoholic beverages; the men were more frequent users. For instance, when asked how often they had drunk beer, wine, or some other liquor during the past month, 27.1% of the women, in contrast to 13.5% of the men, had not done so. At the other extreme 29.3% of the men, in comparison with 12.1% of the women, reported some liquor consumption at least three times a week, including some who drank every day. More men also reported that during the month they had drunk to the point where they felt high. Close to 36% of all the women reported that this had occurred, compared with 62.5% of the men.

Drinking had decreased for many of these young adults. In fact, close to 53% of those who ever drank recalled a time during earlier years when they consumed more alcohol, whereas about 26% recalled a period when they drank less. This was as true for the women as for the men. The latter began drinking at an earlier age, with more than 41% stating that they started before age 16, compared with about 28% of the women. There was also a suggestion that women who had been discharged from group settings began earlier (mean = 16.1) than women who had left foster homes (mean = 17.1). There was no such connection for the men.

Among the men there was no connection between their drinking and the amount they said they worried, whereas among the women there was. Women who reported more drinking tended to describe themselves as greater worriers ($r = .16$), and a connection also existed between frequency of worries and the number of times they had been tipsy recently ($r = .25$). For the women this latter was linked with a poorer sense of well-being ($r = -.27$), while for the men there was no such connection.

The picture of drug use was similar. The young adults were presented with a list of eight drugs and asked to indicate how often during the past year they had used such things as marijuana, amphetamines, cocaine, barbiturates, Quaaludes, or tranquilizers. The respondents completed this on their own. More of the males (81.2%) than females (66.4%) had used some drug during the year. Marijuana and cocaine were by far the most frequently cited by men and women alike, while the use of tranquilizers was rare. The men were more frequent users, and had also used a greater variety of drugs, than the women. Close to 29% of all the males spoke of using at least one drug practically every day, in contrast to 14% of the women. At the other extreme, 48.9% of the males, but 65.4% of the women, had used drugs once or twice a month or less during the past year, including those who reported using no drugs at all. There were no differences in frequency of drug use between those who were discharged from foster homes and group care.

Close to 45% of those who had ever used drugs, whether male or female, said that their drug use had decreased in comparison with earlier years, and a roughly similar proportion (37.3%) spoke of an increase. As in the case of alcohol consumption, the men were younger than the women when they began using drugs. About 43% of the men, in contrast to 29.3% of the women, reported some drug use before age 15. Once again there was a suggestion that the women who were discharged from group settings were somewhat younger (mean = 16.2) than the women from foster homes (mean = 17.5) when they first used a drug, whereas no such difference existed among the men. We did not collect information on what drugs were used while youngsters were in placement, and therefore do not know the extent to which tranquilizers or other drugs were used at that time.

A few other sex differences stood out. Women who spoke of worrying more often described themselves as more frequent users of drugs ($r = .34$). The latter was also linked to a poorer sense of well-being among the women ($r = -.32$). None of these associations existed among the men. Not only did men express fewer worries, but worries also had no bearing on their alcohol or drug use. Or perhaps alcohol or drug use, more acceptable as outlets for men in our culture, worried them less. It is not clear which came first in time. Finally, males who said they were younger when they began to use drugs tended to speak of more frequent drug use ($r = -.18$) at the time of our interviews. For women there was no such connection. Unfortunately, we have no independent corroborative evidence for any of this. It is possible that those men who were the most frequent users were in a sense bragging about their earlier beginnings with drugs. If so, why was this not the case among women? What is reported here is simply what they reported, and our data are flawed to the extent that they reported incorrectly.

Formal Help-Seeking

When people are worried or feel that they have a personal problem, they may seek advice and help from a broad array of professional counselors including psychiatrists, psychologists, social workers, marriage counselors, physicians, and members of the clergy. We attempted to get a rough indication of this by asking the young adults who were interviewed whether, and where, they had sought such help since their discharge from care.

Close to 47% had at one time or another since 1975 turned to a professional for advice or counsel with a personal problem. There were no differences between men and women, nor between those who were discharged from foster homes and group settings. The two largest single sources to whom they had turned were the clergy (18.8%) and professionals at social agencies (16.3%), and most of the latter consisted of staff members of the same agencies that had discharged them. Some young adults had turned to more than one source for help, but they were in a minority (15.1%). We did not ask about the nature of the problems for which they had sought counsel since their discharge, or when they sought help, or the extent of the help provided. However, no matter where they had turned, a majority felt they had been helped. For instance, this was the case for about 74% of those who had sought counsel at a social agency.

We combined various professional mental health and social agency contacts in order to assess the extent to which such sources had been used. Some 30.5% of those who were interviewed had turned to one or more of these sources, the women to a greater degree (37.7%) than the men (24.8%). Men and women turned to social agencies in equal proportions, but more of the women had at some point sought help from psychiatrists and clinics. It can be assumed that this simply reflected sex differences in the use of psychiatric and mental health clinics by the population at large.

Summary Comments

Some final comments are necessary about the sex differences we observed over and over again. Considering the fact that there were no sex differences in the sense of well-being, and that this sense of well-being for both males and females was linked to the frequency of symptoms and to the amount they said they worried, a curious puzzle exists. What meaning should be attached to the fact that women reported more frequent worries and symptoms of various sorts than the men? One obvious answer is that they had more psychological problems by the time of our interviews. This seemed odd since at the time of discharge they had, if anything, fewer problems that were recorded. It is, of course, possible that women, more than men, developed problems in the intervening years. We had no independent measure of this. But if they had more problems by the time we saw them, why was their sense of well-being so similar to that of the men?

Since we were dealing with their own ratings of worries and symptoms, another interpretation of the differences between males and females must be entertained. Perhaps in an absolute sense there were no differences, but women felt freer to express themselves about worries, given the fact that our culture is more accepting of, and even expecting, such expression by women. The women in our sample were certainly not unusual in complaining more frequently than the men. In fact, our data in large measure reflected what has been reported by other investigators about a greater prevalence of health and emotional concerns among women than among men (Campbell 1981; Veroff, Douvan, and Kulka 1981; Wechsler, Rohman, and Solomon 1981).

It is also possible that the women were more apt to label things as problems than the men, and perhaps they used a different yardstick in assessing the frequency of their worries and symptoms. This may have led more of them to seek help from various mental health professionals. Irrespective of the help they received, such guidance may have led them to perceive themselves as worriers. It may have sensitized them to look for strains and tensions, so that they were more likely than the men to label various feelings as worries, and to believe they worried more frequently.

Troubles with the Law

The men predominated in this area of concern. Before describing what was learned, a word of explanation about the procedure: rather than singling out the respondents for discussion, material will be presented on the total population of 421 individuals, including the 117 nonrespondents, the 21 we did not attempt to interview, and the 6 who had died. This should provide the fullest picture possible.

For information I relied on identifications provided to me by the New York State Division of Criminal Justice Services following agreements about confidentiality, and after obtaining all necessary permissions. We provided the Division with information on each of the 421 individuals that included their full name, maiden name (where relevant), sex, date of birth, racial appearance, and (where available) birthplace, Social Security number, and criminal justice identification number. After this information was matched against the division's computer listing, we received the official record of all fingerprintable arrests, charges, and dispositions that had occurred in New York State. Juvenile offenses were not included, as prescribed

by law. I reviewed the identifying material in each of these
records in order to determine a positive match. A listing of
previous addresses, identical to those in our files, was often a
help in such matching. In most instances there was no doubt
about the match. Where there was doubt, as could occur when
an individual's record showed numerous dates of birth or a
plethora of names, I did not regard it as a positive match unless other parameters were identical. If I erred, undoubtedly
I did so on the conservative side. The results are also conservative in that the material we received was generally limited
to New York State. Except in a few instances, we had no official information about individuals who were arrested elsewhere but not in New York State. Even within New York State
my count may not be precise, for some individuals may have
used aliases, or the identifying information may have been entered incorrectly. For all these reasons due caution must be
exercised. Nevertheless, the picture presented can provide a
rough indication of the young adults' troubles with the law in
New York State.

During the four- to five- year period since their discharge
from foster care, 32.7% of the 257 males and 4.9% of the 164
females had been arrested on charges of having committed a
misdemeanor or felony according to reports by police pre-
cincts throughout New York State. All but one of the eight
women had been arrested only once. One-half of the 84 males
had been arrested once, about one-third had been arrested
two or three times, and the remainder, all together 14 males,
had been arrested four to nine times since their discharge from
foster care. More of the men discharged from group settings
(40.2%) tended to have been arrested than those discharged
from foster homes (28.5%), and they had been arrested more
frequently. For instance, of the 47 males from foster homes
with an arrest record in New York State, roughly 38% had
been arrested twice or more often, whereas this was the case
for 64.9% of the 37 arrested males from group settings. Females with arrest records were too few in number for such a
detailed examination. Therefore, in most of what follows the
focus will be only on the males.

One can speculate about why somewhat more males from group care had been arrested than males from foster homes. It was more difficult for them to get settled following their discharge from care, and they had less economic support to fall back on. Their connections with a family were more tenuous, and more of them may have relied on peers as a central source of social support. Perhaps they were for some reason less clever, or were more apt to be booked because they did not have foster parents who might spring into action, and vouch for them vis-à-vis the police if trouble arose.

With respect to the young adults' willingness to speak of arrests in our interviews, we asked only one question about arrests since leaving foster care. A comparison of their responses with the official records of New York State showed that 58.8% of the males and four out of five women with such a record spoke of this in the interview. Obviously the subject was a sensitive one which some had forgotten, denied, or wanted to hide. There were also some who spoke of a run-in with the police but who had no official record. I do not know how to interpret this. Perhaps their run-in was minor, so that they were never arrested for a fingerprintable charge. The question in our interview did not make this distinction. Perhaps they were arrested in another state, although virtually all were living in New York when interviewed. Finally, it is possible that they were arrested in New York State but did not know the precise date of their discharge from care, the date I used for the official recording. In view of all of these problems with their self-reports of arrests, only the data from the official records will be used in what follows.

The Nature of Arrests

A particular arrest frequently included a record of several charges—a mixture of felonies and misdemeanors. For instance, burglary in the third degree—a class D felony—may have been recorded along with a charge of reckless endangerment of property—a class B misdemeanor. We broadly classified each arrest according to whether the most serious charge was a felony or misdemeanor. About two-thirds (67.9%) of the 84 males who had been arrested since their discharge from foster care had been charged with at least one felony, and about one-half of these had been so charged on two or more occasions. Further, using the 1971 Penal Law of the State of New York, I classified each felony arrest according to type, again using the most serious charge listed on each arrest. Most common were property felonies, including burglary, grand larceny, and forgery. Of the 84 men who were arrested, 37 had been charged with such an offense. Next in frequency were charges of personal violence, including murder, rape, robbery, and felonious assault. Twenty-five of the 84 men had been so charged. Victimless felonies, including various narcotics charges, were less frequent. Of course, any individual who had been arrested more than once could have been arrested for more than one type of felony, and could also have been arrested on another occasion on a misdemeanor charge. Among the 84 men who were arrested, 34 were arrested for a misdemeanor involving property, such as petty larceny, criminal possession of stolen property, or unauthorized use of a vehicle. Next in frequency of misdemeanors were offenses that are regarded as victimless, such as criminal possession of a controlled substance, public lewdness, and possession of a dangerous weapon. Nineteen of the 84 men were at some point charged with such an offense. Finally, 5 of the 84 had been charged with a misdemeanor involving persons, for instance, menacing. Overall then, arrests on offenses against property, whether felonies or misdemeansors, were more common than charges involving personal violence.

But what is the significance of arrest figures? This question will not be addressed. Opinions on the subject are many yet a definitive answer is not readily available. At a minimum, and for our purposes that will suffice, such figures mean that some of those who left foster care, for whatever reason, had a run-in with the law. But who were these individuals who had a record of arrest in New York State?

Factors Connected with Arrest

Other things beyond the group care-foster home difference distinguished those with a record of arrest from those with no such record in New York State. They differed in some aspects of their background, their placement experience, and their current circumstances. I examined separately males who were discharged from foster homes and those from group care. Further subdividing them into various ethnic groups sometimes suffered from much reduced numbers, but this allowed me to pursue various leads.

Whether discharged from foster homes or group settings, their level of education distinguished between males with a record of arrest and those without such a record. Close to two-thirds (64.2%) of the latter had at least completed high school by the time of their discharge from foster care, compared with 39.2% of those with a record of arrest since their discharge. One-half of the latter exhibited learning problems at the time of their discharge compared with 25.7% of those with no record of arrest. Furthermore, 41.8% of those who were arrested had been discharged from foster care with a fairly serious social or emotional problem, in contrast to 16.2% of those who were not arrested.

Some additional linkages were apparent for the males from group settings. For instance, 59.5% of those who were arrested had entered placement for reasons such as neglect or abandonment, in contrast to 38.2% of those who were not arrested. Those arrested also had less contact with their biological families during the first or last years of placement than those who were not arrested. For those arrested, contact was more often infrequent or there was none at all. For males who were discharged from foster homes, on the other hand, there were no connections between placement reasons or their contacts with their biological families during placement and records of arrest.

The factors discussed thus far were linked to arrests irrespective of the young males' ethnicity, although this was also an element in who was arrested. Among those discharged from foster homes 37.4% of the black males as compared with 19% of white and 12.5% of Hispanic males had been arrested since their discharge from foster care. Among those from group settings 50% of the black, 13% of the white, and 51.6% of the Hispanic males had been arrested. I looked at this more deeply and tested a number of hypotheses about their backgrounds and placement, but nothing consistent emerged that shed any light on the observed differences. But among those who were interviewed black males who had been arrested spoke of many more extensive periods of unemployment in the years since their discharge from foster care than black males who had no record of arrest. It is, however, not clear to what extent difficulties in finding work led to activities that resulted in arrests, or to what extent arrests resulted in greater problems finding work.

My review of other background and placement variables showed no other consistent connections with records of arrest. For instance, I examined whether arrests were more apt to occur among those whose biological mothers or fathers had been in jail or prison in the past. To the extent that we had information, no connection existed. Elements of placement such as their age at entry or the number of times they had been shifted also were not connected with records of arrest.

But various aspects of the males' circumstances at the time of our contacts were linked to records of arrest. Only the respondents can be discussed here. First, those with a record of arrest had completed on the average 11.3 years of schooling by the time of our contacts. In contrast, males with no record of arrest averaged 12.5 years. Those with a record of arrest were on the whole less apt to be employed, and more of them were receiving public assistance at the time of our interviews than was the case for those without a record of arrest. More had never married, but they were as likely to be living with a partner or spouse as those never arrested, and they were as happy with these relationships. They had lived at more addresses since their discharge from care, and were less apt to be involved with clubs and organizations in the communities where they resided. Whether discharged from group settings or foster homes, those with a record of arrest had more extreme scores on the enlarged Srole scale (Robinson and Shaver 1973), an indication of greater anomia (Srole 1956) or alienation from the society at large.

Males with a record of arrest were as likely to be residing in New York City or its surrounding suburbs, said they attended religious services as frequently, felt they knew as many of their neighbors and generally spoke of having as many friends. Furthermore, their level of contact with, and expressions of closeness toward, their biological and foster families did not differ from that of those who had no record of arrest. They were as satisfied with themselves and how they got along with people as those not arrested, but if discharged from group care they were somewhat more likely to agree with the statement "no one cares much what happens to me." At the same time, arrested males did not describe themselves as greater worriers, they felt as optimistic about their future, and their overall sense of well-being did not differ on the average from that of those who had no record of arrest.

Convictions

Many readers may have been wondering why arrests have been discussed at length here rather than convictions that resulted from the arrests. The official arrest records included some information on the disposition of charges, as well as sentences, but there are many problems with these data. Since the variety of reasons for this have been well reviewed elsewhere (Cosgrove 1979), they will not be detailed here. One major problem is that the data in these records on convictions are drastically incomplete. For instance, some or all of the dispositions were missing for 49 of the 84 males who had been arrested. This may have meant that the dispositions were never received by the Division of Criminal Justice, that some cases were never disposed of, or some were perhaps still in process. In view of these limitations I will omit any discussion of the number of convictions, but will, for whatever it is worth, report on the number of individuals who were ever convicted of a misdemeanor or felony, usually upon a plea of guilty, following their discharge from foster care.

All together there was a record of at least one conviction for 33 of the 84 males who had been arrested on misdemeanor or felony charges. The proportion was virtually identical for the eight females, three of whom had been convicted. It is no surprise that men originally charged with misdemeanors were less apt to be convicted than men whose most serious charge was a felony offense, although the latter was most often reduced. For instance, of the 27 males who had been charged with one or more misdemeanors, but no felony, two were subsequently convicted of a misdemeanor, whereas of the 57 males who were charged with one or more felonies, 6 were convicted of a felony and 25 were convicted of a misdemeanor.

The proportion of those arrested who were ever convicted was similar whether they had been discharged from foster homes (40.2%) or group settings (37.8%), although a larger proportion of the latter had records of arrest. Apparently their relatively more frequent run-ins with the law were not considered more serious in nature.

Summary Comment

There were few factors that distinguished males discharged from foster homes who subsequently had a run-in with the law from those who did not. A more limited scholastic achievement and problems at discharge predominated. If black, the risk of arrest was greater. They said they felt as close to their foster families but were apparently more footloose following their discharge from care, had more difficulty in the labor market, and were more apt to be receiving public assistance.

Similarly, for those from group settings, limited schooling, problems at the time of discharge, difficulties with employment, and greater mobility were in evidence. They tended to be more at risk of arrest than those from foster homes, particularly if they were black or Hispanic. Tenuous ties to their biological parents and extended families were important elements for these males, unlike their counterparts who had foster families for support. For if they were or felt deserted during their placement, on whom could they fall back following their discharge into the community?

I had the impression that among these men there was a fair amount of flailing about, of getting into trouble with the police in an episodic way rather than in a consistent pattern of run-ins with the law. After all, one-half of the 84 males arrested had only one recorded episode, and for one-half the last recorded arrest in New York State was between 1975 and 1977, rather than in the two subsequent years. In any event, by the time of our interviews, despite their general sense of alienation, these men's assessment of themselves and their lives did not differ from that of those who had never been arrested.

Were More of Them Arrested?

Perhaps the most important question is one that has not been addressed thus far. Was a larger proportion of these young adult males from foster care arrested than their counterparts in the population at large? The question is a vital one that requires an answer in view of assertions that jails are overpopulated with those from foster care, and news reports referring to "authorities" suggesting that graduates of long-term care are "much more likely than the average youth to wind up an unemployed adult living off welfare and crime" (Kwitny 1978:1). An answer is also important from the perspective of those who have spent years in foster care; as one young man said: "I used to get into a shell when I heard the term 'foster'—a child should not be called 'foster'—people get the wrong view . . . they think you're a hoodlum."

This question is difficult to answer precisely, but a rough estimate was possible. To arrive at it I singled out male respondents and nonrespondents who had a record of arrest in New York State in 1979. There were 27 in all. In order to compare them with males in the general population, I secured two sets of figures: the number of males of the same age in each ethnic group who had been arrested once or more often on a misdemeanor or felony charge in New York State in 1979, and census estimates of the total number of males of the same age in each ethnic group in New York State. The latter, based on the March 1980 Annual Demographic Survey, was not identical in time but was the closest approximation available. The comparisons between the foster care group and males their age in New York State showed that within each ethnic group (that is, among blacks, Hispanics, or whites) the proportion of graduates from foster care who had been arrested was almost identical to the proportion of males with records of arrest in the general population. For example, 13.1% of the black males from foster care had an arrest recorded in New York State in 1979, compared with 12.6% of black males their age arrested in the population at large. The situation among Hispanics and whites was similar, although the proportions arrested were smaller. It is possible that these comparisons were marred by the fact that the foster care group included some who were living outside New York State. It was not possible to arrive at a more precise comparison since some of those who lived elsewhere had been arrested in New York State in 1979. Nevertheless, I also compared foster care graduates who resided in New York State at the time of our contacts. There still seemed to be no differences between the foster care group and others. I also examined an older group of foster care graduates, discharged in 1970, who will be discussed in the next chapter. This 27- to 30-year-old group was also compared with males of the same age residing in New York State.

Once again there were no differences in the proportion from foster care who were arrested in New York State when compared with their counterparts in the general population, although the numbers were too small to be other than tentatively suggestive at best.

I focused on men since too few women had records of arrest. Furthermore, I did not compare rates of conviction because of the problems inherent in these data. To repeat, the material on male arrests can be regarded only as a rough estimation. Yet this issue was too important to omit. No doubt there are some errors, but they would have to be sizable and all in one direction in order to support the notion that long-term foster care regularly and disproportionately spawns young adults who will eventually be arrested for criminal activity. At a minimum the material presented here calls such beliefs into question. Beyond this I hope that these data will begin to fill the vacuum in which sterotypical ideas have flourished and predominated.

Chapter Eleven

ADULTS WHO LEFT FOSTER CARE
IN 1970

The central focus of this presentation has been on young adults in their early to mid-twenties some four or five years following their discharge from foster care. Selecting this time frame involved several considerations. I wanted to allow time for the young adults to experience something of life, but did not want too much time to elapse for memories about foster care to fade. Despite numerous advantages and disadvantages of using alternative years, in the end reality intruded. The availability of computerized discharge listings limited my choice to a 1975 discharge date. To have chosen an earlier date would have required going from agency to agency in order to identify all relevant cases by hand. Although possible, the task seemed too cumbersome and time consuming.

Nevertheless, I was beset by a nagging curiosity about adults from foster care who were somewhat older, and therefore decided to attempt to locate a group that had been discharged from foster care in 1970, five years before our main sample. I thought that comparisons between the younger and older group could provide useful information on whether more of the older ones had established their own families, were further along in their education, and were more settled in their work. I also wondered whether with time there would be increases in such things as economic dependency and the use of foster care for their children. I also had questions about their sense of themselves and their lives, and whether these differed in comparison with those who had been discharged from care more recently.

In selecting the older group I imposed a number of limitations. For one, only those who had been discharged from foster homes were included. Second, they came from fewer agencies, seven in all, including one borough office of the New York City Human Resources Administration. The other six were agencies of Catholic, Protestant, or nonsectarian affiliation. The choice here was partly guided by necessity, since it depended on who could give us some assistance in identifying all relevant cases, on whose files were organized so as to ease the task, and on the location of those files. That is, we wanted to avoid extensive travel.

Even so, the task was formidable. In addition to identifying every person who had been discharged in 1970, we had to establish their age at that time and whether care had been continuous for at least the preceding five years. This often required a review of the case records in order to determine whether a given individual met the sample criteria. All together 137 individuals were so identified. From this total we excluded eight who, according to their records, were severely retarded, physically disabled, or disturbed, and an additional five who had passed away in the years since their discharge. The job of locating the rest presented greater difficulties than was the case with the younger group because more years had elapsed. Nevertheless, we interviewed 65 of them and received completed questionnaires from another 12, or a 62.1% rate of response. Of those with whom we made contact only two individuals refused to participate and in two other cases the former foster mothers gave us a message to that effect.

In order to see whether those who responded differed in any consistent way from those who did not, I examined all of the information from their case records. In some 125 comparisons there were only four differences. Since one could easily expect that many differences by chance alone, we can assume that with regard to their background and placement the respondents were representative of the total group discharged from the seven agencies in 1970. Of course, one does not know about possible differences in the postdischarge circumstances of those who did not respond, although one area was suggestive. Those who responded were less likely to have had a New York State record of arrest (6.5%) than those who did not respond (27.7%), and it follows that more of the latter also had been convicted of a misdemeanor or felony since their discharge from foster care. Obviously, with this older group, we had more difficulty contacting those who had at some point been arrested. Why this was so is not clear, since we did not have a similar problem with the younger group—those discharged in 1975. For the younger group there were no differences in records of arrest or conviction between those who responded and those who did not.

In comparing young adults ages 22 through 25 (mean = 23.9) with those who ranged in age from 27 through 30 (mean = 28.3), I will focus on the 77 respondents (36 males and 41 females) who were discharged from the foster homes of seven agencies in 1970 and 112 respondents (61 males and 51 females) who were discharged from the foster homes of those same agencies in 1975. I felt it was important to restrict the comparison to the same agencies in order to minimize extraneous factors that could intrude as a result of variations in agency policies and practices that guide decisions at intake and during placement. The concern with a five-year difference in time meant that the two groups overlapped their tenure in these seven agencies to some extent. Since organizations change rather slowly over time, it seemed unlikely that the foster care experience of these two groups would differ vastly.

Yet over the years we have witnessed some demographic changes in the population of children entering placement. This, perhaps combined with less restrictive agency intake policies, is reflected in differences in the ethnic composition of the two groups. Thus, the older group was 50% white, 31.6% black, and 18.4% Hispanic, whereas the younger group was 25.2% white, 51.4% black, and 23.4% Hispanic. Since this eth-

nic difference could have a bearing on the results, I compared
the two groups while holding race constant whenever this factor seemed relevant. In such comparisons the number of cases
in each subdivision were, of course, very small, thus limiting
one to overall impressions. This material will be reported in
detail whenever the ethnic composition of the two groups influenced the results.

Background and Placement

There were greater similarities than differences between the
two groups. For instance, the two groups were alike in the
ages of their parents at the time they were born, their parents'
education, the marital status of their parents, the mental hospital and correctional histories of their parents, in who was
primarily responsible for their care prior to being placed, and
in the whereabouts of their parents at the time they came into
care.

They were placed for similar reasons and were on the average approaching their third birthday at the time. The two
groups were alike in the average number of times they were
shifted (mean = 2.4) and in the number of foster homes in
which they had lived. A minority of each group was placed
solely in foster homes. In both groups most had some experience in one or more group settings, but more of those discharged in 1975 had their first long-term placement in a group
setting than those who left care in 1970. Perhaps this occurred
because more of the younger group entered foster care with
problems. Yet virtually all had their longest placement in a
foster home, and the average number of years spent in that
placement (mean = 12.9) was roughly the same for each group.
Furthermore, the two groups were alike in the proportions
who lived with one or more of their siblings sometime during
their placement, and a similar majority of each group was in
touch with some siblings while they were in foster care. The

two groups did not differ in the proportions that had some contact with other members of their biological families during the early or later years of placement, but at both times more males from the older group had frequent contact with their kin than did males from the younger group. This was so regardless of their ethnicity. Among the women, the two groups were virtually identical in the frequency of their contacts with kin.

Perhaps the main difference between the two groups was the problems they exhibited. Although they did not differ in their average age at the time of placement, a smaller proportion of the older group entered foster care with one or another kind of problem than was the case with the younger group. This difference was particularly noticable among Hispanic and white respondents, rather than among those who were black. This reflects what has been generally observed in recent years in the foster care field, namely, an increase in the proportion of children entering care with problems. However, by the time they were discharged from care, such differences between the two groups had vanished, except in one instance. The older males were less likely to exhibit learning or educational problems during the last years of placement than the younger males. This was so regardless of their ethnicity. It is curious that, despite such differences in educational problems, the two groups of males did not differ in the number of grades they had completed at the time they were discharged. Apparently the younger males had been promoted despite their educational lags and problems. The scholastic achievement for the two groups of women was also equivalent. For the group as a whole, 57.9% of the older and 62.5% of the younger ones had completed high school or gone beyond by the time they were discharged.

In sum, the two groups were more alike than different in their background and in their experiences during placement. But these few differences will be considered in reviewing their lives after their discharge from foster care.

Place of Residence, Mobility, and Living Arrangements

At the time of our contacts about 34% of the older, as compared with roughly 49% of the younger, group resided in New York City. More of the older ones lived in the suburbs and in other parts of the country. Had more of them moved over time? Or had fewer of them lived in New York City in earlier years? The answer was that more of them had moved. We asked the older group where they had lived in 1975, when they had been out of care roughly the same number of years as the younger group. At that time about the same proportion of the older ones lived in New York City as was the case among the younger ones in 1979 or 1980. By the time of our contacts the older group had also lived at more addresses than the younger group, but again such differences were erased when asked about the earlier comparable period following their discharge from foster care. In other words, there were no inherent differences between the two groups to begin with but with the passage of time there had been more relocation.

There were no differences between the two groups in their feelings about their communities. That is, they were quite alike in how pleased they felt about their homes, their neighborhoods, and the services provided there. They were also quite alike in their housing since a majority of each group lived in apartments. But the two groups were not alike in their living arrangements. The older ones were less likely than the younger ones to be residing with their foster parents, and more of them were living with a spouse than was the case among the younger ones. I will shortly discuss this further.

The two groups were much alike in their connections with people in their neighborhoods. They were as pleased with their neighbors, knew as many of them, and got together with them as often. Yet the older group was more involved in community activities. Nearly 67% of them belonged to some social club or other local organization, in contrast to 42.6% of the younger group. But in the spiritual area, whether in regard to attendance at religious services or the satisfaction derived from religion, there were no differences between the two groups.

On a more personal level the two groups were also quite alike. For example, they spoke of the same number of close friends on the average, were as satisfied with the number of friends they had, and tended to see these friends with equal frequency. Furthermore, the two groups were alike in the proportions who felt they had many, several, a few, or no friends or family they felt free to talk with and count on when worries or problems arose, and they were alike in their negative ratings of such statements as: "no one cares much what happens to me."

Marriage, Partnership, and Children

As was to be expected, the two groups differed in the proportions who had ever married since their discharge from foster care. The difference was particularly sharp among the men. Somewhat more than 61% of the older males in contrast to about 25% of the younger ones had married, although some in each group were no longer married by the time of our contacts. There were differences among the women also since nearly 71% of the older women in contrast to about 47% of the younger ones had married. In general these trends existed for all ethnic groups, although among white women the differences were negligible. Were the differences between the two groups simply a function of their age, or were the two groups truly different? I examined this by comparing rates of marriage during roughly equivalent time periods for each group— the four or five years following their discharge from care. More of the older group, particularly males, had married by 1975 than had the younger ones by 1979 or 1980. In other words, the younger group reflected the general national trend in recent years to defer marriage.

By the time of our contacts not only had more of the older group ever married, but more of their marriages had also ended. Thus, 42% of the first marriages of the older group had ended in separation or divorce compared with about 23% of the marriages in the younger group. A few in each group had remarried. Nevertheless the differences in marital breakdown in the two groups reduced the differences in who was married and living with a spouse at the time of our contacts, particularly among the women. Among the men 50% of the older ones and 23% of the younger ones were still married, or had remarried, when we spoke with them. But among the women there were no longer any differences between the two groups since about 36% of each group were living with a spouse at the time of our contacts. Clearly more of the marriages of the older females than of the older males had broken up by that time. In part this occurred because the older women had first married when they were somewhat younger (mean = 20.6 years) than the older men (mean = 22.1 years), and therefore more of their marriages had already arrived at a critical period. It was not that the older women's marriages were more unstable since broken marriages had on the average lasted an equivalent amount of time (mean = 3.8 years) among both older males and females.

In any event, by the time of our contacts the proportion of married men differed in the two groups, whereas the proportion of married females, whether older or younger, were alike. The older adults who were living with a spouse at the time of our contacts, whether male or female, had been married longer (mean = 5.5 years) than those in the younger group (mean = 2.2 years), but there were no differences between the two groups in their descriptions of their marriages. About 90% of each group rated their marital relationships as very or pretty happy.

There were also some in each group who were living with sexual partners to whom they were not married. The full picture of mates still showed some difference between the two groups of males, but it was not as wide. Somewhat more than 58% of the older males and 39% of the younger ones were living with a spouse or partner. The women were again quite alike since about 60% of each group were living with a spouse or partner at the time of our contacts. On the average the two groups were alike in describing their happiness with their mates—roughly 93% felt they were very or pretty happy.

More of the older group had children, particularly the males. Nearly 56% of the older males, in contrast to about 27% of the younger males, spoke of children, and they also spoke of more children. In each group most of these men were either married or living with a partner, and a majority of the fathers said that all their children lived with them. One does not know with any kind of certainty about the accuracy of these figures because some men in each group were probably unaware of children they had fathered and of their whereabouts. Therefore, in some of what follows the discussion will be limited to women.

Four to five years after their discharge from foster care, the two groups of women were alike in the proportion who were mothers. But by the time of our contacts 63.4% of the older ones, in contrast to 45.1% of the younger women, had given birth to a child. Close to 54% of the older mothers had given birth to two or more children, compared with roughly 35% of the younger ones. In both groups most of the mothers were either married or living with a partner. But some 11.5% of the older and 21.7% of the younger mothers, almost all black, had never married nor were they living with a partner at the time of our contacts.

In a previous chapter the extent to which the main sample had placed their children in foster care was discussed. Here one could ask the same question about the older mothers. Since more years had passed, had more of them placed a child? Two of the 26 older mothers had a child in foster care at the time of our contacts. One additional mother said that one of her children, born and placed prior to her own discharge from foster care, had been adopted. The children of four other mothers lived elsewhere—with their former husbands or with godparents. As for the 23 younger mothers, one had placed a child into foster care, and one was living with a child while a second child was living with the mother's former foster family. Although no information is available about comparable groups in the general population, the increase in foster care use between the younger and older groups seems negligible, and the overall proportion who had used foster care was too small to sustain any assertion about repetition through generations.

The two groups of women did not differ in their average age (mean = 20.7 years) when their first child was born. It naturally follows that the older group had children who were on the average older, although a few were still caring for infants. In both groups mothers were primarily responsible for the care of their children when not in school, although both groups used a variety of shared arrangements. There were also no appreciable differences in their self-ratings as parents. A majority in each group of women—77.3% of the younger mothers and 90% of the older mothers—considered themselves to be excellent or good parents. Almost all of the rest rated themselves as fair rather than poor. The men were even more positive in their self-assessment since all but one rated themselves as excellent or good fathers.

When asked about the timing of their children the two groups differed. More of the older group, whether male or female, said that if they could start again they would have preferred to have their first child when they were older, and a few stated that they wished they had not had the responsibility at all. For instance, close to 62% of the younger mothers were satisfied with the timing of their first child, including a few who wished they had been younger, but only 25% of the older mothers were equally satisfied. Similar differences existed between the younger and older males although in each instance a larger proportion of fathers than mothers said they were satisfied with the timing of their first child. Undoubtedly the women were more burdened with the care of their children and possibly felt that such responsibilities had interfered with their freedom, their education, or their career development. As they looked back over the years, most of the older mothers felt this keenly. The wish about later timing did not, however, mean that they did not wish to have children. Most said that if they had it to do over again they would have children. And when asked about the ideal number of children for a family or person, both groups felt this to be two or three.

In both groups of women not all who had been pregnant had given birth, and some who gave birth had had additional pregnancies. There were both miscarriages and abortions. The older and younger women did not differ since 71.4% of the former and 62.5% of the latter had been pregnant, and this had occurred about as often in each group. Furthermore, about 22% had had one or two miscarriages, some 38% had had one or more abortions, and close to 56% of the women, whether older or younger, had had one or the other or both.

Given the extent of unwanted pregnancies and regrets about the timing of children, it is not surprising that both groups felt they had neither been well prepared about family planning, nor been given adequate sexual information prior to their discharge from foster care. Only 2.8% of the older and 8.9% of the younger group felt they had been well prepared.

Education and Employment

Earlier it was mentioned that the two groups did not differ in their scholastic achievement at the time they were discharged from foster care. Furthermore, by the time of our contacts, the average number of grades they had completed (mean = 12.4 years) were identical, and the proportions in each group who had received additional vocational training were alike. At the time of discharge rougly 39% of each group had not completed high school, but by the time of our contacts this had dropped to 24%. At the other extreme, at the time they were discharged no one in either group had completed college, but by the time of our contacts a similar proportion of each—roughly 7%— had a college degree or had gone beyond. Over the years both groups had continued with their formal education, and about 85% of each said they wanted more schooling in the years ahead.

In view of national increases in unemployment during the late 1970s and early 1980s, I expected to see differences between the younger and the older group in their rates of employment at the time of our contacts. The data did not consistently bear this out. Similar proportions of males, 82.4% of the older and 75.9% of the younger ones, were employed. However, among the women a difference existed irrespective of ethnicity, for 76.3% of the older ones in contrast to 56.3% of the younger ones were employed on a full- or part-time basis at the time of our contacts. I speculated about possible reasons for the difference. Perhaps general increases in unemployment made it more difficult for the younger women to find jobs. Alternatively, perhaps more of the younger ones chose not to work because their children were younger. If so, I would have expected the differences to lessen when comparing the employment picture of the younger women at the time of our contacts with the older ones four or five years earlier, when they had been out of foster care for roughly the same number of years, when their children were younger, and when more were married. If their recall was correct, about as many of the older women were employed then as at the time of our contacts. In other words, a larger proportion of the older women were employed irrespective of the time. Rather than positing an inherent difference between the older and younger women, it seems reasonable to think that there were more job opportunities for women in the mid-1970s, and that with increasing unemployment over the years the younger women, those with less experience, had a particularly difficult time competing in the labor market.

There was also more direct evidence of the impact on the younger group of rising unemployment figures. Whereas the older group, men and women alike, had on the whole held more full-time jobs since their discharge from foster care, there were no differences between the two groups in the number of times they had been unemployed and looking for work for as long as a month. On reading this one might think that these periods of unemployment occurred for both groups during the early years following their discharge from foster care. If so, one would be mistaken, for during those early years the older group had considerably fewer periods of unemployment than the younger ones. Clearly, the years following the younger group's discharge from care were more difficult economically. Jobs were not as plentiful and there was more movement from one job to another. Thus, four to five years after their discharge from foster care, those in the older group who were employed had kept their particular jobs longer than the younger ones had five years later. And, in view of the older group's more extensive work experience over the years, it is not surprising that by the time of our contacts the employed in the older group had held their particular jobs considerably longer on the average (mean = 3.1 years) than had the younger ones (mean = 1.4 years).

Those who left foster care in 1970 were employed in numerous kinds of jobs. Somewhat more than 17% of them were in professional or technical positions; 35.7% were engaged in managerial, sales, or clerical jobs; 26.4% were classified as craftspersons; and 18.6% were service workers. In contrast, only about 6% of the younger ones were in professional or technical positions; but 50% held managerial, sales, or clerical jobs; 10.5% were craftspersons; and 23.4% were service workers. Other occupational groupings, including operatives and transport workers were equally represented in both groups. The median gross income of the older group—their own earnings during the year prior to our interviews—was $9,725, in comparison with $6,653 among the younger ones, but there were no differences in their own earned incomes when one examined roughly the same number of years following discharge from care. Shifts in purchasing power over the years would, however, suggest that the younger ones were having a tougher time financially. Yet despite the income differences at the time of our contacts, the two groups, whether male or female, were alike in their satisfaction with the work they were doing; in their satisfaction with the amount of money they had available for such basic things as food, housing, and clothing; in their ratings of their standard of living; and in their feelings about the extent to which they were achieving success and getting ahead.

Some in each group were receiving public assistance at the time of our contacts. The two groups of men were quite alike since only a few received such aid. However, the women differed. At the time of our contacts 27.5% of the younger women, in contrast to 9.8% of the older ones, were receiving public assistance. This difference was particularly apparent among black and Hispanic women. It is noteworthy that the proportion of older or younger women who had ever received such aid since their discharge from foster care did not differ. Roughly 42% of the older and about 35% of the younger women had at some point received public assistance. But among the older women the proportions had dropped within each ethnic group. Furthermore, in most instances such aid began in the four years immediately following their discharge in 1970, and they received public assistance for about the same amount of time, on the average, as the women in the younger group. In other words, economic dependency had occurred mainly during the early years following discharge. It was a temporary rather than a chronic phenomenon. One must, of course, remember that more of the older women were employed four or five years following their discharge from care, and that better employment opportunities at that time were partially responsible for their decreasing dependence on public support. Even if one stipulates this as a factor, our data did not lend support to notions about welfare chronicity, unencumbered by adverse economic trends in the society, for those who were discharged from foster homes.

Contact and Closeness with Biological and Foster Families

Although during their placement a larger proportion of the older males had frequent contact with their biological families, other than their siblings, by the time we spoke with them no differences existed between the older and the younger ones.

The two groups of women were also similar. About 28% of the younger and 22% of the older group were frequently (once a month or more often) in touch with their kin. Others spoke of infrequent contact, but in both groups roughly 57% had no contact at all by the time of our interviews. Since their discharge from care, the proportion of each group with no contact with their kin had increased. This occurred primarily among those who had had infrequent contact during their last years in care. This drop in contact was not a function of time since discharge because the younger and older ones were alike in this regard. Although one cannot say with certainty, it seems reasonable to assume that the situation of the older group resembled that of the younger group, and that contact was dropped during the four or five years after their discharge rather than more recently.

The two groups were also quite alike in their closeness toward their biological parents or relatives. Among those who maintained some contact, about one out of four said they felt very close to someone. In contrast to their contacts with biological parents and relatives, a larger proportion of each group was in touch with, and felt very close to, at least one brother or sister. Again both groups were quite alike. Among the vast majority who knew of a brother or sister, close to 73% of the older and 75% of the younger group were in touch with a sibling, and about 54% spoke of feeling very close to at least one brother or sister. Clearly over time siblings continued to represent a major link to their families of origin.

Both groups were also quite alike in the proportions who had kept in touch with their last or a previous foster family. About 90% had some contact at the time of our interviews. The women from both groups were also alike in the frequency of their contact. Among those who maintained contact, about 89% were frequently in touch and nearly the same proportion in each group—about 75%—felt very close. But with the men the two groups differed. Among those who were in touch, 64% of the older in contrast to roughly 93% of the younger ones maintained frequent contact. There were parallel, but much diminished, differences in closeness. Roughly 76% of the younger and 60% of the older males who were in touch said they felt very close to their foster families. It appears that with time, as the men established their own families, their contact with their foster families diminished. Most kept in touch, but on the whole less frequently than the men who were younger and also less often than the women in their own age group.

Troubles

The older and younger groups were quite alike in their assessment of their own physical health and a variety of symptoms. For instance, a large majority of each group rated their health as excellent or good, and they were equally satisfied with the state of their physical health. Furthermore, there were no differences in how often they complained of such problems as sleeplessness, nightmares, loss of appetite, headaches, stomach upsets, nervousness and tension, and days of feeling sad and blue. They were also quite alike in describing the amount they worried. Close to three out of four persons, 71.4% of the older and 73.2% of the younger ones, said they worried sometimes, a little, or never. They were also alike in their satisfaction with the way in which they handled problems that came up in their lives.

The two groups were about the same age, on the average, when they began drinking alcoholic beverages, and were alike in the amount they drank during the month prior to our interviews. The proportion of each group that had used drugs was similar, but the younger adults began using drugs at a somewhat younger age, on the average, than the older ones. They had used about as many drugs during the preceding year, but among the women the younger women tended to use them with greater frequency. For instance, 31.2% of the younger compared with 14.3% of the older women spoke of having used a drug one or two times a week or more frequently during that time. No differences existed among the men. Although the difference in drug use among the women was not large, it probably reflected the proliferation of drug use among young people generally which showed up in a more pronounced way among the younger women.

Finally, I compared the two groups on their run-ins with the law. As already reported, I used the official New York State Division of Criminal Justice Services records of arrests and convictions for the total groups, including those we never contacted. For males and females alike there were no differences in the proportion of the older and younger ones who had a record of arrest or conviction on misdemeanor or felony charges since their discharge from foster care. Nor were there differences in the number of times this had occurred. In each group a much larger proportion of males (27.6%) than females (5.1%) had a record of arrest, but within each ethnic group older and younger persons were represented in almost identical proportions. The older males had been out of foster care longer yet had not been arrested in larger proportions, although most continued to reside in New York State. This suggested that with the passage of time more and more of those from foster care did not have run-ins with the law. The data supported this line of reasoning. Only a small percentage (2.2%) of the older group of males had their first record of arrest between 1975 and 1979. In other words, there were no differences in the records of arrest between the younger and the older group because such troubles were more apt to begin during the early years following their discharge from care, when they were younger, than later on.

Alienation and Sense of Well-Being

Disaffection with the society in which one lives is to some extent a function of age (Campbell 1981). In many areas of life younger people who are reaching for independence have more of a struggle. If one singles out the economic area alone, one can point to lower earnings and less security of employment. Factors such as these probably played a role in the young adults' attitudes. On the Srole Anomia scale (Robinson and Shaver 1973) the older adults were less disaffected on the average than those in the younger group, and this was so within each ethnic group. Furthermore, the older adults, regardless of ethnicity, were more satisfied with "life in the United States today" than were the younger respondents. Beyond these differences little distinguished the two groups. They did not differ at all in their sense of well-being, and they felt equally optimistic about achieving their personal hopes and goals in the future.

Final Comments

At the beginning of this chapter a number of questions were raised. What has been learned? What can one say about those who have been out of foster care for a longer time than our main sample? Over the course of time they have relocated, have established independent living arrangements, and have become more involved in various organized community activities. They reflected the trends of the culture since more of them had married, even in the earlier years, and having done so more of their marriages had also broken down. More had children. They were more settled in their work, were better off economically, and felt less disaffected from the larger society. With the passage of time, fewer women were economically dependent on public support, and the number of men with first records of arrest decreased. In most other ways the additional years out of care mattered little.

One is tempted to conclude that with the passage of time no deleterious effects of their foster care experience emerged. Of course, some will question the comparability of the two samples, and others will worry about those we never reached. However, I could see few differences between the two groups, and where they existed I tried to take them into account. Some may feel that not enough time had passed for deeper difficulties to appear. If so, I would have expected to see the seeds or symptoms by their late twenties, but I did not. And so, I am led to the conclusion that no harmful effects emerged with the passing years. If anything, they seemed more settled and in control of various aspects of their lives than those who were more recently discharged.

Chapter Twelve

COMPARISONS WITH THE GENERAL POPULATION

From time to time readers may have wondered whether and in what way the young adults from foster care differed from young adults generally. This is a vital question, one that I knew should be addressed when this work began. But what group, could serve as a reasonable comparison? Ideally one would want to use people who had precisely the same background as our sample but who did not, for some unknown reason, enter foster care. If such a group exists, how could one identify them? Initially I hoped to use siblings for comparison. This dream was shattered since one sibling was rarely placed while another was not. Other comparison possibilities that were considered also did not materialize.

But all was not lost. At the time we began, two national surveys were in progress at the Institute for Social Research of the University of Michigan (Campbell 1981; Veroff, Douvan, and Kulka 1981). We purposely asked our sample some of the same questions that were included in those surveys. In time I received the national survey responses of those who were in the same age range as the young adults in our sample who had been discharged from foster care. I secured this material for each ethnic group, separately for males and females. Additional comparison data were available from national surveys conducted by the National Opinion Research Center (1978) at the University of Chicago.

Despite such a windfall, there are a number of problems when one uses such national data for comparison. For one,

the ethnic composition of the national surveys and of our sample differed widely. Therefore, it was necessary to analyze the
material separately for each ethnic group. Even this was difficult since such surveys, based on random samples of the total
United States population, include relatively few black or Hispanic respondents. In the 22- through 25-year age group, for
instance, the number of black respondents varied from 25 to
35 depending on the particular survey, whereas whites were
represented in much larger numbers, ranging from 126 to
more than 250. Hispanic respondents were so few in number
that we could make no comparisons at all. In a few areas, such
as marriage and employment, I obtained general population
data for New York City (Commerce 1979a) that allowed us to
make some comparisons across the three main ethnic groups
in our sample.

Another problem is that the results of national samples are
not always perfectly consistent, at least when one singles out a
relatively small age group from the overall total and subdi-
vides this group even further. For instance, two surveys might
show a difference between young adults in the general population and the respondents from foster care, while there might
be no such differences when one examines a third survey. In
statistical language, results from small samples are simply more
unreliable. No doubt other problems, such as those connected
with nonresponse, also affected various surveys somewhat differently.

It must also be kept in mind that national surveys inevitably
include many people who have grown up and are living in
small towns, whereas the background of our foster care sample was more urban. National surveys include a smaller proportion of East coast residents and a wider range of socioeconomic backgrounds than was the case for the young adults
from foster care. Unfortunately, we could not control for such
differences because doing so would have reduced the sample
size even more. Finally, the timing of the national surveys was
not identical with our study, although they were not too far
apart.

For all these reasons we can use the survey information as a basis for making only rough comparisons. In almost all instances I will report on material we secured by asking the identical questions with the same response formats as had been presented to young adults in the general population. Furthermore, I will not dwell on the details of each survey. If several surveys asked the same question, I will point out general population-foster care differences if the results were all in the same direction, even if some were not as strong as others. The purpose here is to look for general trends—to see what suggestions can be obtained about how the foster care group differed from their counterparts in the population at large.

To repeat, in what follows all comparisons with national survey data concern only black and white respondents, whereas all New York City comparisons include Hispanic respondents as well. All comparisons were completed separately for each ethnic group; however, sometimes the groups as a whole will be discussed in order to avoid clumsiness. This, of course, is done only when the separate ethnic comparisons show the same thing.

Mobility and Community

Since some young adults from foster care had to establish independent living arrangements upon discharge, I expected to find differences in mobility between them and young adults in the population at large. Unfortunately, comparable data were so sparse that we were limited to two comparisons. The first concerned New York City residents only. Furthermore, the only comparable question asked whether they had moved at all during the four or five years preceding the interviews. More foster care respondents who were living in New York City, regardless of ethnicity, had moved at least once than was the case for other New Yorkers their age. This was so whether they had been discharged from foster homes or group settings. Finding suitable permanent housing in New York City was no easy task, so that more of the general population young adults from New York City apparently continued to reside with their own families for an extended period of time.

Nationally I examined the length of time that people had resided at the address where they were living at the time they were interviewed. There were no differences between the two groups on the average. Apparently those who left foster care eventually became as settled in their places of residence as other young adults in the population at large.

Foster care respondents were also as satisfied with their places of residence, such as their apartments, as young adults nationally, but they were less satisfied with their neighborhoods as places in which to live. I do not know what attributes of their neighborhoods displeased them. They may have been more dissatisfied with the upkeep of the buildings, the amount of open space, the level of noise, or the people who frequented the area. Whatever the reasons, they found their larger physical surroundings less attractive than young adults in general. Their more urban existence was undoubtedly a factor here.

Feelings about one's physical surroundings can be an important aspect in the evaluation of one's life. One's personal environment is even more vital in that assessment. Neighbors, social participation in organizations, and spiritual support are all aspects of that environment. The young adults from foster care were as likely to say they knew many or several neighbors, rather than a few or none, as the other young adults. Furthermore, the frequency of their contacts with neighbors did not differ.

Those who left foster care also did not differ from others in the proportions who were members of some club or other community organization, in the proportions who said they had no religious preference, or in the frequency of their attendance at religious services. In sum, the young adults from foster care had settled in their communities and had become as much a part of their neighborhoods as young adults in the general population.

How did they feel about the society at large? Much has been written about the alienation of young people, about their criticism and distrust of American institutions. In view of the foster care group's past experiences, I thought they might feel more disaffected with the larger society than other young adults their age. To examine this I combined three items from Srole's (1956) scale that had also been asked of young adults in a national survey. In our sample as well as nationally young black adults felt more alienated, but this was as true of those from foster care as in the population at large. White young adults also did not differ in their average scores. If anything, the young women from foster care, whether black or white, felt less alienated than the women their age in the general population. I do not know why this was so. In any event, those who had left foster care were no more disaffected than others their age in the general population. This conclusion, however, must be tempered by their answers to another question, for when asked to rate "life in the United States today," those who had left foster care were distinctly less satisfied than other young adults. This was so whether they were black or white, male or female, from foster homes or group care, or whether they resided in New York City or elsewhere. Perhaps their reactions reflected a greater concern about inflation and unemployment, about the ease of finding suitable housing or the state of their physical surroundings, about crime and safety, or other factors. Whatever the case, they were more critical about their country than other young adults, and in this sense were more disaffected.

Friendships and Social Support

The young adults from foster care were on the average as satisfied with their friendships, and with the number of friends they had, as were young adults from the general population. They did not feel they needed more friends, and were as frequently in touch with their close friends as young adults generally. There were also no differences in their wish that people liked them more—their need for acceptance.

When asked whether they had many, several, a few, or no friends or family they felt free to talk with and count on for advice or help if worries or problems arose, there were no differences between any of the foster care and general population respondents. At the same time, black respondents from foster care, but not whites, were less extreme in their disagreement with the statement "no one cares much what happens to me." In addition, those who left foster care, whether black or white, were less extreme in their disagreement with the statement "these days I really don't know who I can count on for help." Thus, while the foster care respondents resembled others nationwide in feeling they had people to turn to, as a group they expressed less certainty about support.

Marriage and Children

The groups differed in the extent to which they had ever married. Whether black or white, male or female, more of the young adults from foster care had never married than young adults nationally. The differences were consistent for all groups, although smallest for white women discharged from foster homes. Depending on the survey, roughly 20% to 40% more of the foster care respondents had never married.

These results were at least in part a function of regional differences as well as differences in the size of the communities where foster care and respondents from national surveys grew up and resided. For instance, U.S. Census data (Commerce 1979b) show that young adults residing in the Northeast were less apt to be married than those in other parts of the United States, and the national surveys I used for comparison included proportionately more of the latter than did our sample. In fact, when I compared New York City residents from foster care with U.S. Census data on those their age in the New York City population, there were no differences in the proportions of never married black, Hispanic, or white males, nor among white or Hispanic females. However, more black women from foster care had never married, but the difference was much reduced over differences that existed nationally.

Further support for the idea that geographic differences were at play came when I compared our sample with national survey figures on age at marriage. More young adults in the population at large had married earlier, at age 21 or less, than young adults from foster care. No doubt, this was influenced by the fact that proportionately more young adults in the general population surveys lived in small towns of the Midwest or West, where early marriage was more common, than in urban areas where most of the foster care respondents had grown up and resided.

It is also important to recognize that the available comparisons, because of their focus on marriage, missed sexual partnerships that had been established on an ongoing basis among those who by choice or circumstance did not travel the legal route. Unfortunately, data about partnerships were not routinely collected in the national surveys, nor was such information available from census data for New York City.

In the 1960s Meier (1962) reported a higher incidence of marital breakdown among 28- to 32-year-old foster home respondents when compared with U.S. Census figures for the state of Minnesota. There was no evidence of this among our younger sample. The proportion of young adults from foster care who had married and had separated or divorced was neither higher nor lower when compared with young adults nationally. Unfortunately, no comparisons were available about the duration of broken or existing marriages. But, having married when younger, the national survey couples who remained together probably had been married longer up to the time they were interviewed.

Unfortunately, some of the numbers became very small when I singled out married respondents in order to examine reported marital happiness. Yet in the material we had available, there were no differences in the proportion that described their relationships as very, pretty, or not too happy. Although a generally smaller proportion of foster care respondents had married, if they had done so they were as satisfied as those their age in the general population.

If one were to adopt a conventional stance, the differences in the incidence of marriage might lead one to expect a larger proportion of young mothers in the general population. This was, however, not the case, for the women from foster care were just as likely to have given birth to a child as young women in the population at large. It is therefore likely, although we had no comparable data on this point, that more young mothers from foster care had no husband. Some, instead, chose to live with, and had a child by, a male partner. In reporting about children, I singled out women since the information about the birth of children was less apt to be accurate among unmarried males.

Did those who left foster care lean in the direction of childlessness? The answer is no. A majority of those who had no children, whether from foster care or in the general population, expected to become mothers or fathers some day. Furthermore, the two groups did not differ in their opinions about the ideal number of children for a family to have.

Education

The three national and New York City census samples reported this information in one of two ways. Some reported the highest year of school completed, as we had done, while others used a less precise classification including such categories as "some high school," "high school graduate," "some college," and so forth. For the sake of consistency I categorized all the data in this manner. Some variations also existed in regard to who was excluded from the national surveys. One survey, I was told, excluded dormitory residents from their sample. This must have resulted in a downward skew on educational level.

An additional and more important inconsistency concerning the results seriously weakens what can be said here. It turns out that the data on educational levels for this age group differed greatly among various population surveys. For instance, one survey included 28.6% white males who were college graduates, whereas another survey reported 10.9%. Our use of statistical tests cannot overcome such a problem, and so this discussion will be limited to general impressions based on my review of all the data. These impressions are offered with due caution, for they are at best suggestive.

On the whole, young women from foster care and those from the general population did not differ particularly, but the men from foster care tended to have completed less education than males nationally. For example, when I combined all national surveys, 11% of the black and white women from our sample had completed college as compared with 20.5% in the general population. Even more striking, 2.3% of the black and white men in our sample had a college degree in comparison with 22.1% of the young men in the population at large. At the other end of the educational spectrum, 62% of the males from foster care had a high school or more limited education, in comparison with 51.6% of the males in the general population. The differences were in part, but not entirely, a function of males who had been discharged from group settings.

There were still differences in scholastic achievement when I singled out residents of New York City. Males and females from foster care had completed less education when compared with young adults their age in the New York City population at large. This was particularly true among black respondents, but the results for Hispanics and whites also leaned in the same direction.

In sum, overall differences in educational achievement existed, but why they were particularly strong in one group and not in another is less than clear. Perhaps some, more than others, had overcome educational lags in the period since their discharge from care. Perhaps some had more of an inclination, or more of an opportunity, to do so. But one consistent theme was found. In each group, whether male or female, whether black, Hispanic, or white, the proportion from foster care with a college degree was smaller. The differences were sometimes sizable, sometimes small, but always present. During their placement they had fallen behind educationally. Once they had been discharged, economic constraints must have slowed up their progress and may have altered their aims. Thus, four or five years later they still lagged behind other young adults their age.

Employment

In view of educational differences, I expected to find some differences in employment, particularly among the men. This expectation was only partly borne out. The young men and women will be reviewed separately and no differentiation will be made between those with full- or part-time jobs since the latter were so few in number. Full-time students were, however, excluded.

The proportion of white males from foster care who were employed did not differ from white males in the general population. This was the case in all national samples as well as when I singled out foster care respondents who resided in New York City for comparison with white males their age in the New York City population. The picture was very different for black males. Proportionately more from foster care were unemployed than black males nationally. The differences were sizable in each survey although not always statistically significant because the number of Black males in such surveys was so small. When black males from these random national samples were combined, which I did in this instance, the difference in employment was sharp. Some 68% of black foster care respondents were employed, in comparison with 93% in the population at large. These results were heavily influenced by black males from foster care who resided in one of the five boroughs of New York City, among whom the level of employment was particularly low. When these New York City residents were excluded in order to single out black males from foster care who lived outside New York City, the proportion that was employed was identical to that of black males in the three national surveys.

Furthermore, a smaller proportion of black males from foster care who remained in New York City was employed (53.1%) than that of black males (74%) their age in the New York City population. This was almost entirely a function of black males who had been discharged from group settings. When I examined black males from foster homes separately, the difference in employment between them and their counterparts in the New York City population was much reduced and no longer statistically significant. A similar situation prevailed among Hispanic males from foster care who resided in New York City. Close to 62% of them were employed, in contrast to roughly 87% of the Hispanic males their age in the New York City population. Further subdivisions resulted in rather small numbers, but once again the difference was in large measure due to those who had been discharged from group settings. Thus, black and Hispanic males from group settings who were living in New York City fared particularly poorly in the labor market. As far as I could discern, no more of them had been discharged with serious social or emotional problems than black or Hispanic males from foster homes, nor did they differ in this regard from white males who had been discharged from group settings. However, all males from group settings, whether black, Hispanic, or white, had completed fewer grades by the time of our contacts than males who had been discharged from foster homes. No doubt, the foster parents had encouraged some to continue with their schooling, whereas those from group settings generally had less support after their discharge. This must have affected white males as well, but they probably had better opportunities to find a job than young black and Puerto Rican males. Thus, less scholastic achievement, coupled with poorer employment opportunities, led to more unemployment for New York City black and

Puerto Rican males discharged from group settings when compared with black and Puerto Rican males in the New York City population.

The situation for the young women was rather different. My focus here, by the way, was on those who were employed or seeking a job, while those who designated themselves as full-time homemakers were excluded, as they were in the surveys I used for comparison. Young black women from foster care did not differ from black women their age in the general population, whether nationally or in New York City, in the proportion who were employed on a full- or part-time basis. There were also no differences for Hispanic women who lived in New York City, the only comparison we had available for this group. White women from foster care who remained in New York City also did not differ proportionately from other white New York women their age. However, nationally a larger proportion of white women from foster care were looking for work than white women in the general population.

There were few other employment-related differences between the young adults from foster care and those their age in the general population. For instance, there were no differences in the proportions that had been unemployed and looking for work for as long as a month. Among the employed there were also no differences in the hours worked in an average week, nor in their level of satisfaction with their jobs. Likewise, there were no consistent differences in their own or their household gross median incomes during the year prior to the time they were interviewed, although one could imagine that in terms of real income the respondents from foster care had less, since more of them were residing in and around New York City. This may have had a bearing on the responses of young black adults in our sample when asked to compare their incomes with those of Americans in general. Roughly 58% of them, in contrast to 40% of the black respondents nationally, felt their incomes were below or far below average. Whites did not differ in this regard. The groups were also alike in assessing improvements in their financial situations during the past few years, and in the proportions that felt their financial situation had recently deteriorated. Given this overall picture, it was not surprising that there were no differences in the young adults' average satisfaction with their own financial situation.

Some believe that foster care inevitably produces people who become economically dependent on public support. Therefore, it was important to test this notion. In a previous chapter one aspect of this was examined among younger and older adults, all of whom had been discharged from foster homes. There, it was pointed out that as time went by such economic dependency decreased, but nothing was said about whether those who had left foster care were more likely to be receiving public assistance than those their age in the population at large. Comparable age-specific figures of public welfare recipients were, unfortunately, not available nationally. Therefore, I singled out New York City, where most of those in our sample who were receiving such aid resided, and obtained age-specific totals of male and female welfare recipients for the last quarter of 1979. These figures included people who were receiving all forms of public welfare except those (such as the disabled) who had been shifted to the Social Security system. An ethnic breakdown of the public welfare figures was, however, not available. But I did have the age-specific ethnic proportions of the male and female population of New York City.

In order to compare the incidence of welfare among New York City residents in our sample with the incidence of welfare in the same age group in New York City generally, it was necessary to weight the welfare figures for black, Hispanic, and white respondents in our sample according to their proportions in the general New York City population. This was necessary because the ethnic proportions in our sample differed from those of the general population of New York City. When I then compared these weighted values, I found a slightly higher proportion of males and females from foster homes who were receiving public aid. Among this age group in the New York City general population, roughly 5% of the males and 17.4% of the females were receiving public assistance, while the comparable figures for those from foster homes were 10.3% and 25.3%. Two factors can easily account for these percentage differences. First, our figures included some people who fell into categories that were excluded from the general population figures because of their shift to Social Security. Second, and perhaps most important, a potential bias was introduced by one of our methods of locating respondents which involved using computerized listings of welfare recipients. Although using these lists assisted us in checking addresses and in locating some New York City residents, it also undoubtedly inflated the proportion of our sample that was receiving public assistance.

These two factors cannot, however, account for differences that were evident when we applied the same weighting system to those in our sample who had been discharged from group settings. In this group close to 19% more of the young men and nearly 31% more of the women were receiving public assistance than men and women their age in the general population of New York City.

Those who had been discharged from group settings constituted only about 27% of our total sample. At the time of their discharge from foster care they faced greater hurdles than those who had been discharged from foster homes. Their transition into the community was more abrupt, inevitably required a relocation, and more of them had to fend for themselves. At the same time, they had been discharged with more limited schooling, a difference that persisted over time. Greater difficulties in their ability to find stable employment and partnerless motherhood affected their disproportionate use of public assistance. With the understandable exception of this group, our data lent no support to the notion that there is a connection between having been in foster care and economic dependence on public support.

Health and Symptoms

No differences existed among young adults in their assessments of their own health. For instance, when asked "do you have any particular physical or health problem," 79.7% of those from foster care and 78.4% of young adults nationally said no. Nor were there differences in the proportions who rated their own health as excellent, good, fair, or poor.

Our sample and the young adults in one national survey were also asked about various troubles and complaints and about the frequency of their occurrence. It will be recalled that these included twelve common symptoms such as problems of getting to sleep or staying asleep, headaches, loss of appetite, difficulty getting up in the morning, dizziness, nightmares, and feeling fidgety and tense. On ten of these twelve common symptoms there were no discernible differences. One of the other two symptoms—having an upset stomach—was cited more often by whites nationally than by whites in our sample. The second item concerned nightmares. Here black respondents from all foster care settings, but only whites from group care complained more on the average than those in the general population. For instance, on a four-point scale where a score of 1 signified "never" and a 4 meant "many times," black respondents from foster care had an average score of 1.8 compared with a 1.3 average for blacks nationally.

They were also asked how often there had been times when they could not take care of things because they "just couldn't get going." Black respondents from foster care but only whites from group settings felt this had occurred more frequently than the young adults from the general population. There were no differences in the proportions in either group that said they drank alcoholic beverages, but black respondents from foster care said they drank more frequently in order to help handle tensions, and they felt there were more times that they drank too much, than black respondents nationally. One does not know whether black respondents from foster care actually drank more; in any event, they apparently worried more about their drinking than young black adults in the general population.

The overarching question is whether young adults from foster care complained of more problems than other young adults.

I was looking for a pattern, but none emerged. For instance, it seemed possible that a number of items clustered together that touched on the tendency to worry, but there was no difference between our sample and respondents in the general population when asked directly about their own nervousness and tensions. In other words, I could find no consistency, although here and there some differences were found between the groups. I was, however, mindful of two dangers. By singling out areas of difference from an array of possibilities, there is a danger of overemphasizing the problem side of the roster. An even greater danger pertains to the likelihood of chance findings. That is, in more than 70 comparisons I reviewed, one could have expected to find' four differences purely on a chance basis. We found few more, and what differences we found were small. They showed up sometimes in one group and sometimes in another, but more often for black respondents where the size of the national comparison groups was skimpy. The overall picture, therefore, suggests that with respect to health and various symptoms the young adults from foster care did not differ from young adults in the population at large.

But one large difference existed. More of the young adults from foster care, whether black or white, whether discharged from foster homes or group care, had, since their discharge, turned to mental health professionals for advice or help with a personal problem than had young adults in the general population. They had turned to social agencies, mainly those from which they had been discharged, and to clinics, marriage counselors, and psychiatrists. The differences were sharp. Close to 32% of the young black or white adults from foster care, compared with 15.1% of those in one national survey, had during the past four or five years sought such advice or help. The magnitude of the differences in reported symptoms that have just been discussed is not at all commensurate with the large difference in the proportion of those who sought formal help. Perhaps they had been effectively helped with various problems since their discharge from foster care, so that by the time of our contacts such problems had subsided. Perhaps they had never had more problems but were more prone to label things as problems than young adults in general. Their past experience in foster care probably sensitized them to look for problems, made them more aware of resources for help, and made them more prone to seek guidance from professional advisers than was the case for young adults their age in the population at large.

Self-Image, Happiness, and Life as a Whole

Much has been written about the self-image of the foster child although systematic studies on this subject are rare (Weinstein 1960). Clinical observations have most often suggested that the self-evaluations of these children suffer, perhaps as a consequence of feeling rejected and abandoned, or because the very fact of placement may have raised questions about their own worth. We could not address the issue of self-evaluation at the start of placement nor during placement. But we could ask how the former foster children, now young adults, evaluated themselves in comparison with young adults in the general population.

One of the national surveys included some questions from Rosenberg's (1965) self-esteem scale, two of which were essentially identical to questions we asked. The respondents rated their agreement on a four-point scale with the following: "I feel that I'm a person of worth, at least on an equal basis with others" and "I am able to do things as well as most other people." A different national survey asked respondents to rate their satisfaction with themselves on a seven-point scale. The data comparing these national samples with the foster care respondents are presented in table 12.1, where I separated those who were discharged from foster homes and those from group settings because of differences that stood out. Among white respondents, the average differences between young adults discharged from foster homes and those from the national

Table 12.1
Self-Evaluation of Respondents From Foster Care and National Samples

	WHITE RESPONDENTS								
	Discharged from:								
	Foster Home			Group Setting			National Sample		
	Mean*	(N)	S.D.	Mean*	(N)	S.D.	Mean*	(N)	S.D.
Person of worth†	3.56	(52)	.61	3.14	(22)	1.13	3.69	(189)	.61
Can do as well†	3.42	(52)	.61	3.00	(21)	.95	3.59	(189)	.58
Satisfaction with self‡	5.41	(46)	1.07	4.35	(20)	1.35	5.37	(257)	1.12
	BLACK RESPONDENTS								
Person of worth†	3.45	(103)	.78	3.43	(30)	.68	3.72	(29)	.65
Can do as well†	3.31	(99)	.77	3.24	(29)	.79	3.45	(29)	.69
Satisfaction with self‡	5.24	(91)	1.29	5.50	(28)	1.23	5.37	(35)	1.68

*A high score signifies a more positive self-evaluation.
†Four-point scale.
‡Seven-point scale.

samples were at best weak and inconsistent. In contrast, the self-ratings of whites from group settings were consistently less positive than those of young adults in the population at large. Among black respondents there was a weak difference on only one question—the "person of worth" question. Those from foster care, whether discharged from foster homes or group settings, tended to assess themselves less positively. On the other questions the average responses did not differ at all and were not consistent. Therefore, with the exception of whites who had left group care, there was little evidence to support the contention that the self-evaluations of young adults from foster care had suffered to any extent.

Further evidence came from comparisons with yet another study (Grow 1979), whose focus was on married and unmarried white mothers. I singled out a similar group from our sample and compared the average scores on Rosenberg's full scale. Whether married or unmarried, there were no differences between the white mothers from foster care and young white mothers with children of roughly comparable ages. To repeat, we cannot say anything about the self-image of these young adults during the time they were in placement. Perhaps events subsequent to their discharge improved their assessments of themselves. Nevertheless, our results did make me wonder about the problem of generalizing from anecdotal reports that are often based on extreme cases that have captured someone's attention.

Finally, the young adults' sense of happiness and their satisfaction with "life as a whole" will be examined. I compared the foster care respondents' ratings of their own general happiness with three national samples, but only one survey was available with which to compare their satisfaction with life. The details will not be presented here, for they were so similar to what has just been presented. On the average, the young adults from foster care did not differ from young adults nationally in their sense of happiness or in their satisfaction with life as a whole, with one exception. Once again the white respondents who had been discharged from group settings regarded both areas more poorly than white adults their age in the general population. One example will suffice to show the extent of this difference among white respondents. On a seven-point scale of satisfaction with life as a whole, white adults nationally scored 5.33 on the average, followed closely by those who had been discharged from foster homes (mean = 5.24) but quite distantly by those from group settings (mean = 4.27).

Why was there a difference for white, but not for black, respondents from group care? For an explanation one must return to what was mentioned earlier. There were probably more placement options available in specialized group foster care facilities for whites who seriously needed such care than for blacks. The latter were, therefore, more likely to be placed in or to end up in other facilities, such as those administered by the correctional system, than in foster care group settings, and thus they didn't become part of our sample. Therefore, greater placement selectivity, rather than diverse reactions to the group care experience, can explain the observed difference.

Adults Discharged in 1970

Comparative material was also available for the adults who had been discharged during an earlier year, all 27 to 30 years old at the time of our contacts. It will be recalled that this was a much smaller group and that all of them had been discharged from foster homes. Therefore, in much of what follows 24 black and 38 white respondents from foster care will be compared with from 17 to 45 black and 132 to 286 white respondents their age from the three national surveys. Little can be said about New York City residents because the numbers in each ethnic group in our sample were too small. Other subgroup comparisons also sometimes resulted in such limited numbers as to be of questionable reliability. In view of these constraints and considerations, the discussion of the older group will be less detailed; broader brush strokes will be used in painting a picture of them.

Overall, few differences were apparent between the older group from foster care and adults their age nationwide. What differences existed sometimes favored, if one can use such a value-laden term, one group and sometimes the other. For instance, the foster care group had settled in their communities and had become as much a part of their neighborhoods as other adults. They had lived at their most recent place of residence for as long and were as satisfied with their surroundings. There were also no consistent differences in the proportions that knew many or several neighbors, rather than a few or none, and the two groups saw their neighbors as frequently. They were as often members of clubs or organizations in their communities, and their religious preferences and practices were similar. Finally, their average scores did not differ on items from the Srole Anomia scale (Robinson and Shaver 1973), but as with the younger group, whites from foster care were more dissatisfied with "life in the United States today" than whites nationally. The average scores of the two black groups, however, differed less and were not statistically significant.

In their close personal relationships there were also few differences between the two groups. Those from foster care were as likely to say they had as many friends as they wanted, were as satisfied with their friendships, saw their close friends as often, and expressed about the same need to be accepted as other young adults. Black adults from foster care felt they had more friends or family they could talk with and count on if they had worries than blacks in the general population. There were no such differences among white respondents, although whites from foster care tended to be less extreme in their disagreement with the statement "these days I really don't know who I can count on for help." The association was, however, weak and was not at all apparent among black respondents. At the same time there were no differences in response to the statement "no one cares much what happens to me."

As was the case with the younger group, differences existed in the incidence of marriage. The differences were almost always consistent, but not always particularly strong. On the whole, roughly 37% of the adults from foster care had never married in contrast to 15% of those nationally. Regional influences once again appeared to play a role. Because of small numbers I could not compare New York City residents, but a comparison of all our black, Hispanic, and white respondents with New York City census data showed no differences within each of these groups. No differences were apparent in their ratings of their marital happiness. Likewise there were no consistent differences between those from foster care and several national samples in the incidence of marital breakdown among this older group. In other words, there was no confirmation of what Meier (1962) reported in the 1960s, although the data here were only suggestive given the small size of some subgroup comparisons.

The women from foster care were as likely to have given birth to a child as women their age nationally, and there was no indication that men or women from foster care leaned in the direction of childlessness. There were also no differences in their opinions about the ideal number of children for a family.

As was the case for the younger group, some educational

differences existed. For example, 6.5% of the men from foster care had completed college in comparison with 29.2% in the general population. A similar differential existed for white women, but the proportion of black women who were college graduates did not differ (there were about 9% in each group); however, a larger proportion of black women from foster care had completed some college than was true for black women nationally. With the exception of these black women, those from foster care were represented disproportionately at the lower end of the educational range—among those who had completed high school or had less schooling.

Despite these educational differences, a majority of all the young adults in this age group, whether from foster care or nationally, were employed in a full- or part-time basis. There were no differences here, nor in the hours worked during an average week. The numbers were too small to assess job satisfaction among black respondents, but among whites close to 36% of those from foster care voiced dissatisfaction, in contrast to roughly 7% of the whites in the population at large. Perhaps their more limited education resulted in their holding less interesting jobs, which in turn influenced their satisfaction. There were, however, no income differences that stood out except that black women from foster care tended to have higher gross median incomes than black women generally. Proportionately more of this group also felt their financial situation had improved during recent years than was true for black women generally, whereas no differences existed among other foster care and general population respondents. Black respondents from foster care also were more satisfied about their financial situation than black adults in the population at large; but when comparing their own incomes with those of other Americans, most rated themselves as average or below, as was the case of black adults nationally. The white adults in our sample did not differ from other respondents on any of these questions about their own financial situation.

A comment is necessary about public assistance among residents of New York City. The numbers were very small since there were only 26 New York City residents from foster care in this age group. Yet the importance of the issue of economic dependency demanded that this subject be considered. In view of the size of the group it was impossible to use weights in accordance with ethnic proportions, as I had done for the younger sample. It was also less important for this older group since they were ethnically more similar to the general New York City population. Therefore, I simply compared the proportion from our sample receiving such assistance with the proportion that received such assistance in the same age range in the New York City population in the last quarter of 1979. There were absolutely no differences for either the men or the women in our sample. For instance, 14.3% of the women from foster care received public assistance, but the figure was 16% for the general population. To the extent that one can overcome wariness about generalizing from a small group, there was no support here for a connection between foster care and continued dependence on public support.

The foster care group considered themselves to be as healthy physically as adults of the same age at large. Furthermore, in their assessment of the frequency of twelve common symptoms, the only differences occurred among white respondents. White adults nationally were more apt to complain of problems in falling or staying asleep, of having headaches, and of having upset stomachs than the white adults from foster care. Thus, on various symptoms, the foster care group either did not differ or complained less. There were also three questions about the consumption of alcoholic beverages. White respondents differed on none, but one item differentiated among black adults. As was the case with the younger sample, black respondents from foster care felt that they drank more frequently to help handle tensions than did black respondents from the general population. Although the few observed differences lead to the overall conclusion that on health and a variety of symptoms foster care and other older adults were alike, one difference did stand out. Roughly 29% of the adults from foster care had at some time since their discharge turned to a mental health professional, including the staff at their agency of discharge, in contrast to about 16% of adults their age in the general population.

On the three questions that dealt with these adults' self-evaluation, a weak difference existed on only one, and only among white respondents. The ratings of adults from foster care of the statement "I am able to do things as well as most other people" tended to be slightly less positive than the ratings of white adults their age in the general population. No differences whatsoever existed for the whites on the other two questions, and the black respondents were alike in their evaluations of themselves on all three. As for their sense of happiness, the average ratings of those from foster care were virtually identical to the ratings of adults from three national surveys. Last of all, there were also no differences in the adults' assessment of their lives as a whole. Taken all together, one can conclude that the adults from foster care did not differ from other adults their age in their sense of well-being.

Final Comments

How do the former foster children, now young adults, fare when compared with others of their age? There is no one simple answer unless one is willing to be trapped into a "good-bad" dichotomy. Rather, there is a continuum of faring. Some fare a little better, some a little worse, but most are functioning in society in about the same way as others their age.

The comparisons that have been presented, although rough, show few consistent differences between those who left foster care and others of their age nationally. At most, those from foster care were more critical of their country and somewhat less sure on whom to count for help. This last may have reflected a greater uncertainty about their sexual partnerships. More of those who left foster care had never married, and these young adults were more likely to express some uncertainty about whom to count on for help than those in our sample who had married. Regional factors were undoubtedly at play in the lower rate of marriage among those from foster care. The data on age at marriage, as well as the New York City comparisons, bore this out. Yet one is left with the uneasy feeling that perhaps other factors as well, such as some hesitation about making a commitment, were involved.

Educational differences also stood out rather consistently. Dissimilarities in the socioeconomic backgrounds of those who left foster care and young adults nationally no doubt had some bearing on the educational lags of the former. However, the scholastic deficits that emerged, and continued to linger, as they were growing up also played a role in their lower educational achievements.

But in the many other aspects of life that I examined, those who had been discharged from foster care and the national samples were more alike than different in what they were doing and in how they assessed important elements in their lives. This was so across the board, with an occasional exception here and there for those from group settings, and especially for whites.

In view of these results it behooves one to ask: why do people tend to make dire predictions about those who have spent many years in foster care? Why is it when I casually inquired of others, the most common response was not positive, or even an "I don't know," but something on the order of "They're probably all a mess." In response, I must pose some questions of my own. Is such a negative view tied to people's tendency to ascribe to all what may describe but a few? Is such a view bound to beliefs about the overriding import of blood relations for people's development? Is there a tendency to blame offspring for the inabilities and role failings of biological parents? Why such a singular emphasis on vulnerability? Is there so little confidence in young people's capacities to come to grips with the reality that no one's world is perfect? Is there so little faith in the strength and resilience of children?

PART THREE

THEY SPEAK ABOUT FOSTER CARE

Chapter Thirteen

THEIR REACTIONS AND SUGGESTIONS

In the preceding pages a picture of the young adults was painted by moving forward through time from their background and placement experiences to their lives when we spoke with them. When we began our search that was one objective, but there was another purpose as well: it was to hear their reactions to foster care, their own feelings about those years. We wanted to know about their satisfactions and dissatisfactions and to learn what from their lives was most closely linked to their reactions. We wanted to hear their suggestions, their thoughts about what might improve foster care for those in placement now or in the future. We wanted to know their assessment of the preparation for independent living they had, or had not, received. Finally, we wanted to know what services they thought would be useful for agencies to provide after they discharged people from placement.

Satisfaction with Foster Care

A number of approaches can be used to learn about people's positive or negative reactions to an experience. I looked at two aspects—the young adults' general satisfaction with their experience in foster care and whether they felt lucky to have been placed. The two are related, yet differ. One can feel fortunate about having had an experience, but dissatisfied with what occurred in it. On the whole, the young adults were quite satisfied with their experience in foster care. With the excep-

Table 13.1
Satisfaction with Foster Care

	Discharged from:			
	Foster Home		Group Setting	
	Males	Females	Males	Females
Generally, I was satisfied with my experience in foster care				
Very true	36.1%	52.7%	36.5%	25.0%
Pretty true	42.6	29.7	36.5	20.8
Not very true	13.9	9.9	15.4	29.2
Not true at all	7.4	7.7	11.5	25.0
Total %	100.0%	100.0%	99.9%	100.0%
Total N	108	91	52	24
All in all I was lucky to be placed in foster care				
Very true	50.5%	60.9%	48.0%	60.9%
Pretty true	40.0	33.7	32.0	21.7
Not very true	4.8	4.3	14.0	17.4
Not true at all	4.8	1.1	6.0	—
Total %	100.1%	100.0%	100.0%	100.0%
Total N	105	92	50	23

tion of the women who were discharged from group settings, a majority said they were very or pretty satisfied. This can readily be seen in table 13.1. The 15 women from group settings who were discharged from group residences and institutions expressed the greatest dissatisfaction. For example, there were large average differences in satisfaction between these women and women discharged from foster homes, whereas the satisfaction of the nine women who left group homes fell in between. The numbers here were, however, very small and therefore are cautiously suggestive at best. The males' hierarchy of satisfaction with the various settings was similar, but the differences were negligible. Apparently the more impersonal atmosphere of larger group settings was especially distasteful to the women. This was reflected in some comments that stressed "in the group home the house parents cared . . . they treated us as if we were their children" and "it was a congenial family atmosphere," whereas comments about larger settings often singled out their impersonality, a "you were kind of a number" feeling, and a loss of individuality and privacy. As one person summarily stated: "It was a collage of kids . . . children of all ages packed in there."

Table 13.1 also shows a consistently higher proportion who felt lucky than those who felt satisfied. The difference was particularly sharp for the women from group settings, 82.6% of whom said they felt lucky they had been placed although only 45.8% were satisfied with their experience in care. In the sample as a whole these two things were linked ($r = .46$), but not perfectly. Those who felt luckier about having been placed also felt more satisfied with their experience, although there were some who felt lucky but were not so satisfied.

Factors Connected with Satisfaction

By and large those who felt their placement was necessary, and this was a large majority, expressed more satisfaction with their experience than those who felt they had been placed un- necessarily. Furthermore, those who, according to their case records, were originally placed for reasons that were perhaps more understandable to them, such as someone's death or a caretaker's mental or physical illness, were more satisfied with their experience than those who entered care because they had been abandoned, neglected, abused, or placed because people could or would no longer cope. These combined factors lead one to the conclusion that satisfaction with foster care was in part a function of who had come to terms with the need for placement, and who had an acceptable rationale for why it had occurred.

There were other important links to the young adults' sat- isfaction with their experience in foster care. I did not exam- ine everything, but rather singled out key elements that made sense conceptually. Among those discharged from foster homes, without doubt the most decisive element in their satis- faction with foster care was their relationship with their foster families. Those who felt closer to their last or a previous foster family were more satisfied with their experience than those who felt less close ($r = .56$). Other factors were intertwined, for the more satisfied had remained in their longest placement for a longer period ($r = .29$), were younger at the start of that particular placement ($r = -.22$), and had been shifted about less frequently ($r = -.35$). Furthermore, those who used their foster family's last name while in care (even if only on occasion) or who said they wanted to do so, were more likely to be satisfied than those who did not ($r = .24$). Such a wish was one indication of their positive feelings about their foster families. Finally, the more satisfied said they felt more comfortable ($r = .23$) talking with people about their experience in foster care.

These links with satisfaction were unique for those discharged from foster homes, although in the case of shifts in placement the connection with satisfaction leaned in the same direction for both those from group settings and those from foster homes. There was nothing I could discern that was uniquely linked to the satisfaction or dissatisfaction of those who were discharged from group settings. Therefore, in what follows the group as a whole will be examined and some of the things I reviewed will be described, many of which were not associated with satisfaction. For instance, demographic factors such as ethnicity or religion were not connected, nor were there differences in satisfaction among those discharged from voluntary agencies of Catholic, Jewish, Protestant, or nonsectarian affiliation, nor between those from the voluntary or the public sector. Their level of education at the time of our contacts was also not linked to satisfaction, but their feelings about the amount and quality of their schooling while in placement were linked. Those who were more positive were also more satisfied with their foster care experience.

It is noteworthy that on the whole the amount of contact with biological parents or adult relatives during placement was not tied to the young adults' satisfaction with care, but their feelings about contact were. Those who were satisfied with the amount of contact they recalled, whatever it was, were more

satisfied with their experience in foster care. So, too, with regard to their siblings. Those who felt they had enough contact
were more satisfied than those who felt their contact was too
limited. There was a common thread that ran throughout, a
kind of halo of satisfaction or dissatisfaction that affected their
answers to a variety of questions. For instance, those who felt
more satisfied with their experience were less apt to say that
they felt lonely ($r = -.36$) or that they had no roots ($r = -.40$)
while in placement, did not think foster children often felt
worthless ($r = -.42$), described themselves as minimal worriers ($r = -.26$), and had a more positive sense of well-being
($r = .19$). Finally, they were more satisfied with the amount of
help provided by their agencies in preparing them to go out
on their own ($r = .21$).

Reactions and Concerns

Although most of the young adults were, on the whole, satisfied with their experience in foster care, this did not deter
them from making suggestions and from speaking critically
about a variety of things they had experienced, had witnessed
happen to others, or had heard in discussions with various
people. Their comments and suggestions flowed forth when
we asked: "From your own experience what do you think
would make foster care better for those who are now in care
or who will be in care?" Some gave no suggestions, but they
were few in number. All together more than 96% responded
with some comments or concerns. In addition, we obtained
more quantitative measures of their reactions to specific aspects of foster care. These results are sometimes based on
fewer respondents since here and there some did not give an
opinion because they felt they lacked information.

In order to portray what they said, I have been selective, for
it is not possible to report the many and varied thoughts of so
many people. Some topics were touched on frequently, while
others were unique. This presentation will make a broad sweep

in an attempt to depict the variety of comments in preference to making a numerical count. Material will be presented simultaneously from those discharged in 1975 as well as 1970, for they expressed similar concerns. One might call it a haphazard selection of remarks filtered through my own judgment. I will act as their mouthpiece in an attempt to capture what they said, using a liberal sprinkling of direct or nearly direct quotes from their interviews and questionnaires. Throughout, interpretations will not be made since it is their turn to speak for themselves. Their thoughts and suggestions will often concur, but will at times appear ambiguous or even contradictory. The purpose is to present an assortment of reactions to a large variety of experiences in foster care. It is hoped that such an approach will spark discussion among those who are most concerned about children in foster care.

Screening and Selection

Many of the young adults called for improvements in the screening and selection of foster families and house or cottage parents: "I know that agencies are anxious to find people . . . that should not get in the way of their being careful about selection." Character assessment and people's principles must be emphasized: "Some cottage parents are hired because the agency needs bodies rather than paying attention to qualifications." More time and care in making evaluations by agencies was a consistent theme: "If agencies expend more energy toward finding good homes, then agencies would not have to expend energies on services later." Investigations should be thorough and workers "should not be intimidated by the foster parents" in their eagerness to find homes for children. In screening families the agency should learn "whether these people are for real or just in it for the money . . . put them through red tape . . . mainly will he [the child] be loved, will he be accepted by that family as their own, will he be treated as their real children are treated?" The agency needs "to be able to tell the difference between the needy and the greedy . . . when the chips get down and dirty it's the foster child it comes down on . . . you need to find secure people . . . financially and emotionally . . . as foster parents . . . or the child will be the scapegoat when things go wrong."

There were numerous suggestions about what the process of screening should entail, some general and some quite specific, including "find out what they want to get out of it, and give to it . . . give them psychological tests." This last was mentioned by some as a way to assess people's motivations and capacities for love, tenderness, and warmth. There was a concern that people's economic background and living accommodations, such as rooms and beds, have been more specifically reviewed than their past experiences with their own or other children, their familial background, their stability, and their "habits of family conduct . . . how they conduct themselves and how they live their lives, how well they take care of their responsibilities," and whether they are involved in their communities. "Get references from neighbors." Some thought that evaluations need to be broadly focused and should include "screening of both parents and all those that live there, and others who spend a lot of time there," including older biological children and relatives of the foster parents.

Educational concerns entered their discussion of the selection process. Some felt that too little emphasis was placed on foster or house parents' interest in schooling or their ability to encourage children to accomplish in school: "People must be chosen who will steer children right, who have an interest in their schooling," who will help motivate children to move ahead and not to be discouraged. The attitude should be "don't let anyone tell you that you can't do," or "my foster mother always said don't let being a foster child stop you from being what you want to be." It was suggested that screening could include a review of the "school records of natural children to see how they are doing." Minimum educational requirements for foster parents were also proposed, such as "at least high school . . . they didn't, and couldn't help us at all" with school work. Finally, the importance of providing models was cited. "Homes should be chosen carefully . . . I was lucky because I grew up around a lot of smart people . . . their children did well and it gave me something to aspire to."

The age of foster parents also received some attention: "Be careful about their age . . . my foster family was too old. Don't have a generation between foster parents and foster children . . . they should be of an age where they can have an open mind and are flexible." Some found it difficult to communicate about a variety of things because of the age differential, while others stressed that people should have "current ideas . . . not antiquated," regardless of their chronological years. This was a particular worry in comments about handling teenagers since those "who are too old and set in their ways" were seen as posing barriers to communication and understanding.

Finally, they commented on the difficulty in evaluating people because they easily "put up a front." Some felt that licenses should be issued for a "trial period of six months," while others thought that agencies should rely more on people who have been in foster care to screen potential foster parents. "Someone with experience in foster care would know and be able to pick up cues. Experience is very important and I know . . . I've been out there." Stricter state regulation of the screening process was also suggested.

Foster Parent Qualities

Many commented on important positive personal qualities and attributes found in foster parents: "Foster parents are angels . . . I always felt at home, like one of her children." Love and affection, sharing everything in their home, the ability to communicate with and listen to a child, acceptance, understanding, providing a sense of security and stability, and having an awareness of a child's needs were some of the qualities cited. "It was a marvelous experience . . . the foster parents went into it with the attitude: we picked you and you're very special." Some also spoke of the foster parents' interest in hearing about the child's feelings about being a foster child. Some did not think of themselves as foster children. As one addressed her foster father in a newspaper on Father's Day some years ago: "I love you my one and only Dad. Thanks for all your love when I was good or bad. Your only daughter."

Many of the young adults felt a sense of family while in foster care. When asked whether growing up in foster care was like growing up in one's own family, close to 63% of those discharged from foster homes felt this was very or pretty true. In contrast, most of those who were discharged from group settings disagreed.

Offspring

The presence in the home of the foster parents' biological children can affect the foster care experience in positive or negative ways and caused some to refer to the old saying "No matter what, blood is thicker than water." Much depended on the foster parents' attitude and behavior, as well as on the young person's sensitivities. "Foster parents treat their own blood differently than outsiders . . . I always felt like an outsider," or "She took care of her own children and tolerated us," or "I was never part of the family . . . always on the outskirts . . . but I was strong . . . because of my own self-respect." We heard descriptions of foster parents who gave more attention, privileges, or gifts to their own children. Sometimes these children "never let me forget that I was in foster care . . . that I was not as good as they." Some, therefore, suggested that children should be placed in homes where there are no biological children. At a minimum the presence of such children and the attitudes toward them require careful review. Positive aspects were also stressed. When there was a sense of equitable treatment, having these children in the home "made it more of a family." And when asked whether foster parents treated their own children better than they treated foster children, about 58% of those discharged from foster homes disagreed. Favoritism occurred, but it was clearly not the norm. It is important to say that I do not know precisely how many of those who agreed were speaking from their own experience; some may have heard about this from others, or simply thought this was likely to be true.

Their Own Siblings

There was little disagreement among those who spoke about their brothers and sisters. Siblings "should not be separated" was a consistent theme. People viewed siblings as allies, a ready-made support group, so that "if there are problems, you could talk to each other" or "could depend on the strength of one another." If it is necessary to separate siblings, there should be ample opportunity for contact from the start, and there should be flexibility. For instance, some questioned why appointments and special arrangements were necessary in order to see a sibling; they felt this was a barrier to contact. Others stressed the importance of telling foster children about the identities of all their brothers and sisters, or else "the child can be wondering for years whether or not he has any brothers or sisters." Some spoke of surprise meetings in their teens, and of worries about incest. "He was placed by a different agency and was living just a few miles away . . . he had a different last name . . . I might have met him and dated him without knowing."

Their Background and Placement

Even greater concern was expressed about foster children being given adequate information about their family background—their heritage. About seven out of ten agreed that they wished they had known more about their family background during their placement, and 50% said they had felt they had no roots. They spoke strongly about their right to know about their ancestry, their heritage, or their roots. "A person has a right to know early on about their own family or else they make up all kinds of things in their heads." They believed that "a lot of foster children wonder about where they came from" and that at the very least photographs should be provided. As one person summed up the predicament: "I wouldn't know my mother if she walked right by me." They thought that accurate information about ethnic background should be provided, and some felt strongly that children ought to be placed with those of similar ethnicity in order to help maintain a cultural identity and sense of their heritage. "I regret that I don't know any Spanish . . . my fosters are white and I was raised as a white child . . . no attention was paid to maintaining my cultural background." They emphasized that not only their own histories but "the past history of one's people" were important information to impart. "For when the child is grown he or she won't know how to speak or understand the Puerto Rican language or culture, as in my case, and that's hell to live with."

They also stressed that relevant medical history items should be given. They spoke of discomfort at being unable to answer questions posed by their children, by doctors, and by others. Some thought that foster parents "should be given more information about a foster child's biological background so they can answer questions" as they arise, and that foster parents need to understand that children's questions are quite natural. "They made me feel that I was hurting them with my questions . . . though I had no bond with my natural parents . . . just natural curiosity." They also emphasized that social workers "should not be evasive in response to questions . . . I could never get an answer . . . people were not direct." They recognized that the truth could be upsetting, but less so than imaginary information used to fill in gaps, and that evasiveness by social workers was sometimes translated by the child

into "they don't care about me . . . so when I had questions
later on about other things like sex information I felt I had no
one to turn to."

Not only did they advocate increased information about
family background, but some spoke specifically about the importance of explaining to young children that they had been
placed, and why this came about. "I wasn't aware of being a
foster child until age seven . . . I learned then because my
name was different . . . but at one time I thought this was
true for everyone, that the last name didn't mean anything."
Some singled out clear discussions about the reasons for their
placement: "Most children could understand what went on . . .
it's bad to be left in the dark." Their suggestions about the
timing for such discussions ranged from age seven to nine.
Some went further and suggested that discussions include a
consideration of "realistic future alternatives . . . that is,
whether he will go back to the parents or remain in placement
. . . natural parents often give children false hopes."

Contact with Kin

Contact with biological parents and relatives was frequently
touched on. Some suggested there should be more contact;
others thought there should be less. "If the family wants to
keep in touch from the beginning of placement fine, but not
just show up in the middle years . . . it messes up a child's
head . . . visiting should not be allowed unless there is some
continuity." Perhaps the most recurrent theme was the importance of consulting with the foster child "about what they want
or need." Phrases like "don't force" or "don't insist" on contact
were frequently used, for "there are some who really feel their
parents are strangers." Others stressed the same point but for
different reasons: "You are never asked if you want contact
with your family . . . they seem to forget all about your parents." Perhaps their desire for consultation was a factor in their
assessment of the role of the agencies. More than six out of

ten thought that agencies wielded too much control over visiting arrangements. A few also commented about the time allowed for contacts and stressed greater flexibility about weekend visits with biological family members. Others singled out
the quality of the visits when they were held at the agency.
They felt that the atmosphere was impersonal with "everyone
running around"; many foster children were there at once,
and there were too many people in a room. "The visiting
schedule was too rigid and arbitrary . . . as one got older it
became more and more meaningless . . . superficial . . . you
got candy and gifts and it was a waste of time."

Some spoke about contact as a source of bewilderment, stir-
ring up questions about who was a parent. "When my biological mother came to visit, I couldn't call my foster mother
mommy . . . I had to address her as Mrs. X . . . I should
have been asked before my biological mother was thrown back
into my life when I was seven." Others were bothered by references to "your mother" by the social worker: "At home it
was mommy and daddy when I talked with my foster parents
. . . but the worker used 'mother' to refer to my biological
mother . . . it leaves a child confused about who really is my
mother."

One other aspect of biological family contact received attention. If children wanted to have contact with their biological
families, the agencies should not only assist in every way possible, but "try to help the child find his natural parents after he
reaches a given age." An "agency mechanism for tracking down
natural parents" and the provision of all birth records to a
child were suggested.

Services for Kin and Prompt Decisions

Some also spoke of the role agencies could play in providing
services to biological family members. "Rehabilitation," helping families with their problems, the "need to work with them
about how they feel about having a child in foster care," and

preparation for a return home were mentioned. "Provide help to understand what it is like to live together after being separated for a long time." Some spoke about much broader issues: "Change social conditions . . . alleviate poverty, provide and plan for each family so that they can stay together, do away with unemployment . . . create social service agencies designed to keep people together," and in those situations where a biological family's difficulties are primarily financial, why not give the money allotted for foster care directly to the family instead?

Others voiced impatience with biological parents "who waver back and forth," and with the outcome of judicial proceedings: "Does the child belong to the biological parents? My mother would not release us . . . the best thing is to be able to define the situation early . . . children go down the tubes while the court decides if the parent has a heavy problem." Foster care should be reserved for those whose biological families maintain contact and "quickly establish how much involvement the family wants." Time limits for decisions were proposed: "Give the parent a time limit to decide . . . give them information to help them decide . . . make clear to them the pros and cons of their actions . . . make clear what their responsibilities are . . . instead of allowing them to waver . . . they shouldn't be allowed to latch onto a child." Time limits for foster parent and agency decisions were also mentioned, as was consultation with the children themselves: "If a foster child, why not an adopted child . . . so you get rid of the label of foster" and so "you'd feel more secure . . . because I never knew whether or not the agency would move me from the foster home."

Economic Advantages and Motives

Somewhat more than 66% of the young adults said they had benefited in that they felt they had material things in foster care that their biological families could not provide. But they stressed that other aspects of foster home and group care environments were more important. They cited a long roster including love, patience, understanding, and involvement with the child, as well as people's ability to guide the young person and to set limits. "You can live in a nice house but if you don't get love what good is it? . . . but maybe it's a place to live . . . if you get a good family with affection for you then you're lucky . . . my foster mother had a nice house, wall-to-wall carpet, but drank and said some terrible things." They expressed strong opposition to anyone who provided foster care for their own financial gain and thought this needed to be closely monitored. Nearly 45% of the young adults who were discharged from foster homes felt that a lot of foster parents "are just in it for the money." Some spoke on the basis of what they heard from others and some from their own experience: "To some the foster child is a dollar sign," or "It was like a children's factory . . . children were always coming and going . . . when some left others soon took their place . . . it seemed more like a profit scheme." They wondered how many families would "take in children if there was no payment"; some felt that funds that were provided were not always used for the benefit of the children, and others complained of being made to feel they were a financial burden for the family—"as if they [the family] were counting every meal." Certain agency rules "like the foster parents getting separate receipts when they shop for you" made some wonder about financial motives.

At the same time, some suggested that the funds for foster care were not adequate. "A child doesn't need a silver spoon environment, but he does need opportunities." Whether talking about foster homes or group settings, higher budgets for clothing, for food, and for personal allowances were suggested. Special circumstances that can arise, such as the illness or death of a foster parent "need to be taken into account . . . have some differential payments" based on reevaluations of the changed needs of the foster family.

Foster Parents and the Agency

They also suggested greater flexibility in allowing foster parents to make a variety of decisions. "I think my foster mother should have had a free hand and not had an iron glove thrown at her" in arranging for the place of visits with the biological family. Some felt that agency rules about such things as permissions for trips, vacations, and school conferences had the effect of removing parental responsibilities and seemed overly restrictive and intrusive, "when in other ways they never looked upon themselves as foster parents . . . they were just my parents." Sometimes agency rules were interpreted as limiting the freedom of the foster child when compared with the biological offspring of foster families, and "making the situation different to a real family." One young man, after stating that he realized that ultimate responsibility rested with the agency, commented at length: "Foster parents should be given more leeway if they are considered responsible adults . . . they had to inform the worker about numerous things . . . every weekend they wanted to go away they had to inform . . . this doesn't allow for anything spontaneous as occurs in ordinary families . . . it spoiled a lot of good times . . . and maybe discouraged other families . . . it's not that the agency didn't give the ok, they always did . . . it's the fact of always having to do it . . . and one can't always find the worker . . . why should they always have to hunt for that one person? . . . at a minimum, someone else should have the authority at the agency . . . a family just can't operate spontaneously if they always have to check in."

On the other hand, the agency should assume an active role in providing assistance in areas where problems can arise. "Have group meetings for foster parents and their foster children to clear up problems before they become a big hassle." They also spoke of the value of having foster parents meet with each other "so they can talk about what being a good foster parent is." Family sessions for foster parents and the children in placement; sessions that include the foster parents' biological children; and joint meetings for foster parents, biological family members, and the foster child were suggested. Training sessions on child rearing should be available. "Foster parents need a group on how to handle adolescents . . . or children at different stages of development . . . there's a need for seminars where they can ask questions . . . and talk with people who have been in care themselves."

Feeling Set Apart

Children who are in foster care want to be treated like others. But there is a difference. They are foster children and feel different because of that. " 'Foster' sounds like a disease," said one, whereas others spoke of a positive experience as one in which the word "foster" was not used. "We wanted to feel part of the society and so we didn't let on we were in foster care." This was not an isolated incident, for nearly 58% of the respondents said that it was very or pretty true that at times they did not want to acknowledge being a foster child. Some even refused to participate in this study on this ground. Furthermore, close to 63% felt that children in foster care feel different or set apart from other young people.

They spoke of numerous situations that served as reminders of how they differed. "The money you get is not enough for more than necessary items . . . it makes you feel out of place . . . not having the same things makes you feel different . . . you don't feel like an average kid." They spoke of "agency controls" over children, of "all those strange faces in the agencies," and of rules and procedures that other children did not have to be concerned with. "Clinic days every month made you feel different . . . you had to miss school . . . I didn't want the school to know and asked my foster mother not to tell . . . so she wrote to the school that I was sick for the day." Others wondered, "Why couldn't we go to a regular doctor?"

One felt that "having to call the agency doctor and not the family doctor just pointed out the difference between you and others . . . it was also quite demeaning."

Some lied to friends who were inquisitive. Some spoke of other children and adults teasing or ridiculing them about being a foster child and said that "it is very hard growing up with a different name . . . children make fun of you . . . it's a lot of heartache." They spoke about children in school who asked them about different names on their homework, "then they would ask why I was in foster care . . . why didn't relatives take care of me . . . it made me feel very different . . . at registration there were different names too . . . why does everyone have to know? . . . it's like you are marked." Some changed the foster parent's initials on homework "to conform to my last name . . . I was embarrassed about being in care . . . I felt different, I didn't want to have to explain to people . . . being a foster child was my largest secret."

Some singled out caseworker visits to a school or a foster home: "The main thing that would remind me that I wasn't part of the family was when the worker would come and ask me questions that I knew I'd better have the right answer for." Some recalled adolescence as being a particularly uncomfortable time, and of worries about friends or neighbors knowing about foster care. They commented about people's stereotypes, and of being confronted with assumptions and predictions about behavior "because it's in your blood . . . it's hereditary." Some suggested that agencies should stress that "you're like every other child . . . even kids who live with their own families have problems . . . it's just that your mother couldn't care for you . . . then I wouldn't have felt so different." Some thought that agencies overgeneralize by assuming that children in foster care have problems and felt agencies would do well to be more discriminating about attaching "a label of emotionally disturbed." Others made comments to the effect that "the child should be treated like a person, not like a client" and "not like a general pattern." Some from group settings also expressed concern about general attitudes in the com-

munity and school system when "a place takes on the reputa-
tion of a few bad children . . . because then everyone suf-
fers." Some felt that more and better communication between
group settings and the surrounding community could lessen
the existing stereotypes, and perhaps "there should be a cam-
paign that publicizes that foster children are people too . . .
like black is beautiful." After all, "being a foster child is not
such a terrible thing."

Shifts of Placement

Over and over again agencies were admonished for moving
children around: "There has to be a greater understanding
that one is moving people, not furniture" and "Children are
not objects . . . like merchandise" were common refrains.
Shifts, whether from one foster family to another or from
"cottage to cottage," are unsettling and confusing. "Once you
get settled in school, comfortable with a family . . . with
friends . . . as soon as I got situated I had to move . . . the
hardest thing about foster care was the movement." They spoke
of the confusion "when things you were taught to do in one
home were not accepted in the next one." They spoke from
their own experience and from what they had heard from
others, or had witnessed; although they recalled situations
where "it was best to move," more than seven out of ten young
adults felt that children are moved around too much. They
thought more time and care needed to be invested in selecting
placements in the first place, and that shifts be considered only
"when absolutely necessary."

Some questioned the reasons for certain decisions and complained that "they didn't like my getting too close to my foster
parents" and that some "foster parents were afraid to get too
close" because they worried that a child would be removed.
They felt that children and foster parents need reassurance,
and should be told "that when the social worker comes to visit
a child it's not to take them away." Children also need reassur-

ance that a move will not occur suddenly. When another child in a home or group setting leaves without warning, it is frightening to the children who remain and sends them an unintended message. "This other younger child left . . . it just suddenly happened . . . it scared me, made me insecure." Others advocated clear explanations to those who are shifted, as well as to those who remain, about "why he or she couldn't stay . . . to this very day I don't know why she left or where she is . . . I felt close to her . . . we should have been allowed to stay in touch with her."

Some spoke of explanations given as overly vague: "If all the social worker can say is that it's best for you to move, then the child can't understand why he or she is being moved." Unclear explanations are a source of confusion and can lead some to blame themselves—to feel they were responsible. The experience of a shift, or witnessing the movement of others, was seen by some as punishment for unacceptable behavior. Thus, more than six out of ten, and more from group settings than foster homes, felt that "children in foster care have to behave well" or else they will be moved. Some who felt this because they feared a return to their biological families gave the following advice to children: "Be natural; don't be afraid that if you did something wrong you'll be sent back."

Education

Some thought that shifts, when they necessitated transfers to new schools, had interfered with their progress in school. Others complained about the variety of schools they attended: "I had lots of problems with school, but instead of dealing with them I was moved from one school to another." A central concern, however, was with the level of education provided for foster children and with how much, or little emphasis was placed on this by agency staff and foster parents. "Provide better education" and "give children the best education possible" and "don't allow teachers involved with foster children to pass them by" were common themes.

School progress needs to be carefully monitored and the children's potential carefully assessed. "Education should be a main priority." They felt that "education needs to be stressed more" during the time children are in placement, that steps should be taken to "develop an interest in school . . . help the kids to value school" and to "push the kids." Some gave specific suggestions, such as "set up routines to follow . . . set limits . . . start people off with books . . . start young." Others mentioned their regret about not having "spent more time on academics." One complained about being labeled: "They thought I was slow so they kept me down." At the same time some spoke positively about their experience. "In seventh grade I didn't know how to read . . . they made me . . . I failed everything but I came back . . . they encouraged me." Others cautioned about the influence of staff expectations: "The social worker gave me the impression I should accept limitations about training . . . just because I had had problems . . . it freaked me out." Finally, some stressed that education and training were essential in preparing foster children for independent living, so they would be able "to help themselves."

Agency Staff

An atmosphere needs to be developed where children feel free to express themselves. Some regarded the relationship between staff and children as impersonal, even officious. "They'd come in with an attaché case and notebook and would write things down . . . you never knew what they were writing or what they'd do . . . there was no parent image . . . not like a friend . . . we were afraid to get too close." Some were afraid they would be moved: "She always threatened to take me away . . . then she'd ask why I was so quiet . . . or so skinny . . . I just had no one to turn to." Those in charge "who make all the rules" were looked upon as distant and removed. "If somehow people in higher positions would come down and talk to the kids rather than just oversee."

They spoke at length about the importance of careful screening and selection of caseworkers, counselors, and cottage parents, and suggested periodic reevaluations of staff members: "You need mature people . . . and people who really care about children," who are serious, empathic, and "trained to enable them to understand more about the foster care experience." Trust and friendship, character and principles, "people you can go to and count on . . . parental figures," ability to listen, responsiveness and directness were among the qualities mentioned. "Much depends on the social worker. Some are not into their jobs . . . they didn't spend more then their hour . . . they need to take you out and really talk . . . it's a job you have to be involved in . . . . not 9 to 5."

They emphasized training and experience, and raised questions about the age of some staff members "who were just kids themselves." Some were concerned about "student workers who let their own problems get in the way." Some from group settings stressed strength, the ability to impose controls and limits, "but don't give away drugs like candy." They felt the agency staff should be prepared to handle fights "and not allow kids to walk over them." They spoke of protections that are needed "to stop older kids from bullying around the young ones," and that workers "should not side with adult counselors just because they're adults," nor should they take sides with biological or foster families but "they should be in tune with kids' needs." A few singled out the assignment of social workers and suggested that the sex of worker and child should be the same for ease of communication, particularly for an older child. They stressed the importance of understanding and sensitivity to needs and problems, but also criticized an overemphasis on problems. "Have social workers who aren't always looking for something to be wrong," and "they shouldn't act like they feel sorry for you or pity you." Finally, staff members should be selected who are knowledgeable, who "will be informative" about community resources, and who "will be more involved in people's plans for their future." Perhaps, some suggested, former foster children would be an asset as staff members, or could be asked to meet with children in groups "to discuss the good and bad things they are experiencing . . . and be of some help in giving them advice firsthand."

Suggestions about staff selection mainly concerned the quality of interactions. There were also suggestions about the quantity of contact between social workers and children. They advocated more frequent visits but also expressed concern about excessive intrusion "on a child's privacy . . . it should depend on what the child allows . . . shouldn't force themselves on a child." A central theme concerned the social worker's understanding of the child's environment. "The social worker should be around more and not wait 'til something happens to come by." Some thought that agencies are at times misled by "false fronts" that are put up. "If there was fighting in the home it seems like everything would clear up the day before the social worker came . . . my foster father would say now you'd better be good . . . she's coming." Some spoke "of a complete change of atmosphere . . . the big act," or of dressing up children when on other days "they looked like shit." They felt that a greater investment of time, or even occasional unannounced visits, could provide social workers "with a truer picture . . . once a month any foster parent can make a child happy with a new toy . . . so the child looks happy . . . it can be a false impression."

Some spoke about the importance of social workers "remaining neutral" and not taking sides: "I always saw her in the presence of the foster parents. I never felt she was there to help me . . . she was there to help them." Some regarded their contact with the social worker as too superficial, "a 'hi, how are you' thing." Workers need to work more closely with the children, and should listen more to what children have to say: "I knew they didn't want to hear my feelings . . . they didn't believe me and thought I was doing awful things . . . I wasn't, I just was trying to be a bit more independent."

Many commented that meetings with the social worker in the presence of a foster parent did not allow them to speak freely "because one is too afraid to say anything." They spoke about "it being thrown up to you afterwards" and about the fear of being moved. "But the social worker should get a child's view of things in private," for otherwise "a child will just give them the right answers." In this context some spoke of having been sexually molested by a foster father or counselor, and about instances of physical abuse, but the suggestion for private sessions was much more general. On the other hand, some thought they never would have felt free to talk because "I would have felt disloyal to my foster parents."

They were also concerned about confidentiality. "Foster children should have the chance to speak out without fear of reprisal." It was clear from their remarks that they felt that foster children worry that a social worker or psychiatrist may divulge things they have discussed, and some gave examples of how "I got hell" afterwards from a foster parent. They suggested "there should be someone at the agency to hear complaints without informing on anyone." They thought that those in placement can serve as a resource for others. "Agencies should introduce foster children of the same age living in the same area . . . they can help each other out . . . relate better to each other." One person suggested setting up "a hot line . . . for complaints and to discuss problems."

When a good understanding existed between a child and a social worker or other staff member, when communication was direct and open, "when she was there if I needed her," the staff member was seen as an extremely positive influence, "like a parent." But "I always found it hard to say anything to a social worker . . . I had a lackadaisical attitude . . . because they always sent a different person." Some thought that "the constant changing of social workers was the main problem" in their experience in foster care. "Once I finally was able to trust one they were transferred, and then I would have to start all over again." They spoke of it as "nerve racking to have counselors coming and going," felt it interfered with the likelihood of establishing rapport, and said "it became a joke to see how long a social worker would last." Some spoke of attempts to obtain information about biological relatives: "I was always told they'd try . . . but they didn't tell me and the social workers kept changing . . . after a while I gave up." One person suggested the assignment of two social workers to a child to ensure continuity of staff and to alleviate the feeling of desertion when a worker leaves. These reactions were summed up as follows: "Social workers often talk about the issue of abandonment and then they end up doing the same thing."

Inclusion in Decisions

Some felt left, and others felt left out: "They always had conferences and you weren't in on it and they don't tell you what they discussed about you . . . then they write a report and you don't know what they've said." Some felt that general statements such as " 'it's in your best interest' makes you feel like a client, not like a person." A recurrent theme in their comments was the importance of consulting with children and allowing them to share in, and contribute to, decisions that need to be made. By age ten or the early teens "children should be able to have a voice in where they are placed . . . if a kid is old enough to be transferred around like a ping-pong ball he's old enough to decide where he's happy . . . children in foster care grow up very quickly." They advocated inclusion in decisions about the type of placement, changes in placement, visiting with or return to the biological family, and issues connected with their schooling. They suggested more input following trial visits in foster homes. One suggested "trial periods in more than one foster home when kids are at least ten years old so they can compare two places and help in deciding the final placement," whereas another thought "the trial and error placement method is too abrupt . . . a weekend isn't long enough to know . . . a month would be proper . . . the benefits would outweigh the negative aspects" and would allow mutual decisions to be made. Some singled out consultation about the location of a placement. "I was out of my element . . . I was placed in a foster home in Brooklyn . . . I'd never been in Brooklyn in my life . . . so I ran away," and another spoke about "not isolating kids from their neighborhoods." Some spoke in a more general way about feeling "a loss of control" over what happened to them, that foster children should be allowed more control over their lives, and "children must have certain rights . . . these need to be defined."

Privacy, Individualization, and Control

They spoke of the desirability of more privacy. Roughly 37% of those from foster homes, in contrast to 64% of those from group settings, felt they had not had enough privacy while in care: "It was like living in a goldfish bowl." They spoke of overcrowding, of staff members watching foster care children shower, and of mail that was screened. They complained about group care as impersonal: "It's like a herd of cows." Some spoke of "so much structure that you feel caged in," and suggested greater freedom to socialize, "don't treat children like a regiment," and felt that rules should be interpreted with greater flexibility. They advocated a more individualized approach to children in order to bring out their special qualities: "Institutions should permit people to be individuals . . . and not copies."

At the same time some from group settings felt that adults needed "to be in control . . . rules are necessary . . . now there's not enough of that . . . it's a jungle . . . staff is too weak and the kids are in control." They spoke of the importance of discipline and supervision, gave examples of drug and alcohol abuse, of children hitting counselors, and of being sexually molested by other foster children. Some were frightened by what they described as "a boiling pot" atmosphere when

you "have a kid who's a delinquent under the same roof as a
kid who is there just because he didn't have good parents."
They felt that there should be greater emphasis on "giving
kids moral values," spoke positively about staff who "kept kids
in line" because "if you let the kids get away with too much
it'll catch up with them in time . . . they can't get away with
things once they get out in the world." They thought education about drugs and alcohol needed increased attention while
youths were still in placement. An expansion and greater di-
versity of recreational activities were suggested "to keep you
on the go . . . keep you doing something" on the assumption
that "more activities during leisure time will help keep kids
out of trouble," and one added emphatically "especially when
it rains."

Preparation for Life and for Discharge

A recurrent theme touched on the role that could be played
by foster care graduates and youths in placement. "Former
foster people should be asked to go back and talk with current
foster care kids . . . to present a positive image . . . that they
too can make a success of their lives." They suggested discussion groups between foster care graduates and children in
placement. They thought older children could be given more
responsibility for developing peer groups and for serving as
"activity guides" for others.

Throughout their teens foster children should be given more
responsibilities and duties, including part-time jobs after school
and "handling money . . . be encouraged to budget." Some
felt they were overly protected and "when it came time to leave
I had no sense of responsibility because everything was done
for me," and "they gave things to us without helping us to
understand that in real life you need to earn them." They suggested that "agencies should let go a little" and do everything
imaginable prior to discharge to "teach young people to be

responsible for themselves . . . because if you're working your boss isn't going to tell you to do this or that . . . if you're wrong he'll just fire you."

Close to eight out of ten felt that children in foster care "worry a lot" about their own future. Although mentioned earlier, it is worth repeating that 52% of the young adults stated that they had received a little, very little, or no preparation for discharge from their agencies, 23.1% said they had received some preparation, and about one-quarter spoke of a lot of preparation. "A person being discharged should not be left out in the street . . . that's how they left me." They spoke of "teaching kids what they need to know to make it in life . . . they should be oriented about what they can expect of the future" and of "helping kids understand that things will not be handed to them but that they have to work to earn them." They stressed that preparation and "making a child aware of alternatives" should begin years before the final discharge date, and should be a high priority for agencies. Some complained that "they only ask 'are you happy?' " while others said such things as "taking you out shopping is good but not enough." Over and over they spoke of the importance of spending time on, and of sorting out people's interests, aspirations, and goals. They advocated improved counseling to provide children "with an upward goal direction."

All young adults were given a list of nine broad areas, including job preparation and career planning, money management, and preparation for obtaining training and schooling, and were asked to select those for which they thought the agency had prepared them well. They were then asked to choose the three areas they thought most important for agencies to provide prior to discharging young people from foster care. Close to 71%, males and females alike, chose job preparation and career planning as one of the most important, but only 23.4% thought their agency had prepared them well in this area. They felt that for many "the world is remote when you're in placement." Prior to discharge a heavier emphasis should be placed on vocational training, on providing young people with specific skills, on encouraging or "pushing" people to work during placement, on giving them specific information about employment options and job placement services, and on helping people to find employment. "After 18 I shouldn't have been put on welfare . . . they should have prepared me with a vocation so I could support myself."

Somewhat more than 65% of the young adults selected the financial area as one of the three most important for agencies to stress in preparing young people for discharge. Some 25.5% thought their agencies had prepared them well in this regard. The dissemination of information on resources for obtaining financial aid, including financial assistance for continued education, was seen as one aspect of such preparation. They were concerned about money management and income. "They should have taught the value of money . . . saving for the future . . . money management." They spoke of the importance of learning how to budget, of "helping young people to save some money while still in foster care," and of teaching young people how to handle money, for instance, by giving them responsibility for purchasing clothes. Some wondered whether "agencies could give money directly to the foster children when they are older." Others were concerned about financial problems following discharge, and spoke about providing discharge grants for everyone. There were suggestions for creating a fund for each child: "Where the agency doesn't succeed in getting a child adopted, they should set up a bank account and deposit a minimum of $50 a year . . . just like a mother would do . . . to be given to the person at discharge." Some spoke of the difficulty of "getting credit." One raised the issue of foster parents' wills and the legal problems that can ensue for a foster child who is not a blood relation, yet may have known no other family.

"There should be more stress put on areas dealing with the foster child's future . . . such as education, jobs and careers" was a constant refrain. They spoke of the importance of improving educational preparation, and of providing more counseling services to help with vocational issues and career plans. Close to 51% thought that preparation in how to get training or schooling was one of the three most important areas. About 37% stated that they had been well prepared in this regard. Some stressed that "education is essential" and suggested that "an educational fund should be established for kids so they can get other training or go to college if they want." Furthermore, specific information should be given to everyone about training programs, about stipends and grants, "and they should be helped in how to apply." Some complained that "you were just given the idea that you wouldn't have money to go on with school" while others stressed that "young people often don't know the facilities of their agency that could help them . . . it's a social worker's job to know these things and to educate the foster child." They felt that more information should be provided about various educational resources and services in the community as well. "The thing that was stressed was that one had to worry about basic things in life like food and clothes rather than emphasizing that one should think about a career . . . and one's motivation toward such a goal . . . but maybe they did that [stressed basic things] with girls more than with the guys." Complaints such as this may be one reason that the women on the whole felt less well prepared for discharge than the young men; close to 51% of the women said that they had very little or no preparation for their discharge from foster care, in comparison with about 37% of the males.

"They made sure I got an education and that I had some place to live before being cut off." Slightly more than 16% said that they had been well prepared in how to find a place to live. Such preparation was probably not emphasized by agencies in cases where, upon discharge, a young adult planned to reside with foster or biological family members, in a college dormitory, or had enlisted in the armed forces. Yet nearly 55% of those from group settings and roughly 38% of those from foster homes thought it was one of the three most important areas for predischarge preparation by agencies. In addition to finding housing, several stressed that "to prepare kids to function outside the agency, provide open settings in the community" as a means of learning about independent living. Six months to a year before discharge "arrange for small groups to live together in an efficiency . . . with their own budget . . . because as it is now one goes from total support to total nothing." Another suggested that "at discharge there should be a community where kids can go 'til they find their own place . . . some low-cost temporary residence to turn to." At a minimum young people need to be provided with information to enable them to find such temporary housing.

"There should be better preparation for growing up and for discharge . . . I received no preparation about sex, for instance, from anyone." Only about one out of ten young people said they had been well prepared, or given information on sexual matters and family planning, although one out of four thought this area should be given high priority. Nearly 33% of the women, in comparison with about 19% of the men, selected such preparation as one of the three most important areas for an agency to emphasize. "Due to archaic rules an adolescent still must go to the agency doctor who is a pediatrician . . . who in the world would ask a doctor who treated you as a two-year-old for birth control?" The young adults thought that agencies should make certain that each person was provided with adequate information. "They should go over the basics that any parent would teach a child . . . like menstruation . . . I was never told about it and when it happened I cried." They felt that agencies should not assume that foster parents will adequately prepare children about sexual matters: "They shouldn't take it for granted that foster parents will teach all . . . the agency should not leave it up to foster parents to teach family planning . . . they should make sure that the child is not left dangling in midair." Prior to leaving foster care young people should be given a roster of community facilities that could be used after discharge. Preparation for marriage and parenting was given high priority by 11.8% of the young men and women, whereas 4.4% felt they had been well prepared in this regard. More (14.2%) thought they had been well prepared for shopping, cooking, and household care, but only 7.7% considered this a high-priority item. One young adult suggested that in group care "they should rotate cooks . . . older kids should be cooking instead of agency cooks . . . and smaller children could watch and learn . . . it's part of preparing people for independence."

About 17% thought that the provision of information about medical coverage should be a high-priority area prior to discharge, and 19% felt well prepared in this regard. During placement "you do receive medical care, but once discharged medical coverage is not continued . . . and if I get sick it's just my tough luck . . . there's need for a health plan that goes beyond 18 and 21." At a minimum young people should be made aware of medicaid provisions and other insurance possibilities prior to their discharge.

The discussion of discharge led some to advocate open records. As young adults they wanted to know about their past and about brothers and sisters. Some spoke of wanting to know whether their recall of past events was correct, or wanting medical information, and of wanting to know why they had not been adopted. One young person captured the feelings expressed by others: "I'm old enough and can take it . . . I've managed . . . files should be available to you at 18 . . . after all, you're an adult . . . rather than their sitting with a big file in front of you and writing things down to give you . . . they make such a mystery of it and you end up with questions that you carry with you . . . it's my life after all in the files."

Some described discharge as a sharp separation, as "being cut off" or as "cutting you loose," and stated that agencies "should be more interested in what happens after." Some did have contact with someone at their last agency in the intervening years since their discharge. Close to 59% of those from group settings, in contrast to roughly 29% of those from foster homes, said they had spoken with someone since they were discharged. In each group a majority had but a few contacts. All together 13.7% stated that the purpose was to obtain information of various sorts, 4.6% said they discussed one or more problems, an additional 9% said they had done both, and another 9% described their contact as social. We asked those who had sought information or had talked over a problem whether they felt they had been helped with what they wanted. Four out of ten were helped "a lot," whereas roughly 34% spoke of some, and about 26% of not much help. In this last group was one, for instance, who spoke of calling the agency some years ago for some information about housing "and they acted as though once you're out that's it . . . we don't want to have anything more to do with you."

Their ongoing ties with their agencies were mixed. When asked whether they would feel comfortable about turning to the agency in the future if they wanted to talk with someone, about 52% of the men, but less than 39% of the women, answered in the affirmative. This sex difference existed both among those who had been discharged from foster homes and group settings. Those who felt better prepared for discharge were more likely to regard the agency as a resource to which they could turn ($r = .38$). This was perhaps one reason why the women were less inclined than the men to say they would turn to their agencies, for they were on the whole less satified with their preparation for independent living.

After Discharge

The young adults wished that their agencies could have offered a variety of supplementary services to them following their discharge from foster care. Once again we asked them to select those areas in which, if services had been available, they would have wanted to avail themselves in the intervening years. For each area they were also asked to indicate whether they had consulted with someone in their own or another agency since their discharge.

Nearly three out of four young people said they would have liked to discuss employment and career planning, but only about one out of four had had such a discussion with someone

at their agency or elsewhere. Close to 60% said they would
have liked to ask for advice about education, but only 21%
said they had had such a discussion at some community facility. Since it is easier to say that one wanted something than to
take steps in the direction of pursuing advice, one could imagine that some were not overly inclined in that direction. But
it is also clear that they lacked information. In the words of
one: "I managed because I was aggressive but others aren't
. . . material should be provided to inform people" about
programs and where to turn for counsel. In addition to employment and education, they said they would have liked to
discuss financial matters (48.2%), housing (38.6%), family
planning and parenthood (32.4%), legal information and insurance (31.4%), personal relations and marriage (26.1%), and
health and nutrition (21.3%). In each instance the proportions
who had had such discussions were far lower.

"Continue services after discharge . . . a discharged person
should always be allowed to return to the agency for advice or
counseling services regardless of the number of years passed."
Some felt that "a follow-up program to assist if needed" was
important to consider, and suggested that agencies might reach
out to people at various points in time after they are discharged. At a minimum during the first year "they should
reach out . . . people need support when they are first out on
their own . . . and need to be told they're doing a good job."
Agency-sponsored social activities were also mentioned. "The
agencies should consider a reunion of foster care alumni on
occasion . . . I wonder what has happened to some of the kids
I knew."

Finally, we asked each young adult to select that area he or
she considered the most important one for agency attention
following discharge, if agencies had the wherewithal. Two areas
stood out—education and work. Among the men, 41.1% selected education and 36.2% chose services that dealt with employment and career issues. It is noteworthy that among the
women this order was reversed since 40.5% felt work and career planning were the most important, whereas 24.3% se-

lected education. Those from foster homes and from group settings were quite alike in this regard. All other areas received much smaller "votes" by comparison.

Fewer women selected education, but men and women both stressed employment and career planning in equal proportions. Perhaps this occurred because by the time of discharge the women had received more education than the men. One does not know whether those who selected employment as the most important area were more concerned about job placement or career planning. Whatever the case, the general similarity in emphasis among the men and women, both here and in their choices of predischarge preparation, must be regarded as a signal to agencies that on matters concerning employment and career choice women want services provided them to be on a par with those provided to the young men.

Closing Comment

In presenting a potpourri of comments, it is easy to overdramatize some things at the expense of others. It is hoped that readers will not come away with a lopsided impression. In thinking about all this material, the reader needs to bear in mind the wide variety of experiences and reactions of these former foster children. Experiences ranged from those who felt they had been victims, whose reaction was "my God, it was terrible . . . awful" to those who spoke about having been "saved," or who stated "they did a million-dollar job with me as I look at other people." On the one hand, some complained about restrictions and having been forced to do labor, while others cast such limitations and expectations in a positive light: "We got clothes on occasions only, and an allowance only after working clearing trees . . . but hard work made me what I am today . . . one family made the cake, but the last family put the icing on it." There were those who viewed foster children as helpless and those who said: "Much depends on the child . . . if the child really wants to make it work, most of the time it will." In addition to such varied reactions, one must bear in mind that our question concerned improvements in foster care, and that even those with a positive experience had suggestions to make. These young adults approached that task thoughtfully, seriously, and with frankness. They wanted someone to listen; they wanted to help. They, and I, hope that their comments will be received in the spirit of that intent.

Chapter Fourteen

WHERE TO NEXT?

Among the general public, and even among some professionals, there is a prevalent belief that foster care spawns people most of whom are psychologically damaged, economically dependent, and engaged in criminal activities. There are expectations that graduates of foster care will mirror their own past by becoming excessive users of placement for their own offspring. At a minimum, people assume that those who grew up in foster care will be quite different from other people. Foster care seems to have become a convenient hitching post for people's complaints about many unsolved social problems.

Foster care has had, in common parlance, a very bad press. Hardly a month goes by without another prediction being made about the dire consequences of having been in placement. Only recently a brief newspaper account of a research project described it as a census of "children who haunt public places . . . hangouts for runaways and the homeless . . . parks, docks, arcades . . . the researchers will explore their recruitment into drug pedling, numbers running, prostitution and pornography, but they also want to examine psychiatric and family factors, in particular how many street children had been in foster care" (N.Y. Times 1982:3). Why "in particular"? Why is foster care singled out as responsible for so many of the troubles of such youths? Foster care . . . as compared to what, or whom?

The assumptions and expectations that abound concerning the dire fate of foster care children seem to have little validity. The products of foster care—the young adults whom we followed in this study—did not measure down to such dire predictions. They were not what might be described as problem ridden when they were discharged nor did they become so in subsequent years; there was no support for the generational repetition of foster care; there was no evidence of undue economic dependence on public support; and their records of arrest were not excessive. Overall, they were not so different from others their age in what they were doing, in the feelings they expressed, and in their hopes about the future.

The differences that occasionally stood out were in the main confined to young adults who had been discharged from group settings, but even there, such differences did not pertain to most of them. When compared with those who had been discharged from foster homes and with young adults in the population at large, those from group settings fared more poorly; this was particularly true for young adults from group residences or institutions. Although over the years there has been a decline in the use of these larger facilities in the United States, the question remains whether the reduction has been sufficient.

One is left with some nagging doubts about the basis for deciding to place some children in group settings. Such decisions have been predicated on the idea that group placements may be appropriate for children who are older, for those who have a limited emotional capacity to develop a satisfactory relationship with a surrogate family, and for those who are emotionally disturbed or whose behavior is assessed as deviant. Group placements have been used in situations where it has been felt that a family placement would threaten the biological family or would arouse loyalty conflicts in the child between two sets of families. Although this last can sometimes be a problem, our data raised questions about the premise. In the long run I could see no evidence of a conflict of loyalties, at least among those who had been discharged from foster homes. It is possible, but not plausible, that this finding simply attests to the accuracy of the placement decisions that were made. At the same time, there are surely foster families who can turn a situation of potential conflict into one of peaceful coexistence.

One was also left with the impression that some of the decisions about placement into group settings were based on expediency because no other place had been found. However, the main point is that the young adults expressed less satisfaction with their experience in group facilities, particularly institutions and group residences, than was expressed by those who grew up in family environments. Their perceptions did not accord with professional reasoning about the positive aspects of group care. This, in addition to the data about their poorer sense of well-being and poorer educational achievement, suggests that greater efforts must be made to provide suitable family environments regardless of the age of the children or their ongoing ties with kin.

Although my stance about foster care graduates is, on the whole, optimistic, any generality must be tempered. I have not researched all of foster care. Rather, this report is based on a highly selected, particular group of young adults, most of whom were in placement for a very long time, much of which was spent in a stable placement. Therefore, most of them grew up as part of another family. They had not been adopted, nor had they returned to their biological families. There were many reasons why they grew up in foster care and eventually "aged out" of the system: a lack of resources of, and for, their biological families; the indecisiveness of the adults responsible, whether professionals or family; the absence of clearly directed goals for the children in the responsible social agencies; and conflicts over, and the legal power of, parental rights. In addition, changes in statutes that allowed new grounds for the freeing of children, and made adoption subsidies possible, were only on the horizon when so many of these young adults entered foster care.

But even with the new laws, some of these young adults would have grown up in foster care, just as some who are now in placement will do so. That is not the ideal situation. It is to be hoped that shifts in practice, including the recent emphasis on clarity in planning for either a discharge to families of origin or adoption, will diminish the likelihood of children remaining in foster care for prolonged periods. But, to repeat, for some the ideal will not, or cannot, be achieved. For others, even if placement is shortened, there are aspects of the situation that require serious attention.

All of the concerns touched upon by the graduates of foster care will not be repeated here. It is hoped that their explicit comments will alert those engaged in providing and overseeing foster care to examine the policies, standards, and practices followed throughout the United States. But some questions need to be raised about three aspects of foster care that have received far too little attention: the contribution of those in foster care to decisions made about their own fate, their education, and their preparation for independent living.

Contribution to Decisions

The remarks and suggestions made by foster care graduates contained a recurrent theme—the importance of consultation with the young people themselves. They felt like pawns—subject to the many powers of others. They felt disregarded, that it did not matter what they wanted or had to say, because too often they were never asked. Whether it was a decision about a foster home, about changes in placement, about visiting arrangements with kin, or about their goals in life, they felt they should have been heard.

The decisions in foster care often involve many, and sometimes conflicting, interests. The viewpoints of the children themselves are, therefore, not sufficient alone but need to be seen as a necessary part of the considerations that determine the recommendations that are made. Such a practice can be beneficial in the long run since it is almost axiomatic that those who participate in making decisions are more concerned about making things work out. The process cannot begin when young people are in their late teens; it must begin earlier. Just when, and under what conditions, such consultations should occur requires much more thought and discussion than it has received. Surely a field that stresses the self-determination of clients needs to take steps to avoid drowning out the voices of children.

Education

Although in most respects foster care graduates were more alike than different from others of their age in the general population, our results showed that they lagged behind in scholastic achievement. During their placement many fell behind in school, and once a lag developed it was difficult to make up for lost time.

Much too little attention has been given to education, or when given it has been too late. Once children begin to fall behind, a vicious cycle too often develops. Incipient learning problems need to be detected quickly. All too often such problems have apparently been allowed to fester. Earlier some likely reasons were suggested. For one, expectations about school performance have probably been lowered by those who adopted a protective stance vis-à-vis children in foster care. Furthermore, foster care agencies have placed a greater emphasis on the emotional, rather than the educational, needs of children. The assumption has been that psychological problems lead to problems in school, and the reverse process has largely been disregarded. Training programs for workers, where they exist, lay heavy stress on sociopsychological matters to the detriment of the educational assessments of children. Foster care agencies hire psychiatric or psychological, but rarely educational, consultants. In other words, education has been given short shrift.

Education needs to be viewed as one element in preparing youths for independent living; optimal school performance is one ingredient in determining future employment options.

There are a variety of things that can be done: (1) The academic potential of children needs to be assessed accurately and over time; a single test at age seven can lead to a distorted picture. (2) Expectations about work at school need to be clearly communicated to children, foster parents, and personnel in group settings. (3) Problems in school need to be identified as early as possible and prevented from simmering; tutorial help needs to be readily available, and could include recruits from among others in placement. (4) Consultation with educational psychologists and others so trained should be a vital aspect of achieving all of these ends. (5) Finally, guides and standards for foster care practice need to address the educational development of children with more than a passing phrase. Unless additional weight is attached to education, foster care cannot approach the goal of developing each individual's full potential.

Preparation for Independent Living

Roughly 34% of the young adults in our study were officially discharged from foster care sometime during their eighteenth year. Somewhat fewer (19.5%) were discharged within nine months following their twenty-first birthday, and the rest left sometime in between. I do not know precisely what determined the timing of discharge, although ongoing attendance at school or in a training program was certainly a factor in a later date of discharge. New York "State and City policies are vague and inconsistent . . . regarding the provision of foster care beyond age 18" (Task Force 1980:51), and so it is likely that, with so many agencies involved, a variety of criteria were applied in reaching decisions.

Over the years following their discharge from placement, the young adults by and large learned to cope with the world and to establish their independent patterns of life. But the period immediately following their discharge was, we can assume, a struggle for many. It was a particularly difficult time for those who left group facilities since, unlike many from foster homes, they were obliged to leave their places of residence, which made their transition into the community more abrupt. But regardless of whether they were discharged from group or foster family care, the road was most difficult for those who had to fend for themselves because of limited or tenuous ties to adults in the community, whether kin, foster families, or others. Although all youths must be prepared for independent living, particular care should be taken to identify youths with only limited ties in order to provide them with whatever they need to make it on their own, or at least to have a good start.

Preparation for independent living needs to be viewed as an ongoing process that begins many years before the date of discharge. Just as children do not suddenly, magically, turn into adults, so independence gradually develops as they are given, and accept, increasing responsibility for themselves. Expectations need to be communicated, experiences provided, and information given. The young adults in our study complained a great deal about the preparation they had received. Their complaints cannot be regarded as unimportant grumbles; they point to much work that needs to be done.

Throughout the United States the components of adequate discharge preparation need to be spelled out and their implementation monitored by those in positions of responsibility. The following is a partial list of general aspects of preparation that must be considered.

— Counseling that addresses educational, work, and career objectives and choices: assessments of interests and skills; information about work and career options; information about educational opportunities, high school equivalency and vocational education programs, college programs and financial aid possibilities; and assistance with enrollment procedures.
— Vocational training and employment: the ABCs of applying for a job; assistance in finding work experiences during placement; training in marketable skills and trades; information on commu-

nity resources for finding employment; assistance in locating
postdischarge employment.

— Training in independent living skills: providing experiences in
handling money and information on budgeting; information and
assistance on establishing savings accounts for earnings; information on various types of financial assistance; availability of supervised independent living settings prior to final discharge; information about how and where to find living quarters and temporary
housing; assistance in finding housing; training and experience in
shopping and cooking.

— Sex education and family planning: education on sexual matters,
family life, and community facilities that provide information and
counseling on family planning.

— Information about kin and other ties: providing an opportunity
to discuss specifics of background; assistance in locating biological
family members and others of the youths' choosing; information
about various community groups that could provide companion-
ship and links to adults.

Some broader questions also need to be addressed as part
of a review of practices and policies that govern the discharge
of young adults: (1) Do young women receive the same kind
of preparation for independent living as the young men? The
women in our study felt less well prepared. I do not know
whether in fact this was so, but one should be sure that there
are no sex differences in any aspect of preparation. (2) Do
state policies place a limit on what youths may retain in savings
from earnings during their placement? New York State law
(Soc. Serv. 398) includes a maximum on earnings retention of
$50 a month, and other restrictions set an annual limit of $600
(HRAa). Apparently amounts earned in excess of this are to
be contributed toward child care. Such policies should be reviewed since they punish youths who have very limited financial means upon discharge. They fly in the face of one aspect
of discharge preparation—the objective of encouraging employment experience and earnings. (3) Do state policies include provision for a discharge grant and what are the conditions and amounts? In New York State a grant of up to $500

is provided for such things as furniture or rent if an application is submitted and a need is established. A "doctrine of reasonableness" is used as the basis for approval. Although one might think that such a grant would frequently be used to tide young people over after their discharge, only a minority of our sample received such a grant. Most commonly no application had been submitted by an agency, and many of the young adults were quite unaware of this possibility. I do not know to what extent such grants are used today. Since the amount of the maximum grant has not changed for many years, its value has surely eroded. This suggests a need for review so that adjustments can be made for increases in the cost of living. Furthermore, the provisions make no distinction between the discharge of a young child back to his or her family and of an 18-year-old attempting to become independent. This too requires reconsideration.

Adolescents who are growing up in foster care need information about the policies that affect them, about discharge planning responsibilities, and about a variety of community resources. It is their life and they must be entrusted with information that will allow them to make choices, to decide what they want to do. Brochures have been recommended that would detail "payment for room and board for college . . . the requirements for receiving a discharge grant . . . policy regarding age for discharge . . . planning responsibilities" and would list resources "for college scholarships, job training, vocational educational programs and supported work programs" (Task Force 1980:53). Such information could be useful if regularly updated and annually disseminated to all adolescents in placement. If some of the information were gathered, assembled, and issued by adolescent recruits in the form of a news bulletin or chain letter, it would have heightened visibility.

Furthermore, states need to review their policies on age for discharge. I would argue for a flexible standard with extensions of placement readily available up to age 21 for youths who are continuing with their education or other vocational or technical training, and for others who are "still poorly equipped educationally, emotionally, and vocationally for self-direction and self-maintenance" (HRAb:52). Agency goals during such extensions need to be spelled out, along with time frames for their achievement and a specification of services to be provided. This is not to suggest that all youths remain in foster care for extended periods. Many do not want this because they are motivated, are mature enough, and have the resources to try their own wings. But for those who are not, extensions of care need to be creatively used. Along this line, the finality of discharge policies also needs to be reviewed. Just as young children are discharged on a trial basis, so a trial period of six months to a year should precede the final discharge of some young adults to independent living. Such a test period could be used to assess their ability to maintain themselves, and it would permit replacement if it became evident that additional preparation was necessary prior to age 21.

Post-Discharge

The end of foster care is the beginning of a new phase of life. During the first several years there are no doubt times when personal crises need to be faced and when questions arise for which information is lacking. The young adults in our sample thought that foster care agencies could serve as useful resources. Some agencies did offer assistance, but the picture was far from uniform. In view of fiscal constraints, this is understandable. At the same time one could imagine the ultimate benefit that could be derived from the establishment of agency information centers, akin to alumni offices. These could provide foster care graduates with a place to turn for information and referral during the first several years following final discharge. Such offices could even provide graduates with brochures containing information on community facilities that address various needs. The nature of requests flowing into such offices could, in turn, be used as a source for ideas about how better to prepare youths for independent living.

These questions and suggestions are a fitting end to this long account. They evolved from the words and thoughts of those with first-hand experience—the young adults who had lived in foster care, who had graduated from it, and who were coping with life. I cannot do justice to their many concerns, for in the end I singled out only a few issues. It is hoped that they will serve as a springboard for discussion, for review, and for action.

At the beginning of this account, it was not clear how it would end. The account is a long one, traversing through time. The full story stimulated questions and provided some answers. Above all, it is a testament to the resilience and strength of children. It is a response to the doomsayers of the world, the prognosticators of inevitable human tragedy.

The young adults gave generously of themselves. They wanted to speak about their experiences and their lives. They were serious, thoughtful, and searching. They spoke for no personal gain, but in the belief that they could help others. They have spoken . . . they have raised questions . . . they are waiting for answers.

APPENDIXES

Appendix A

RESPONDENTS AND NONRESPONDENTS

The 277 respondents and 117 nonrespondents were compared on all data from the case records as well as on official figures for arrests and convictions. In roughly 125 comparisons, four statistically significant differences were found, using a two-tailed .05 criterion.* That many differences could have been expected on the basis of chance alone.

Two of these differences distinguished female nonrespondents from female respondents. At the time the nonrespondents were born their mothers were younger (mean = 24.1 years) than was the case for female respondents (mean = 27.1 years). The mothers of the female nonrespondents were also on the average younger at the time their children entered foster care (mean = 27.5 years) when compared with the mothers of female respondents (mean = 30.4 years). No differences existed among the males. I do not know what meaning to attach to the observed differences among the women. They were probably chance differences.

On the other hand, the other two differences are quite understandable. For one, male and female nonrespondents were more likely to have been discharged from group settings than from foster homes. These data are in the table on page 308. We had fewer leads to pursue for those who had left group settings. For example, biological family members were frequently more difficult to find than foster parents because the case records contained less precise and less up-to-date infor-

*A two-tailed .05 criterion has been used for all analyses completed and reported in this book.

	Discharged From:			
	Foster Home		Group Setting	
	N	(%)	N	(%)
Respondents	201	(73.6)	76	(62.8)
Nonrespondents	72	(26.4)	45	(37.2)
Total	273	(100.0)	121	(100.0)

mation. Hence, it was much more difficult to locate those who had been discharged from group settings.

Second, there was a difference between respondents and nonrespondents in scholastic achievement, but only among those who had been discharged from group settings. At the time of their discharge from foster care, the nonrespondents from group facilities had, on the average, completed 10.7 years of schooling, compared with an average 11.5 years completed by the respondents. Among those discharged from foster homes there were no differences between respondents and nonrespondents in the average number of grades completed. Thus, in addition to the more general difficulty in reaching those who had left group facilities, we seemed to be least successful in reaching them if they had completed less education.

Appendix B

SENSE OF WELL-BEING INDEX

This index consisted of three components: (1) The average score on a seven-point scale of two administrations of the idential item that asked "How do you feel about your life as a whole?" The two questions were separated by 10 to 20 minutes of interview time. Mail questionnaire respondents were asked the question only once. (2) The response to a question that asked "Taken all together, how would you say things are for you these days—would you say they are very happy, pretty happy, or not too happy?" (3) Rosenberg's 10-item self-esteem scale. These three items were combined after z-score transformations. The Pearson product-moment intercorrelations of the three items for the respondents are as follows:

	1	2	3
1. Life as a whole	—	.57	.50
		(N = 272)	(N = 271)
2. Happiness these days	—	—	.39
			(N = 270)
3. Self-esteem	—	—	—

Appendix C

INTRODUCTORY LETTER

WHAT'S HAPPENING: Young Adults in Society Today

New York University
3 Washington Square North
New York, New York   10003
(212) 598-7606

[Addressee]

Some people think that young adults are having a tough time these days, others think young adults are having an easy time. No one knows. We at New York University are conducting a study to find out the answer to this important question. You have been specially selected to be in this project on WHAT'S HAPPENING: Young Adults in Society Today. The project concerns the quality of life, past and present, of young adults who spent many years living away from their families. Your participation in this study will involve giving us an interview, for which we are going to pay you. Your help with this important project will ultimately benefit others who are now growing up away from their families.

We plan to interview many young adults, all of whom have been chosen with the permission of the Office of Special Services for Children and the New York State Department of Social Services. Participation is, of course, entirely voluntary. We hope you will agree with us that we need the cooperation of everyone in giving us an interview. In that regard I want to assure you that everything in the interview will be held in strictest confidence by our project staff. The results will be summarized and presented in statistical form without ever using a name so that no individual can be identified.

A member of our study staff will telephone you shortly to arrange a convenient time for the interview. He or she will be happy to answer any questions you may have about the project. I hope you will welcome the opportunity to talk about your experiences, for I am confident that you will find the interview interesting. Your support of this important work is greatly needed as it will help other young people now and in the future.

Thank you in advance for your cooperation.

Sincerely,

Trudy Festinger, D.S.W.
Project Director

References

Allardt, Eric. 1976. Dimensions of Welfare in a Comparative Scandinavian Study. *Acta Sociologica* 19:227–239.

Andrews, Frank M. and Stephen B. Withey. 1976. *Social Indicators of Well-Being*. New York: Plenum Press.

Baylor, Edith and Elio Monachesi. 1939. *The Rehabilitation of Children*. New York: Harper.

Boehm, Bernice. 1958. *Deterrents to the Adoption of Children in Foster Care*. New York: Child Welfare League of America.

Bohman, Michael. 1971. A Comparative Study of Adopted Children, Foster Children, and Children in Their Biological Environment Born After Undesired Pregnancies. *Acta Paediatrica Scandinavica* (Supl. 221):1–38.

Bohman, Michael and Soren Sigvardsson. 1980. Negative Social Heritage. *Adoption and Fostering* 3:25–34.

Bowlby, John. 1951. *Maternal Care and Mental Health*. Geneva: World Health Organization.

Bremner, Robert H., ed. 1970. *Children and Youth in America: A Documentary History*. Vol. 1: *1600–1865*. Cambridge: Harvard University Press.

—— 1971. *Children and Youth in America: A Documentary History*. Vol. 2: *1866–1932*. Cambridge: Harvard University Press.

—— 1974. *Children and Youth in America: A Documentary History*. Vol. 3: *1933–1973*. Cambridge: Harvard University Press.

Buchwald, Art. 1973. Reminiscences. In Jacqueline Bernard, *The Children You Gave Us*, pp. v–vii. New York: Block.

Campbell, Angus. 1981. *The Sense of Well-Being in America*. New York: McGraw-Hill.

Claburn, Eugene and Stephen Magura. 1977. *Foster Care Case Review in New Jersey: An Evaluation of Its Implementation and Effects*. Trenton: State of New Jersey Foster Care Research Project.

Commerce. 1979a. U.S. Department of Commerce. *1979 Current Population Survey: New York City Data Tapes.*

Commerce. 1979b. U.S. Department of Commerce. *Current Population Reports: Marital Status and Living Arrangements,* March 1979, Series P-20, no. 349, table 9, p. 45.

Cosgrove, Colleen. 1979. Memorandum on "Interpretation of Rap Sheets." New York: Vera Institute of Justice.

Cowan, Edwina and Eva Stout. 1939. A Comparative Study of the Adjustment Made by Foster Children After Complete and Partial Breaks in Continuity of Home Environment. *American Journal of Orthopsychiatry* 9:330–338.

CWIS. 1976–1980. Child Welfare Information Services, Inc. Special Report Series D for New York City for December 31, 1976 to 1980.

Derdeyn, Andre P. 1977. A Case for Permanent Foster Placement of Dependent, Neglected, and Abused Children. *American Journal of Orthopsychiatry* 47:604–614.

Encyc. SW. (Encyclopedia of Social Work). 1977. 17th ed., vol. 1. Washington, D.C.: National Association of Social Workers.

Fanshel, David. 1966. Child Welfare. In Henry S. Maas, ed., *Five Fields of Social Service: Reviews of Research,* pp. 85–143. New York: National Association of Social Workers.

—— 1975. Parental Visiting in Foster Care: Key to Discharge. *Social Service Review* 49:493–514.

—— 1977. Parental Visiting of Foster Children: A Computerized Study. *Social Work Research and Abstracts* 1:2–10.

Ferguson, Thomas. 1966. *Children in Care—and After.* London: Oxford University Press.

Festinger, Trudy. 1974. Placement Agreements with Boarding Homes: A Survey. *Child Welfare* 53:643–652.

Giovannoni, Jeanne M. and Andrew Billingsley. 1970. Child Neglect Among the Poor: A Study of Parental Adequacy in Families of Three Ethnic Groups. *Child Welfare* 49:196–204.

Grow, Lucille J. 1979. *Early Childrearing by Young Mothers.* New York: Child Welfare League of America.

Gruber, Alan R. 1978. *Children in Foster Care—Destitute, Neglected, Betrayed.* New York: Human Sciences Press.

Holman, Robert. 1975. The Place of Fostering in Social Work. *British Journal of Social Work* 5:3–29.

HRAa. Revised 1968. New York City Human Resources Administration. Special Services for Children. *Inter-Agency Manual of Policies and Procedures*. Section 33.

HRAb. Revised 1966. New York City Human Resources Administration. Special Services for Children. *Inter-Agency Manual of Policies and Procedures*. Section 21.

JCCA. 1959. In re Jewish Child Care Association, 5 N.Y. 2nd, 222.

Jenkins, Shirley and Elaine Norman. 1975. *Beyond Placement—Mothers View Foster Care*. New York: Columbia University Press.

Kadushin, Alfred. 1978. Children in Foster Families and Institutions. In Henry S. Maas, ed., *Social Service Research: Reviews of Studies*, pp. 90–148. Washington, D.C.: National Association of Social Workers.

—— 1980. *Child Welfare Services*. 3d ed. New York: Macmillan.

Kwitny, Jonathan. 1978. "Foster-Care System Is Accused by Critics of Harming Children." *The Wall Street Journal*, September 6.

Lash, Trude W., Heidi Sigal, and Deanna Dudzinski. 1980. *State of the Child: New York City II*. New York: Foundation for Child Development.

Littner, Ner. 1971. The Importance of the Natural Parents to the Child in Placement. In *Preliminary Conference Report, First National Conference of Foster Parents*. Publication No. 72-5. Washington, D.C.: Department of Health, Education, and Welfare.

Maas, Henry and Richard Engler. 1959. *Children in Need of Parents*. New York: Columbia University Press.

McAdams, Phyllis J. 1972. The Parent in the Shadows. *Child Welfare* 51:51–55.

McCord, Joan, William McCord, and Emily Thurber. 1960. The Effects of Foster-Home Placement in the Prevention of Adult Antisocial Behavior. *Social Service Review* 34:415–419.

Meier, Elizabeth G. 1962. *Former Foster Children as Adult Citizens*. DSW dissertation, Columbia University.

—— 1965. Current Circumstances of Former Foster Children. *Child Welfare* 44:196–206.

Mizio, Emelicia. 1974. Impact of External Systems on the Puerto Rican Family. *Social Casework* 55:76–83.

National Opinion Research Center. 1978. *General Social Surveys, 1972–1978*. Ann Arbor, Mich.: The Inter-University Consortium for Political and Social Research.

N.Y. Times. 1982. Children Who Hang Out: Who, Where, and Why. *New York Times*, July 16.

Polansky, Norman A., Mary Ann Chalmers, Elizabeth Buttenwieser, and David P. Williams. 1981. *Damaged Parents*. Chicago: University of Chicago Press.

Polier, Shad. 1959. Amendments to New York's Adoption Law. *Child Welfare* 38:1–4.

Reid, Joseph. 1959. Action Called For—Recommendations. In Henry Maas and Richard Engler, *Children in Need of Parents*. New York: Columbia University Press.

Robinson, John P. and Phillip R. Shaver. 1973. *Measures of Social Psychological Attitudes*. Ann Arbor: University of Michigan Institute for Social Research.

Rosenberg, Morris. 1965. *Society and the Adolescent Self-Image*. Princeton, N.J.: Princeton University Press.

Salo, Reino. 1956. *Kunnallinen Lastensuojelutyo Sosiaalisen Sopeutumisen Kasvattajana* (The English Summary: Municipal Child Welfare Work As Promoter of Social Adjustment). Finland: Vaasa.

Shapiro, Deborah. 1975. *Agencies and Foster Children*. New York: Columbia University Press.

Sherman, Edward, Renee Neuman, and Ann W. Shyne. 1973. *Children Adrift in Foster Care: A Study of Alternative Approaches*. New York: Child Welfare League of America.

Shyne, Ann W. and Anita G. Schroeder. 1978. *National Study of Social Services to Children and Their Families*. Rockville, Md.: Westat.

Soc. Serv. 398. New York State Social Services Law. Section 398(6)(j).

SW Year Book. 1933. Fred S. Hall, ed. *Social Work Year Book*. New York: Russell Sage Foundation.

—— 1943. Russell H. Kurtz, ed. *Social Work Year Book*. New York: Russell Sage Foundation.

Srole, Leo. 1956. Social Integration and Certain Corollaries. *American Sociological Review* 21:709–716.

Task Force. 1980. New York City, Mayor's Task Force on Foster Care Services. *Redirecting Foster Care*. New York.

Theis, Sophie Van Senden. 1924. *How Foster Children Turn Out*. New York: State Charities Aid Association.

Van Der Waals, Paula. 1960. Former Foster Children Reflect on Their Childhood. *Children* 7:29–33.

Vasaly, Shirley M. 1976. *Foster Care in Five States: A Synthesis and Analysis of Studies from Arizona, California, Iowa, Massachusetts, and Vermont*. Washington, D.C.: Social Work Research Group, George Washington University.

Veroff, Joseph, Elizabeth Douvan, and Richard A. Kulka. 1981. *The Inner American.* New York: Basic Books.

Wechsler, Henry, Mary Rohman, and Leonard Solomon. 1981. Emotional Problems and Concerns of New England College Students. *American Journal of Orthopsychiatry* 51:719–723.

Weinstein, Eugene. 1960. *The Self-Image of the Foster Child.* New York: Russell Sage Foundation.

Zimmerman, Rosalie B. 1982. *Foster Care in Retrospect.* New Orleans: Tulane Studies in Social Welfare, Tulane University.

Index

Abandonment or desertion of child caring person, as factor in placement, 41-42, 45-46; and arrests after discharge, 203; and contact with biological family during placement, 77; and contact with and closeness to biological family at time of study, 175, 178-79, 181

Abortions among women participating in study, 146, 220

Abuse of child, as factor in placement, 41-42; and contact with biological families at time of study, 175

Adoption: children's wishes about, 62-63; deterrents to, 49, 81

Age of participants in study
—at discharge, 298, 301-2
—at final placement, and sense of well-being, 69
—at first long-term placement, 54, 57; and sense of well-being, 69
—at first placement, 50-52; and contact with biological families during placement, 76, 82, 84-85, 95; and contact with and closeness to biological families at time of study, 174, 180, 183; and educational achievements, 154; and placement history, 55-57; and problems during placement, 102, 104, 110-11; and satisfaction with care, 260; and sense of well-being, 69
—at time of shifts in care, 56

Aging out, xiii

Alcohol use by adults discharged from foster care, 7, 194-95, 225; compared with general population, 243, 251

Alcohol use by child caring person, as factor in placement, 43

Alienation from society, 205, 226-27; general population–foster care differences, 233

Allardt, Eric, 12

Andrews, Frank M., 23, 121

Arrests and convictions after discharge from foster care, 6-7, 200-9, 212, 226-27

Baylor, Edith, 3

Behavior of child: as factor in placement, 41; and shifts in care, 59; *see also* Social and emotional problems during placement

Billingsley, Andrew, 35

Biological family, *see* Family, biological

Birth order of participants in study, 37

Birth weight of children of women in study, 140

Birth weight of participants in study, 33-34

Black participants in study, 30-31, 212; alcohol use, compared with general population, 243, 251; alienation from society, 233; arrests after discharge, 204, 206-8; compared with natural surveys, 230-31, 248; contact with biological families at time of study, 175; education, compared with general population, 237, 250; employment, 163, 168-69; employment, compared with general population, 238-40; financial situation, compared with general population, 250; health problems, compared with general population, 243; marital status at time of study, 136, 218; marital status, compared with general population, 235; older

Intellective and learning problems during placement, 98, 100-3, 107-10, 113-15; and arrests after discharge, 203; and employment, 164, 169; and motherhood, 141-43

Intelligence test results, 101; and functioning of adults following foster care discharge, 6-7

JCCA, 49
Jenkins, Shirley, 73
Jewish agencies, 63
Jewish Child Care Association (JCCA), 49
Jewish participants in study, 31-32, 126

Kadushin, Alfred, xi-xiii, 3, 42, 49, 56, 58
Kin, see Family, biological
Kulka, Richard A., 150, 191, 199, 229
Kwitny, Jonathan, 207

Lash, Trude W., 42
Law, troubles with, after discharge, 6-7, 199-209, 212, 226-27
Learning problems, see Intellective and learning problems during placement
Length of longest placement, 213; and contact with foster parents at time of study, 182; and satisfaction with care, 260
Length of placement, 51
Life as a whole, participants' feelings about, at time of study, 133; compared with general population, 247, 252; see also Well-being, sense of
Littner, Ner, 73
Living arrangements of participants at time of study, 121-23, 133, 215; predischarge preparation for, 286-87

Maas, Henry, 49
McAdams, Phyllis J., 73
McCord, Joan, 5
McCord, William, 5
Magura, Stephen, 73

Male participants in study, 30
—age of parents at birth and placement, 32-33
—age at time of placement, 51-52, 57
—alcohol use at time of study, 195
—closeness to foster families at time of study, 183, 225; and sense of well-being, 189
—contact with biological families during placement, 75-76, 78, 80, 84, 90, 95, 214, 223
—contact with and closeness to biological families at time of study, 178, 181, 223; and sense of well-being, 186-87
—discharge destination, 63
—drug use at time of study, 195-97, 226
—educational achievements: compared with general population, 237, 250; following discharge, 152-53; participants' assessment of, 156-57; during placement, 151-52, 214
—employment, 159-65, 168-70, 221-22; compared with general population, 238-40
—fatherhood, attitudes about, 147, 219
—formal help-seeking after discharge, 198
—health problems and symptoms: income, 165; during placement, 100; at time of study, 191-94, 198-99
—intellective and learning problems during placement, 100-3, 214
—length of longest placement, 57
—length of time in care, 51
—marital status and children at time of study, 136-37, 139-40, 147-48, 216-19; compared with general population, 235
—mobility after discharge, and sense of well-being, 127
—placement characteristics, and sense of well-being, 65, 69-70
—placement history and age at entry into care, 55, 57
—post-discharge advice, need for, 290-91
—post-discharge ties to agencies, 289
—predischarge preparation, 286-87